D0919183

A GUIDE TO FIELD IDENTIFICATION

WILDFLOWERS
OF NORTH AMERICA

by
Frank D. Venning

illustrated by
Manabu C. Saito

GOLDEN PRESS • NEW YORK
WESTERN PUBLISHING COMPANY, INC.
RACINE, WISCONSIN

FOREWORD

For more than ten years, readers of Golden Field Guides have asked that the series include *Wildflowers of North America*. But unlike its companion volumes (*Birds, Trees, Seashells, Amphibians, Reptiles*), there is no precedent for a wildflower guide to treat so vast an area: nearly 15 percent of the earth's unglaciated land surface. Nor is there precedent for a single book to deal with the huge number of plant families, genera, species, varieties, forms, and natural hybrids that make up its wildflowers. In fact, no single technical work covers more than a fraction of the area and its flowering plants, as only regional floristic studies have been published.

Work on this Golden Field Guide began by compiling a catalog of all herbaceous wildflowers described for North America north of Mexico, omitting trees, shrubs, cacti, and woody vines. Plants not usually thought of as wildflowers (such as grasses, rushes, milfoils, most sedges) were excluded, as were plants with inconspicuous or unattractive flowers, like nettles, goosefeet, plantains, and ragweeds. Yet within these limits our catalog lists more than 10,000 species of herbaceous North American wildflowers, comprising over 1,300 genera in 115 families! Such an abundance of species obviously precludes encyclopedic coverage, but how many readers are interested in knowing 50 kinds of Sunflowers, 79 Wild Onions, 81 Buttercups, 120 Groundsels, 150 Lupines, or 375 Milk-vetches? A field guide is feasible, however, at the generic level, and this approach was adopted in writing this book.

With the Golden Field Guide *Wildflowers of North America*, the reader is introduced to our wealth of native and naturalized herbaceous wildflowers, represented by 1,553 of the more common species in 826 wide-ranging genera of 101 families, all illustrated in full color. The text contains data pertinent to identification, including family and generic characteristics, and descriptions of flowers, leaves, size, habitats, and known ranges.

Frank D. Venning

The artist thanks all those who helped locate specimens, drawings or photographs, loaned him their books, or gave ideas, criticism or encouragement in the preparation of the illustrations. His greatest debt is to the following, without whose generosity, patience, and help the paintings in this book could never have been completed: Elizabeth Hall, Dr. John T. Mickel, Dr. Elizabeth Scholtz, Dr. Benjamin Blackburn, and Dr. John P. Craig, for his constant encouragement.

TABLE OF CONTENTS

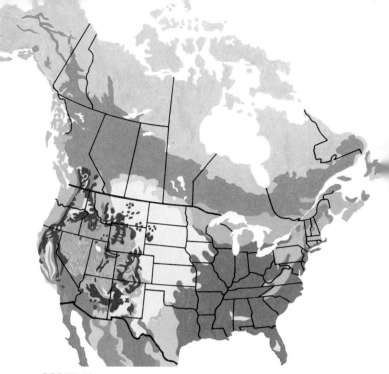

SCOPE: This guide covers a continental land mass of 7,441,049 square miles, from within the Arctic Circle southward over the North Temperate Zone to the edge of the Tropics. The land varies from valleys below sea level to high mountains; soils range from organic peats to slightly decomposed rock. The vegetation includes large areas of the earth's four principal plant climaxes: tundra, forest, grassland, and desert. Geography, topography, and soils combine to provide a rich diversity of environments within each climax; the major divisions are mapped above. The distribution of wildflowers is influenced by these natural areas. Keep in mind that each division may include a number of specific habitats, such as bogs, sea or lake shores, rock outcrops, salt or alkali flats, or mountain meadows, each with different kinds of wildflowers.

Tundra	Pacific Rain Forest	Mesquite-Grassland
Boreal Forest	Deciduous Forest	Piñon-Juniper Woodland
Northern Forest	Grassland	Chaparral-Oak Woodland
Aspen Parkland	Northern Desert Scrub	SE Evergreen Forest
Montane Woodland	Southern Desert Scrub	Mexican Pine and Pine-Oa

AN INTRODUCTION TO WILDFLOWERS

Spanish, French, and English explorers and the colonists who followed them were amazed and delighted by the abundance, beauty, and variety of the wildflowers in North America. Official reports and private letters sent to Europe in the 16th and 17th centuries were filled with lists describing the new plants from the New World. As the wilderness was explored and settled during the 18th and 19th centuries, more and more kinds of wildflowers were discovered and described. But not until the present century, after detailed botanical exploration and study, has the astonishing magnitude of our heritage of native wildflowers been revealed.

The settlers cleared land for farming, cut trees for shelter and fuel, exploited native plants for food, medicine, and dyes. They accidentally brought along seed of European weeds and field flowers with crop seed, and planted Old World pot herbs and garden flowers in their dooryards. But the composition of our flora remained relatively unchanged until about 100 years ago. The Homestead Act of 1862 and the completion of the Union Pacific Railway in 1869 and the Canadian Pacific in 1885 opened the western half of the continent to the plow. The seven-fold increase in North America's population since 1862 and the accompanying agricultural revolution that met the ever-increasing demand for food and fiber brought profound environmental changes. Today, over 788,000 square miles of the continent are cropland, 160,450 square miles of wetland are drained, 53,000 square miles of arid land are irrigated, 800,000 square miles are used for pasture or grazing, only remnants of the vast original forests remain, and more than 1,000,000 acres are lost to urban sprawl each year.

Our flora reflects these rapid environmental changes. Many once-common native wildflowers, unable to thrive if their habitat is modified, are now uncommon or rare; a few are extinct. Others, once restricted in range, are now widespread. Foreign field and garden flowers, adapted to flourish in disturbed soil, escaped into the countryside and became naturalized; today, over 165 species of our most common field and wayside wildflowers are aliens.

North America has pioneered in saving wilderness areas and their wildflowers. Alarm first came from exploitation of Yosemite Valley and the senseless cutting of Sequoias. Congress gave the Valley and Mariposa Grove to California in 1864, to be held in their natural condition for public enjoyment; it was the first time any government anywhere set aside public lands purely for scenic values. The Yellowstone Act of 1872 created the world's first national park; Canada followed in 1886. North America now has 43 national parks (51,281 square miles) where native wildflowers are conserved; some national monuments and state parks are also wildflower sanctuaries.

HOW WILDFLOWERS ARE CLASSIFIED

Plant classification, or taxonomy, is a sort of "street directory" for the plant kingdom; it provides a framework on which all other knowledge of plants is arranged so that it can be readily found when wanted. Each species is placed in a definite position on this framework, based on its natural relationships to all other plants.

Classification begins by studying a plant's characteristics: the kinds of cells, tissues, and vegetative organs it has or lacks, and how its reproductive structures resemble or differ from those of other plants. It is then placed in six categories of descending rank (division, class, order, family, genus, and species), starting by grouping it with other plants that have the same fundamental characters, ending with the features that make it a distinct entity, or species. Sub-categories (sub-class, subfamily, tribe, etc.) are sometimes used to make relationships clearer. Finally, the plant is given a two-word Latin name: its genus and species.

With over 350,000 species of living plants known, it is no small task to provide an accurate usable framework. The classification has been done by many workers, with differing backgrounds and abilities; but it is within a usable, constantly improved framework.

In accordance with this framework, the flowers in this guide are arranged by family and genus. All wildflowers have fundamental characters in common; the most widely accepted way of positioning them within the plant kingdom is:

DIVISION: SPERMATOPHYTA The Seed-bearing Plants
Plants that normally reproduce by seeds containing an embryo, or minute plant.

SUBDIVISION: ANGIOSPERMAE The Flowering Plants
Plants with the seed or seeds enclosed by an ovary, which at maturity becomes the fruit. In all Angiosperms, the pollen is deposited on the stigma of the flower.

CLASS I: MONOCOTYLEDONEAE The Monocotyledons
The embryo has one cotyledon, or seed leaf; the flower parts are usually in 3's; leaves are chiefly parallel-veined. (The first 19 families, 121 genera, and 190 species in this book, pp. 16–53, are Monocotyledons.)

CLASS II: DICOTYLEDONEAE The Dicotyledons
The embryo has two cotyledons, or seed leaves; flower parts are mostly in 4's or 5's; leaves are mainly netted-veined. (The 82 families, 705 genera, and 1,363 species on pp. 54–327 in this book are Dicotyledons.)

SCIENTIFIC NAMES

The concept of the genus, as a group of related species, dates from Theophrastus' *Inquiry into Plants*, c. 310 B.C. But until A.D. 1753, scholars named plants by using a one-word generic name, followed by a descriptive phrase to indicate the species. Thus, when just two species of white roses were known, one was named *Rosa alba, caule aculeato, pedunculis laevibus, calycibus semipinnatis glabris*, the other *Rosa alba, caule petiolisque aculeatis, calycis foliolis indivisis*.* As new species were added, the names became incredibly complex. No one could remember or work with such clumsy names.

In 1753, Carolus Linnaeus devised a binomial, or two-word, system of naming plants (also animals), by using one word after the generic name to indicate the species. This permitted referring to a species without having to quote its full description as a part of its name. It revolutionized the naming of plants and animals and continues in use today. The following points explain how this system applies to the scientific names of wildflowers:

1. Every genus has a unique one-word name. Generic names are nouns, capitalized, and italicized—for example, *Aster, Canna,* and *Phlox.* Sometimes a genus is named in honor of a person (*Brodiaea* for James Brodie, *Brickellia* for John Brickell).

2. Every species has a two-word name; the second word is often an adjective, preferably not capitalized—for example, *Aster macrophyllus* (large-leaved), *Phlox carolina* (of the Carolinas). Rarely, the second word is a hyphenated word—*Aster novae-angliae* (of New England). Some species are named in honor of persons—*Phlox hoodii* for Robert Hood, *Lilium grayi* for Asa Gray.

3. The word indicating the species is used only once within a genus, but the same word can be used again to indicate a species in a different genus—as examples, *Dalea aurea* and *Zizia aurea.*

4. The binomials are written in Latin or in a Latinized form, and are italicized. All scholars wrote in Latin when Linnaeus proposed this system. Latin is still used for scientific names; hence, the names are the same everywhere, irrespective of local languages.

5. A species is conceived as "a population of individuals that are sufficiently alike and closely enough related to be considered one kind." If parts of this population show persistent minor character differences, botanists indicate these by using the sub-categories *variety* and *form.* But in some genera, authorities differ in how they interpret these sub-categories, and shift the rank of some varieties to species, or vice versa. When differences of opinion exist, the text states "about" how many species are in N.A.

*"White rose with prickly stem, smooth peduncles, and smooth semipinnate calyx," and "White rose with prickly stem and petioles, the leaves of the calyx undivided."

COMMON OR COLLOQUIAL NAMES

In this book, flowers are listed by their common names (in boldface), followed by their scientific names. If the flower has no common name, it is listed by its scientific name (in boldface). No attempt was made to manufacture artificial vernacular names for flowers that had none.

Genera often have common names that apply to all species in the genus—for example, all species of *Xyris* are called Yellow-eyed Grass. Some genera have two or more common names that apply to all the species—for example, all species of *Impatiens* are called Jewel-weed or Touch-me-not. Occasionally, different common names apply to groups of species within a genus: Onions, Garlics, and Leeks are three distinct groups within the genus *Allium*.

Rarely, two genera have the same common name; for example, all species of *Listera* and *Liparis* are known as Twayblades. The common name of a species, however, may differ from the collective common name of its genus: *Liparis lilifolia* is a Twayblade, but this species is called Purple Scutcheon; all plants belonging to the genus *Cypripedium* are Lady's-slippers, but *Cypripedium acaule* is called Moccasin-flower.

Completely different wildflowers sometimes have the same common name, and the common name of the same flower may change from one locale or region to another. The common names in this guide are those that appear to be widely established in the literature and in general use. The text does not include all local common names.

ARRANGEMENT OF THIS BOOK

This book is designed as a field guide to the major genera of North American wildflowers. Criteria for selecting genera described and illustrated include range, abundance, attractiveness, and distinction. The species representing the genera were chosen by the same criteria. In genera with large numbers of species, the criteria included species that show the limits of diversity in these genera.

By arranging the flowers in natural groups according to form and structure, the similarities within groups as well as the diversities can be noted. This helps one to become ever more familiar with the common characteristics of the families and of the groups within them—an important aid to identification—and helps in recognizing flowers not illustrated in the guide. In both the Monocotyledons (pp. 16–53) and the Dicotyledons (pp. 54–327), the families follow in a natural progression, from those with simpler to those with more complex flower structure and form.

By grouping genera with similar characteristics together under families, the need for endless repetition of common characteristics is avoided, and it narrows the need to search for groups similar to the specimen. Since identification is largely a comparative process, this

nakes comparisons easy, and places just two requirements on the user:
(1) to know the parts of flowers and kinds of leaves (these are illustrated
on pp. 12–13), and (2) to be able to count the parts—how many petals,
how many stamens, etc.

HOW TO USE THIS BOOK

Some wildflowers are so distinctive they can be identified at a glance;
others may first require careful study of their flowers and foliage. When
an unfamiliar flower is found, the following steps to identification are
suggested:

(1) Scan the illustrations for one that matches or is close to the specimen. This may result in immediate identification of the genus or of both
genus and species. Some variation will be found, and the picture may
not match precisely in color, hairiness, or exact proportion of parts.
However, the form, number, kind, and arrangement of the flower parts
and leaves should agree with the illustration.

(2) Read the text that appears on the facing page to confirm the
identification and to learn more about the plant. Make sure that the
specimen agrees with the generic description as to number and kind of
flower parts and leaves, size, and range, if given.

(3) Some may find identification easier by following the same steps
that the botanist took to classify the flower:

(a) determine if the specimen is a Monocotyledon or a Dicotyledon
(see the descriptions on p. 8 to do this).

(b) determine the family of the specimen by comparing it with
family descriptions in the text; if a family is divided into subfamilies
and tribes, read these descriptions to narrow the search.

(c) from the generic descriptions, locate the specimen's genus. The
illustrations of representative species in the genus will help confirm the
identification and may lead to identifying its species as well.

(4) Although it is not always easy to make an identification, it becomes increasingly fast and accurate with study, practice, and experience. You can identify many common wildflowers at once by the pic-
ture-matching method suggested in steps (1) and (2) above. But do not
rely only on this method. Scan the pages of the book in spare moments
to become familiar with the families, subfamilies, tribes, and genera of
wildflowers; get familiar with the parts of a plant (pp. 12–13) and with
the terms used to describe them (pp. 14–15). If you are just beginning
to study wildflowers, don't become discouraged; it quickly becomes a
joy as you learn more and gain in experience.

(5) If a flower cannot be identified readily by reference to this guide,
consult the more technical regional studies listed in the Selected Refer-
ences on p. 329.

LEAVES

ARRANGEMENT

Opposite:
2 leaves per node

Alternate:
1 leaf per node

Whorled:
3 or more leaves
per node

margin

petiole

stipules

axillary
bud

blade

Petiolate

Sessile

Clasping

MARGINS

Entire

Toothed

Lobed

Lobed
& toothed

Pinna[te]
lobe[d]

COMPOUND LEAVES

Palmate

Ternate

leaflets

petiol[e]

petiole

Pinnate

Bipinnate

Trifoliate

Dissected

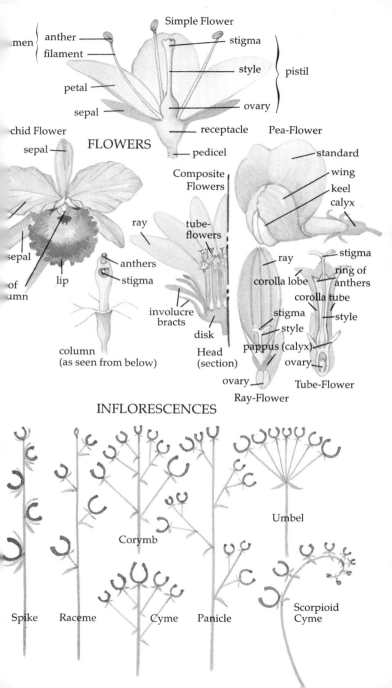

Simple Flower

men { anther
filament
stigma
style } pistil
petal
sepal
ovary
receptacle
pedicel

FLOWERS

chid Flower
sepal
sepal
of umn
lip
column
(as seen from below)

Composite Flowers
ray
tube-flowers
involucre bracts
disk
Head (section)

Pea-Flower
standard
wing
keel
calyx

ray
corolla lobe
stigma
style
pappus (calyx)
ovary
Ray-Flower

stigma
ring of anthers
corolla tube
style
ovary
Tube-Flower

anthers
stigma

INFLORESCENCES

Spike
Raceme
Corymb
Cyme
Panicle
Umbel
Scorpioid Cyme

GLOSSARY

Alternate: one leaf per node.

Annulated: made up of rings.

Anther: the pollen-bearing part of a stamen.

Aril: a fleshy covering at the base of or surrounding a seed.

Awn: a terminal bristle.

Axil: the upper angle between a branch or leaf and the stem.

Axillary: located in an axil.

Bifid: two-cleft.

Bipinnate: twice pinnate.

Bract: a leaf much reduced in size, often scale-like.

Calyx: the outer circle of floral envelopes, made up of the sepals; often green.

Caudex: the woody base of an otherwise herbaceous plant.

Ciliated: with tiny marginal hairs, forming a fringe.

Cleistogamous: small closed self-fertile flowers.

Corm: a short, solid bulblike underground stem.

Corolla: the inner circle of floral envelopes, made up of separate or united petals.

Corona: a crown of appendages between corolla and stamens, or on the corolla or stamens.

Corymb: a short broad flower cluster in which the outermost flowers open first.

Cyme: a short broad flower cluster in which the central flowers open first.

Deciduous: not persistent; falling off at maturity or at certain seasons.

Decompound: more than once compound or divided.

Decumbent: reclining on the ground, but the tip ascending.

Dissected: divided into many slender segments.

Entire: with a continuous margin, without toothing or divisions.

Epiphyte: growing on other plants, but not parasitic.

Even-pinnate: a pinnately-compound leaf lacking a terminal leaflet, hence with an even number of leaflets.

Extra-axillary: arising on side of stem outside of or opposite to an axil, not within or from axil.

Fascicled: in a close bundle or cluster.

Filament: the stalk of an anther.

Flagellae: tiny whiplike appendages, capable of movement.

Florets: tiny flowers that make up a dense head or cluster.

Herbaceous: not woody; leaf-like in color and texture.

Inflorescence: flower cluster; arrangement of flowers on the plant.

Involucel: a small secondary involucre.

Involucre: one or more whorls of small leaves or bracts close beneath a flower, flower cluster, or head.

Keel: a central ridge on the back, like the keel of a boat. In Legumes, the two lower united petals of a flower in the Pea Subfamily.

Node: the place or joint on a stem that normally bears a leaf or leaves.

Odd-pinnate: a pinnate leaf with a terminal leaflet, hence having an odd number of leaflets.

Opposite: paired; having two leaves at one node.

Ovary: the lower ovule-bearing part of the pistil; typically, the ovules develop into seeds, and the ovary into a fruit.

Palmate: with the lobes or divisions attached at a common point, like fingers on an outspread hand.

Panicle: a branched raceme.

Pappus: in Composites, the modified calyx of the florets, usually of hairs, bristles, plumes, scales, or the like.

Pedicel: the stalk of one flower in a flower cluster.

Peltate: a shield-shaped body with its stalk attached to the lower surface, not at the base or margin.

Perianth: the calyx and corolla together; used when there is no clear difference between sepals and petals, as in a Lily.

Persistent: not deciduous; remaining long attached to the plant (even after withering).

Petal: one unit of the corolla.

Petiole: leaf stalk.

Petiolule: the stalk of a leaflet.

Pinna: a leaflet or a primary division of a pinnate leaf.

Pinnate: feather-formed; with lobes or leaflets placed on each side of an axis.

Pistil: the female part of the flower; its basal ovary becomes a fruit; the terminal stigma is the pollen-receptor; the style connects the stigma with the ovary.

Procumbent: trailing or lying partly on the ground, but not rooting.

Raceme: a simple elongated stem bearing stalked flowers, the lower ones opening first.

Rachis: the main stalk or axis of a compound leaf.

Ray: a primary branch of an umbel or umbel-like flower cluster; in Composites, the corolla of a ray-flower.

Ray-flowers: florets of Composites in which the corolla is a short basal tube and an expanded blade, like a single petal of an ordinary flower.

Receptacle: the end of the stem bearing the flower parts.

Rhizome: an underground stem.

Saprophyte: a plant lacking chlorophyll, living on dead organic matter such as humus.

Scape: a leafless flower stalk arising from ground level; it may bear bracts or scales, and be one- or many-flowered.

Sepal: one unit of the calyx.

Sessile: not stalked.

Simple: unbranched, as a stem; not compound, as a leaf.

Spadix: a fleshy spike subtended or surrounded by a spathe.

Spathe: a bract or modified leaf subtending or surrounding a spadix or flower cluster, often colored and flowerlike.

Spike: a simple elongated stem bearing sessile flowers or heads, the lower opening first.

Stamen: a male flower part, typically consisting of a pollen-bearing anther and its stalk, or filament.

Staminode: a sterile stamen; at times showy and petal-like.

Standard: in Legumes, the upper broad erect petal of a flower in the Pea Subfamily.

Stellate: starlike; hairs with radiating branches.

Stigma: the pollen-receptor at the top of the pistil.

Stipel: a stipule of a leaflet.

Stipule: a basal appendage on the petiole, usually in pairs.

Style: the part of the pistil connecting stigma to ovary.

Subtend: to be just below and close up to or enclosed in its axil, as a bract might embrace a flower.

Ternate: arranged in or divided by three's.

Trifoliate: with three leaflets.

Tube-flowers: florets with tubular corollas, usually five-lobed or five-toothed at the tip, in the center of the heads of most Composites.

Umbel: a flower cluster in which the flower stalks arise from a common point, like the ribs of an umbrella.

Umbellet: a secondary umbel.

Whorled: three or more leaves (or flowers) at one node.

Wings: thin or flat extensions or appendages; in Legumes, the lateral petals of flowers in the Pea Subfamily.

CAT-TAIL FAMILY (TYPHACEAE)

TYPHA, a single genus, comprises the family. Perennials of shallow water, forming dense upright stands 6–12' high; tiny flowers in a dense cylindrical terminal spike; male flowers at the tip and soon shed; female below, forming a velvety sausage-like "cat-tail." There are 4 species in N.A. **Common Cat-tail** or **Reed Mace,** *T. latifolia,* of marshes, ditches, or ponds, grows throughout N.A. **Narrow-leaved Cat-tail** or **Nail-rod,** *T. angustifolia,* prefers alkaline water at low elevations; it ranges from e Canada to Ky., Neb., and cen. Calif.

BUR-REED FAMILY (SPARGANIACEAE)

BUR-REED (SPARGANIUM), the only genus. Aquatic plants, 3–5' tall; about 12 species in N.A. Flowers are tiny, in globular heads; upper heads male, lower heads female, developing into hardened beaked burs. *S. americanum* ranges from e Canada to s B.C., s to Ohio, Mo., Kans., Colo., and Utah; mainly e of the Cascades in Wash., Oreg., and Calif.

WATER-PLANTAIN FAMILY (ALISMATACEAE)

Aquatic herbs; lance-like or arrow-shaped leaf blades on long petioles that sheathe the stem at the base; flowers with 3 persistent sepals and 3 white or rosy deciduous petals.

WATER-PLANTAIN (ALISMA) Flowers in whorls of 4 or more at tips of a many-branched panicle; 4 species in N.A. *A. subcordatum* ranges over much of N.A.

FRINGED WATER-PLANTAIN (MACHAEROCARPUS), with a single species, *M. californicus;* grows in shallow water or mud, from se Oreg. to cen. Calif., e to se Ida. and w Nev.

BUR-HEAD (ECHINODORUS) Simple or somewhat branched flowering stems; flowers in whorls of 3–6 or more; fruit a bur; 3 species in N.A. *E. cordifolius* grows in quiet water, from nw Fla. to Tex., n to se Va., s Ind., Ill., Mo., and e Kans., and s from San Joaquin Valley in Calif.

ARROW-HEAD (SAGITTARIA) To 3' high; leaves lance-like or arrow-like; racemes with flowers in whorls of 3, the lower female, the upper male with many stamens; about 16 species in N.A. *S. latifolia* ranges from s Canada southward.

LOPHOTOCARPUS resembles *Sagittaria* but lower flowers are perfect; only 9–15 stamens; 3 species. *L. calycinus* grows from Mich. to S.D., s to Tex. and N.M.

Sparganium americanum

T. latifolia

Typha angustifolia

Echinodorus cordifolius

Sagittaria latifolia

Machaerocarpus californicus

Alisma subcordatum

Lophotocarpus calycinus

SEDGE FAMILY (CYPERACEAE)

Grasslike plants of moist ground; stems often 3-sided. Flowers tiny, ir heads; perianth lacking or of scales or bristles.

COTTON-GRASS (ERIOPHORUM) bears masses of white or tawny silk in the spikelets; about 15 species, chiefly boreal. **Slender Cotton-grass,** *E. gracile,* ranges from s Alaska to Lab., s to Del., Pa., Ill., Ia., Neb., Colo., Ida., and Calif.

WHITE-TOP SEDGE (DICHROMENA) Low tufted plant with the bracts resembling petals; 3 species in N.A. *D. colorata* ranges from se Tex. to Fla., n to se Va.

ARUM FAMILY (ARACEAE)

Plants of wet, damp, or shady places, with acrid or pungent juice. The flowers are crowded on a spadix subtended by a spathe.

SWEET FLAG (ACORUS) Rhizomes aromatic; leaves 2–6' long, less than 1" wide; spadix 2–4" long, the spathe leaflike. One species, *A. calamus,* grows from e Canada to Wash., s to Fla. and Tex.

JACK-IN-THE-PULPIT and **GREEN DRAGON** (ARISAEMA) Plants with 1–3 compound leaves; the spathe encircles the spadix below, flattens into a hood over it. In **Green Dragon,** *A. dracontium,* the leaf has 5–15 leaflets; spadix extends beyond the spathe; ranges from Fla. to se Tex., n to e Canada. Four species of **Jack-in-the-pulpit** are in N.A.; *A. triphyllum* grows from e Tex. to Ga., n to Ky., se N.Y., se Mass., and Conn.

ARROW-ARUM or **TUCKAHOE** (PELTANDRA) Spathe elongated and rolled, or flattened at tip; 2 species with many forms, from se Canada to Fla. *P. virginica* grows in n N.A.

WILD CALLA or **WATER-ARUM** (CALLA) prefers bogs and pond margins. One native species, *C. palustris,* grows from Nfld. to Alaska, s to N.J., Wisc., Minn., B.C., Colo., and n Calif.

SKUNK CABBAGE (SYMPLOCARPUS) One species, *S. foetidus,* of wet meadows or swampy woods; ranges from Que. to se Man., s to upland Ga., Tenn., W.Va., Ohio, Ind., cen. Ill., and Ia.

YELLOW SKUNK CABBAGE (LYSICHITON) One species, *L. americanum;* grows in swamps, from Alaska to Sta. Cruz Mts., Calif.

GOLDEN CLUB (ORONTIUM) One species, *O. aquaticum;* the spathe is rudimentary. In shallow water, from Fla. to La., n to W.Va., Mass.

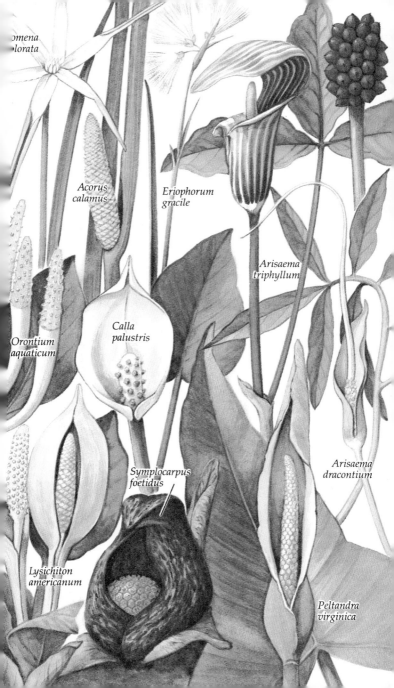

*...omena
...lorata*

*Acorus
calamus*

*Eriophorum
gracile*

*Arisaema
triphyllum*

*Orontium
aquaticum*

*Calla
palustris*

*Arisaema
dracontium*

*Symplocarpus
foetidus*

*Lysichiton
americanum*

*Peltandra
virginica*

BOG-MOSS FAMILY (MAYACACEAE)

BOG-MOSS (MAYACA) is the only genus. Low mosslike plants of wet places; flower parts in 3's; 2 species in N.A., both of the se Coastal Plain. *M. aubletti* grows from Fla. to Tex. and Ga.

YELLOW-EYED GRASS FAMILY (XYRIDACEAE)

Rushlike plants; leaves narrow, in basal tufts; flowers in a headlike spike on an unbranched scape; flower parts in 3's.

YELLOW-EYED GRASS (XYRIS), the only genus in N.A.; 19 species in damp or wet soils, mostly of se Coastal Plain, a few to e Canada and the Midwest. *X. baldwiniana* ranges from N.C. to n Fla. and Tex.; *X. torta*, Ga. to Ark., Tex., n to s N.Eng., upland W.Va., Ohio, Minn., Ia.

PIPEWORT FAMILY (ERIOCAULACEAE)

Low marsh plants with basal tufts of grasslike leaves; male or female florets mixed in dense heads on unbranched scapes.

PIPEWORT (ERIOCAULON) has white-bearded or woolly leaves; florets with 2–3 sepals and petals, 4 or 6 stamens. **White-buttons,** *E septangulare*, occurs in ne N.A.; several species are on the se Coastal Plain.

BOG-BUTTONS (LACHNOCAULON) Florets have 3 sepals, no petals, 3 stamens; 2 species, of se U.S. *L. anceps* inhabits low pine barrens and bogs, from Fla. to e Texas, n to se Va.

HATPINS (SYNGONANTHUS) Florets of 2–3 sepals and petals, males with 2–3 stamens. One species, *S. flavidulus*, in N.A., on the Coastal Plain, N.C. to Ga. and Fla.

PINEAPPLE FAMILY (BROMELIACEAE)

Mostly epiphytes with stiff whorls of leaves; flowers are usually in dense heads or panicles with showy colored bracts. Four genera in s U.S.

AIR-PINE (TILLANDSIA) About 12 species in N.A., mostly in Fla. **Wild-pine,** *T. fasciculata*, is common on cypress in s Fla. **Needle-leaved Wild-pine,** *T. setacea*, is abundant in s Ga. and Fla. **Ball-moss,** *T. recurvata*, grows on wire fences and telephone lines as well as on trees, from Fla. to se Ariz. *T. pruinosa*, less than 6" tall, with its leaves covered by hoary scales, grows on deciduous trees in s Fla. **Spanish Moss,** *T. usneoides*, the least typical species, ranges from Fla. to Tex., n on the Coastal Plain to e Va.

Mayaca aubletti

Xyris baldwiniana

Xyris torta

Eriocaulon septangulare

Lachnocaulon anceps

Syngonanthus flavidulus

Tillandsia usneoides

Tillandsia fasciculata

Tillandsia pruinosa

Tillandsia recurvata

Tillandsia setacea

SPIDERWORT FAMILY (COMMELINACEAE)

Stems knotty and succulent, sheathed by the bases of the simple alte[r]nate leaves; flowers have 3 sepals, 3 petals (free or in a tube), 6 or few[er] stamens. Six genera in N.A.

DAY-FLOWER (COMMELINA) Stems becoming prostrate, rooting a[t] the nodes; flowers with 2 broad and 1 reduced petal, 3 stamens, withe[r] about noon; 8 species in e and s U.S. **Hierba del Pollo,** *C. erecta,* range[s] from Fla. to Tex. and Ariz., n to s Ill., Mo., Neb., and se N.Y.

SPIDERWORT (TRADESCANTIA) Usually 2–3' tall, flowers in um[-] bels, petals all alike. About 21 species in e and s U.S. **Common Spider-wort,** *T. virginiana,* native to meadows, roadsides, and woods, fron[m] Conn. to Wisc., s to nw Ga., Tenn., and Mo.; often cultivated an[d] escaped elsewhere. *T. rosea* inhabits sandy barrens and woods, from n[w] Fla. n to se Va.

ANEILEMA resembles *Commelina,* but the flowers have 3 equal petals[.] *A. nudiflorum* ranges from s Tex. to Ga. and Fla.

WIDOW'S-TEARS or **FALSE DAY-FLOWER** (COMMELINANTIA) ha[s] 2 broad and 1 reduced petal, 6 stamens. One species in N.A., C[.] *anomala,* grows on the Edwards Plateau of cen. Tex.

PICKERELWEED FAMILY (PONTEDERIACEAE)

Aquatic plants with alternate leaves that sheathe the stem; flowers single or in spikes or panicles, the 3 sepals and petals alike, 3 or 6 stamens. Four genera in N.A.

WATER-HYACINTH (EICHORNIA) From S.A.; floats in quiet water on inflated petioles. *E. crassipes* is established from Fla. to Tex., n to Va. and Mo.; also in s Calif.

WATER-PLANTAIN (HETERANTHERA) Grows submerged, floating or anchored in mud; 4 species in N.A. **Mud-plantain,** *H. limosa,* ranges from Fla. to Ariz., n to Colo., Neb., Minn., and Ky.; **Water-stargrass,** *H. dubia,* from sw Que. to Oreg., s to Mexico, Ariz., and Fla.

PICKERELWEED (PONTEDERIA) Stout plants to 3' high, with spikes of funnel-like 2-lipped flowers. *P. cordata* is common from Que. to Fla., w to Mo., Okla., and Tex.

EURYSTEMON, with a single species, *E. mexicanum,* to 16" tall; grows in mud in s and nw Tex.

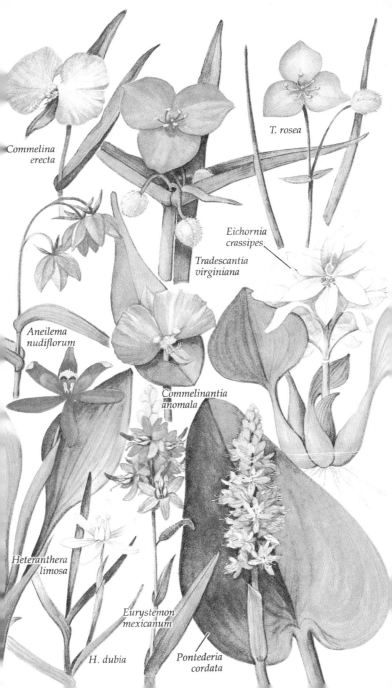

Commelina erecta

T. rosea

Eichornia crassipes

Tradescantia virginiana

Aneilema nudiflorum

Commelinantia anomala

Heteranthera limosa

Eurystemon mexicanum

H. dubia

Pontederia cordata

LILY FAMILY (LILIACEAE)

A large family with 58 genera in N.A. Perennials, withering afte:
flowering to a bulb or crown of fleshy roots. Flowers showy; usuall:
6 but sometimes 2 or 3 perianth parts, all alike; 6 stamens and a 3
celled ovary. In a few genera, flowers are small but borne in dens:
inflorescences.

BOG-ASPHODEL (NARTHECIUM) Inhabits marshy ground; 3 spe
cies in N.A. *N. californicum* grows in the Sierra Nevada and n Coas:
Ranges of Calif., n to sw Oreg.; **Yellow-asphodel,** *N. americanum* (no:
shown), on the Coastal Plain, from N.J. to S.C.; **Mountain-asphodel**
N. montanum (not shown), only in the Blue Ridge of N.C.

TURKEY-BEARD (XEROPHYLLUM) A tuft of narrow stiff 6" leaves,
central stalk 1–5' tall bears needle-like bracts and a dense floral raceme
X. asphodeloides grows in sandy pinelands, N.J. to se N.C., and in
mountain woods, Va. to Tenn. and Ga. **Elk-grass,** *X. tenax,* is found on
dry open ridges or meadow borders in the mountains, from n half of
Calif., n to B.C. and Mont., e to Yellowstone Park.

SWAMP-PINK (HELONIAS), with 1 species, *H. bullata,* bears many
flat evergreen leaves from a tuberous rhizome. In early spring a stout
hollow bract-bearing 1–2' scape develops, topped by a short dense
raceme. Grows in swamps and bogs, Staten I., N.Y., to e Va.; in mountains from Pa. to nw Ga.

BLAZING-STAR or **DEVIL'S-BIT** (CHAMAELIRIUM) Flat lance-like
or spatulate leaves; a short erect stem bearing a 4–12" raceme of small
flowers; male and female flowers borne on separate plants, the female
plants leafier. Only 1 species, *C. luteum;* grows in meadows and woodlands, from Fla. to Ark., n to w Mass., N.Y., s Ont., Ohio, Mich., and
Ill.

FALSE ASPHODEL (TOFIELDIA) Tufts of grasslike leaves and simple
stems, leafy at the base; flowers in racemes or spikes. About 6 species
in cooler N.A. *T. glutinosa*, the most widespread, has pedicels glutinous
from dark glands; ranges from Alaska s to Calif., e to the Atl. Coast, s
to Wyo., Ida., Mont., Minn., Ohio, Ind., Ill., N.Eng., and in the Appalachians to n Ga.

FLY-POISON (AMIANTHIUM) One species, *M. muscaetoxicum*, which
is poisonous; white flowers, becoming green or purplish with age.
Grows from Fla. to s Mo. and Okla., n in the mountains to W.Va. and
Pa., and on the Coastal Plain to L.I., N.Y.

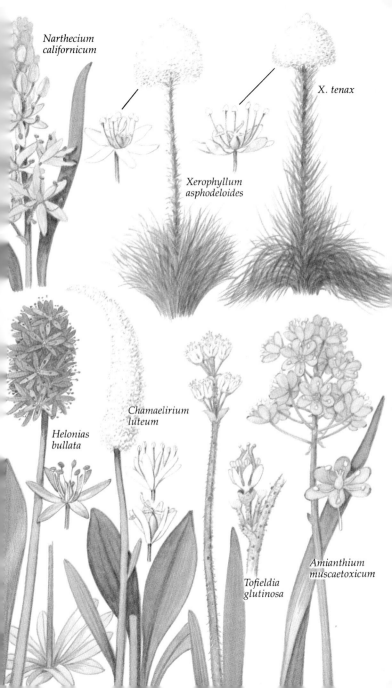

Narthecium californicum

Xerophyllum asphodeloides

X. tenax

Helonias bullata

Chamaelirium luteum

Tofieldia glutinosa

Amianthium muscaetoxicum

FEATHERBELLS (STENANTHIUM) A sheathed bulbous base; 2–4 basal leaves; an erect leafy stem to 6' with a long panicle of flowers in compound racemes; 2 species in N.A., the flowers of both varying from white or greenish-yellow to bronze-purple. *S. gramineum* grows in moist soil, from nw Pa. to Ill. and Mo., s to se Va., upland to nw Fla. **Western Featherbells,** *S. occidentale,* grows on mossy stream banks from B.C. to n Calif., e to Alta., Mont., and Ida.

DEATH CAMASS (ZIGADENUS) Leafy stems from bulbs or rhizomes; large panicles or racemes of white to yellow, green, or bronze flowers, the perianth segments with a gland near the base; all parts poisonous. 14 species in N.A., widespread. **Death Camass,** *Z. nuttallii,* inhabit prairies and limestone, from Tenn. to Kans. and Tex. **White Camass** or **Alkali Grass,** *Z. elegans,* of similar habitats, grows from Alaska to Ariz. and Tex., e to Man., Minn., Ia., and Mo.

CRAG-LILY or **AMBER LILY** (ANTHERICUM) A tuft of grasslike leaves from thick fleshy roots; stem 1–3', with simple or compound racemes; 2 species, in Tex. and sw U.S. *A. torreyi* grows in canyons and on rocky hills, from cen. Tex. to Ariz.

FEATHER-SHANK (SCHOENOCAULON) Plant base with blackish fibers and scales; leaves all basal, keeled, grasslike, with toothed margins; the unbranched scape with a simple flower spike; 3 species, in s and sw U.S. *S. dubium* grows in pinelands on the Coastal Plain, Ga. and Fla. **Green Lily,** *S. drummondii,* is found in sandy or gravelly areas in cen. and s-cen. Tex.

BUNCHFLOWER (MELANTHIUM) Leafy plants 2½–6' tall, from a thick root; upper stem and panicle scurfy; flowers ivory or greenish, aging to purplish or black; stamens attached to the stalklike base of the sepals and petals; 2 species, in e and se U.S. *M. virginicum* grows in meadows, savannas, and thickets, from n Fla. to e Tex., n to s N.Y., Ohio, Ind., Ill., and Ia.

FALSE HELLEBORE (VERATRUM) Like *Melanthium* but leaves 3-ranked and plaited on the stem, stamens not attached to the perianth. Seven species, mostly poisonous, in the cooler parts of N.A. **False White Hellebore,** *V. viride,* grows in moist ground, from Alaska s to n Oreg., e to Rocky Mts. from B.C. and Alta. to Mont. and Ida. and from Que. to Minn., s in the Appalachians to n Ga. **Corn-lily,** *V. californicum,* grows on wet flats and meadows and around springs, from Wash. to Mont., s in the mountains to N.M., Ariz., and Calif.

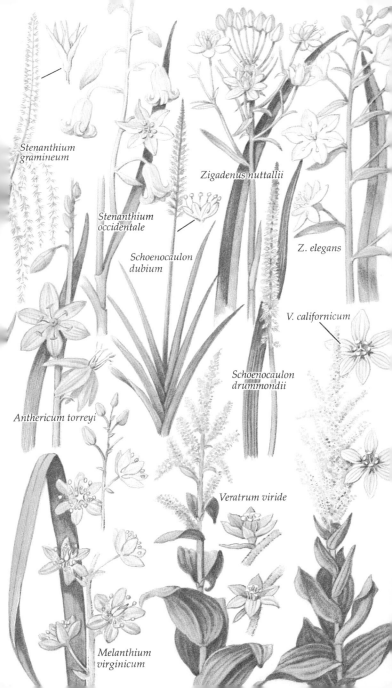

*Stenanthium
gramineum*

*Stenanthium
occidentale*

Zigadenus nuttallii

Z. elegans

*Schoenocaulon
dubium*

V. californicum

*Schoenocaulon
drummondii*

Anthericum torreyi

Veratrum viride

*Melanthium
virginicum*

ONION, GARLIC, and **LEEK** (ALLIUM) Leaves basal, linear, solid or hollow, from a coated bulb; flowers on slim unjointed stalks in a simple umbel on a solid or hollow scape; some or all flowers occasionally replaced by bulblets. The umbel is first enclosed in a 2- or 3-valved spathe, which opens at flowering but remains attached. Leaves give onion or garlic odor if bruised. About 80 species in N.A., widespread.

Nodding Onion, *A. cernuum,* has soft channeled leaves, the margins smooth or toothed. It grows on ledges, gravels, rocky or wooded slopes in mts. or cool regions almost throughout N.A.

Wild Garlic, *A. canadense,* has few flowers; most are replaced by bulblets, which may bear secondary umbels, and in meadows, from Fla. to Tex., n to N.B., s Que., s Ont., Wisc., and Minn.

Yellow-flowered Onion, *A. coryi,* has bulbs of a single fleshy bulb-scale, tasting mildly of garlic. Endemic on rocky slopes and plains in mountains of the Trans-Pecos, Tex.

Crinkled Onion, *A. crispum,* grows in heavy soil of the inner s Coast Ranges, s to Santa Barbara Co. and in the foothills of the Sierra Nevada in Kern Co., Calif.

Wild Onion, *A. stellatum,* is similar to *A. cernuum* in appearance but holds the umbel erect. On rocky prairies, slopes, shores, and ridges, Ohio to Sask., s to Ill., Mo., Kans., and Tex.

BRODIAEA, about 37 species, all of w N.A., has scaly deep-seated corms, 1–5 elongated linear leaves, the scape terminating in a headlike or open umbel. Flowers with jointed pedicels; petals and sepals joined to form a tube up to half their length; 6 stamens, or the 3 alternates reduced. Leaves may appear before the scape, withering at flowering.

Harvest Brodiaea, *B. coronaria,* usually grows in heavy soils on prairies, slopes, and rocky bluffs, from w B.C. to the Mexican border, w of the Cascades and the Sierra Nevada.

Blue-dicks, *B. pulchella,* with very short pedicels, flowers in a headlike umbel. On mesas and open slopes, from w Wash., s to Baja Calif., e to Utah and Ariz.

Snake-lily, *B. volubilis,* is the only twining *Brodiaea*; the 2–8' scape climbs on bushes. The pedicels, to 2" long, often droop when in bud, often curve upward after the flower opens. On bushy or open slopes, inner n Coast Ranges; cen. Sierra Nevada, Calif.

Pretty-face, *B. lutea,* is variable in height, 6–30", and in color, from ivory to pale yellow or gold. Grows in sand or loam, s Coast Ranges, Calif., and the Sierra Nevada to s Oreg.

B. hyacinthina, from 1–2' tall, has white or blue petals and sepals with green midribs, the tube very short. On grassy or rocky open flats or mt. meadows, s B.C. southward, e to Ida. and e Oreg.

A. canadense

A. coryi

Allium cernuum

A. crispum

A. stellatum

Brodiaea coronaria

B. pulchella

B. volubilis

B. lutea

B. hyacinthina

GOLDEN-STARS (BLOOMERIA) Resembles *Brodiaea* but has 2-toothed hairy appendage at base of each stamen, fused into a little cup; 2 species in s Calif. **Common Golden-stars,** *B. crocea*, ranges from Monterey Co to Baja Calif.

FALSE GARLIC (NOTHOSCORDUM) Plants resemble *Allium* but are odorless. Three species in N.A. *N. bivalve*, with 12- to 16-flowered umbel, grows in sandy woods, prairies, Fla. to Tex., n to Va., s Ohio Ind., s Ill., and Neb.

BELLWORT (UVULARIA) Leafy stem, 20–30″, from a rhizome; leaves sessile or stem appearing to pass through them; 6 species in e N.A. *U perfoliata* inhabits open woods or clearings, from Mass. and s Vt. to s Ont., s to n Fla., Ala., Miss, and n La.

FIRE-CRACKER FLOWER (BREVOORTIA) Herb with 2–3 grasslike leaves from a corm; scape 1–3′, bears an umbel of 5–20 nodding flowers 1″ long; 2 species, both of Pac. Coast. *B. ida-maia* grows in sw Oreg. and nw Calif.

MARIPOSA-LILY, STAR-TULIP, or **GLOBE-TULIP** (CALOCHOR-TUS) has 46 species in w and sw U.S. Umbel with few or solitary flowers on a simple or branched stem; sepals and petals not alike—the 3 sepals narrow, the petals broad with a depressed gland, often hairy, near the base.

Desert Mariposa, *C. kennedyi*, has bright red, orange, or yellow petals, with purple or black markings at the base; the gland is circled by a ciliated membrane. In dry soil, from Ariz. to s Nev., se Calif.

Purple Globe-tulip or **Purple Lantern,** *C. amoenus*, has deep pink petals that become purple with age. Flowers nodding or held erect. Grows on the foothills of the w side of the s Sierra Nevada in Calif.

Cat's-ear, Beavertail-grass, or **Blue Star-tulip,** *C. caeruleus*, has white petals tinged with blue, bearing pale blue hairs. On wooded slopes of the inner n Coast Ranges s to Lake Co., w Sierra Nevada s to Placer Co., and in the Greenhorn Mts., Kern Co., Calif.

Dwarf Star-tulip, *C. elegans*, has 2–6″ scapes bearing 1–2 flowers, rarely up to 7 flowers. On shaded or open grassy slopes, se Wash. and ne Oreg. to mts. of cen. Ida. and w Mont.; and mts. of sw Oreg. and n Calif.

San Luis Obispo Mariposa, *C. obispoensis*, 1–2′ tall, has the most extraordinary flower form in the genus. It grows on rocky hillsides of the s Coast Ranges, principally in San Luis Obispo Co., Calif.

Sego Lily, *C. nuttallii*, varies in color, from white, to pale lilac with green midribs, to rose-violet, or yellow. On dry soils, open pine-lands, mesas, or slopes, e and sw Mont. to w N.D., s to e Calif., n Ariz., n N.M., and w Neb.

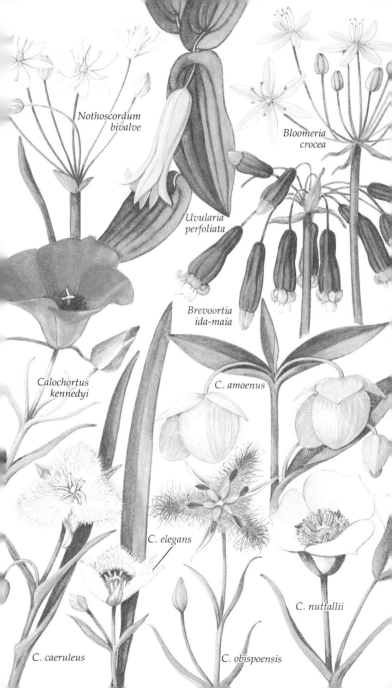

Nothoscordum bivalve

Bloomeria crocea

Uvularia perfoliata

Brevoortia ida-maia

Calochortus kennedyi

C. amoenus

C. elegans

C. nuttallii

C. caeruleus

C. obispoensis

LILY (LILIUM) Plants with unbranched leafy stems rising from fleshy scaled bulbs or scaly rhizomes; leaves sessile, alternate to whorled; showy flowers, solitary or clustered in an open terminal raceme. Flowers are funnel-form or bell-shaped; petals and sepals alike, separate, deciduous, each with a nectar groove at the base; 6 stamens; pistil with a long style and 3-lobed stigma. About 25 species in N.A.

Thimble Lily, *L. bolanderi,* has stems to 3½', broadly ovate or lance-like leaves in whorls; 2 to many nodding to horizontal flowers. Dry hills or wet places, s Oreg. to Humboldt Co., Calif.

Alpine Lily or **Small Tiger Lily,** *L. parvum,* 1–3' tall, has leaves in a few whorls or spread along the stem. It grows about mountain springs and streams, s Oreg., s through the Sierra Nevada.

Chaparral Lily, *L. rubescens,* has 2–5' stems, upper leaves in whorls of 3–7. Flowers white or pale lilac, aging to rose-purple with brown dots. Wooded slopes, s Oreg., s to Marin and Lake Co., Calif.

Turk's-cap Lily, *L. superbum,* has 3–8' green-purple stems, the upper leaves in whorls of 3–8; many nodding flowers. In peaty meadows, swales, swampy woods, Ga. and Ala., n to se N.H., Mass., N.Y.

Tiger Lily, *L. tigrinum,* is 2–6' tall with narrow leaves crowded on the stem. Few to many nodding flowers, spotted with black. Native to Asia, it has escaped N.Eng. to N.D., s to Va.

Washington Lily, *L. washingtonianum,* 2–5', has 5 or 6 whorls of 6–12 leaves; 2–20 flowers, aging to purplish, dotted. Grows in chaparral or openings, sw Oreg., s throughout Cascades and Sierra Nevada.

Field Lily or **Canada Lily,** *L. canadense,* 2–7' reddish-green stems; 1–20 yellow, orange, or red flowers, with dark spots. In meadows, damp woods, thickets, Minn. to Que., s upland to Va. and Ala.

Leopard Lily or **Pine Lily,** *L. catesbaei,* 1–3', leaves scattered on the stem, diminishing upward; usually a single erect flower. In damp pinelands, bogs, or swamps, Fla. to La., n to s Ill. and se Va.

Columbia Lily, *L. columbianum,* 2–4', leaves whorled to scattered on the stem; flowers 2–20 (rarely 1); in meadows, open woods, coniferous forests, s B.C., s in the Cascades to n Calif., e to n Ida., Nev.

Gray's Lily or **Roan Lily,** *L. grayi,* 1½–3', with 3–6 whorls of 3–9 leaves each; 1–4 flowers, horizontal to nodding. In meadows, swamps, and low woods in the mts. of Va., N.C., and Tenn.

Panther Lily, *L. pardalinum,* 1–7'; leaves in whorls of 9–15, fewer above, rarely scattered; flowers few to many, on long pedicels. In moist areas, Coast Ranges and Sierra Nevada, n to s Oreg.

Wood Lily, *L. philadelphicum,* 1–3' tall; 2–6 whorls of leaves plus a few scattered ones; 1–5 flowers, erect, yellow to brick red. In meadows, woods, B.C. to Me., s in mts. or uplands to N.M., Ariz., Neb., Ky., and N.C.

Lilium bolanderi

L. rubescens

L. parvum

L. superbum

L. tigrinum

L. washingtonianum

L. columbianum

L. canadense

L. catesbaei

L. philadelphicum

L. grayi

L. pardalinum

DAY-LILY (HEMEROCALLIS) Lilylike 5" flowers along a 2–6' scape; perianth bases joined in a tube, with 6 stamens attached to its throat; stigma unlobed. Each flower withers after opening for 1 day. Eurasian; 2 species escaped in N.A. **Tawny Day-lily,** *H. fulva,* occurs along roadsides, edges of fields, Fla. to Tex., n to Va., s Ohio, Ind., Ill., and Neb.

CHLOROGALUM has long narrow leaves with wavy margins, rising from a coated bulb; scape with a terminal raceme of flowers 2" wide or less; 5 species, 4 confined to cen. and n Calif. **Soap-plant** or **Amole,** *C. pomeridianum,* the most widespread, produces nocturnal flowers on 2–9' scapes; the bulb contains a saponin used by early settlers for shampoo. Grows on open valleys and foothills, s Oreg. to s Calif.

ALP-LILY (LLOYDIA) One species, *L. serotina,* in N.A. Plant 2–6" tall from short rhizome; bulblike base from dry brownish bracts, basal leaves stringy; flowering stem with 2–4 shorter leaves; single or few flowers in an open terminal raceme. Gravelly ridges, rock crevices, Alaska, s in mountains to nw Oreg., e to Alta., s to N.M. and Nev.

DOG'S-TOOTH-VIOLET, ADDER'S-TONGUE, or **FAWN-LILY** (ERYTHRONIUM) Plants nearly stemless, with 2 flat leaves tapering to petioles that sheathe the base of the scape. Flowers single or 2–5; the 3 petals often with a callous tooth at each side of the base. About 18 N.A. species. **White Dog's-tooth-violet,** *E. albidum,* grows in woods and thickets, from s Ont. to Minn., s to Ga., Ky., Mo., Okla., and ne Tex. **Yellow Fawn-lily,** *E. grandiflorum,* grows in open mountain forests, B.C. to n Calif., e to Mont. and Utah. **Alpine Fawn-lily** or **Avalanche Lily,** *E. montanum,* is found in subalpine and alpine forests and meadows, from s B.C. to n Oreg.

FRITILLARY (FRITILLARIA) Unbranched stems from small bulbs; leaves alternate to whorled; flowers single to few, nodding; sepals and petals free, alike, bearing glands near the base; about 19 species, in w N.A.

Purple Fritillary, *F. atropurpurea,* to 2' tall; on slopes, ridges, in forests, mts., se Oreg. to N.D., s to Ariz., N.M.

Scarlet Fritillary, *F. recurva,* is in open chaparral or woods, s Oreg. to cen. Calif. in the Coast Ranges and Sierra Nevada.

Kamchatka Fritillary, *F. camtschatcensis,* to 2' tall, likes moist soil. In coastal Alaska s to n Wash.

Siskiyou Fritillary, *F. glauca,* 1–3' tall with yellow-green or red-purple flowers; grows on barren slopes, s Oreg. and n Calif.

Hemerocallis fulva

Chlorogalum pomeridianum

Erythronium albidum

E. grandiflorum

E. montanum

Lloydia serotina

Fritillaria atropurpurea

F. recurva

F. glauca

F. camtschatcensis

ODONTOSTOMUM is 1–3′ tall, with racemes of 1″ flowers. The perianth segments are tubular half their length; 6 fertile stamens, 6 infertile. Only 1 species, *O. hartwegii;* on dry hillsides, Sacramento and n Napa valleys, Calif.

ANDROSTEPHIUM, with 2 species, has scapes to 1′ tall, flowers 1–2″ wide, in an umbel; perianth segments fused for half their length; filaments fused in a crown, 6 fertile stamens. *A. breviflorum,* with white to violet flowers, grows in sandy soil, from sw Colo. to s Utah, n Ariz., and se Calif.

DESERT LILY (HESPEROCALLIS) Wavy-edged leaves, 1–4′ stem, raceme of 2″-long flowers. One species, *H. undulata,* in N.A.; on sandy soil of deserts, sw Ariz. and se Calif.

SAND LILY (LEUCOCRINUM) is stemless: the pedicels originate underground. Flowers fragrant, tubular at base, with 6 stamens. One species, *L. montanum;* its habitat varies from sagebrush desert to mountain forest, in sandy to heavy soil, from Oreg. to Mont. and S.D., s to n Calif., Neb., and in the Rocky Mts. at lower elevations to N.M.

EREMOCRINUM, with 1 species, *E. albomarginatum,* produces a dense 12″ raceme from a tuft of long narrow white-edged leaves. Grows in sandy soil, s Utah and n Ariz.

MEXICAN STAR (MILLA) One species, *M. biflora.* Leafless stem to 30″, with 1–6 fragrant flowers, funnel-form at the base. In mts., w Tex. to n N.M., Ariz., s to Oaxaca.

CAMASS (CAMASSIA) Scape and linear leaves from a coated bulb; racemes unbranched, to 28″ tall, a bract below each flower; 5 species in N.A. **Common Camass,** *C. quamash,* prefers moist mountain meadows, B.C. to Mont., Utah, and the Coast Ranges, n Calif. **Wild Hyacinth,** *C. scilloides,* grows in low fields, open woods, meadows, s Ont. to s Wisc., s and sw to Ala. and Tex.

STAR-OF-BETHLEHEM (ORNITHOGALUM) Scape and narrow channeled leaves from a coated bulb; racemes unbranched, bracted. Native to Europe; 2 species escaped in N.A. **Nap-at-noon,** *O. umbellatum,* inhabits roadsides, grasslands, thickets, Nfld. to Ont. and Neb., s to N.C., Miss., Mo., and Kans.

GRAPE HYACINTH (MUSCARI) is European; 3 species are escapes in N.A. They have dense racemes of globular flowers. *M. botryoides* is locally abundant, N.Eng. to Minn., s to Va., Mo., and Kans.

*Hesperocallis
undulata*

*Odontostomum
hartwegii*

*Androstephium
breviflorum*

ucocrinum
montanum

*Camassia
scilloides*

*Camassia
quamash*

*Eremocrinum
albomarginatum*

*Milla
biflora*

*Muscari
botryoides*

*Ornithogalum
umbellatum*

CLINTONIA A few broad leaves, 1 to few bell-like flowers; 4 species, 2 in e N.A., 2 in w N.A. **Corn-lily,** *C. borealis,* has leaves to 1' long, scapes longer than leaves, umbels of 2–8 flowers; grows in woods, up to subalpine meadows, Lab. to Man., s to Minn., Wisc., Mich., N.Eng., mts. of Tenn. and Ga. **Queen Cup,** *C. uniflora,* has scapes shorter than leaves, 1–2 flowers; grows in moist areas, coniferous forests, Alaska s to Calif., e to Alta., Mont., Ida., and e Oreg.

FALSE SOLOMON'S-SEAL (SMILACINA) Stems unbranched, leaves alternate, mostly sessile; flowers fragrant, in terminal panicles or racemes. Five species in N.A. *S. stellata* grows from moist woods and stream banks to rocky exposed hillsides, Alaska to Nfld., s to Calif., Ariz., N.M., Kans., e to Va.

WILD LILY-OF-THE-VALLEY (MAIANTHEMUM) To 1' tall; 1–2 heart-shaped leaves; tiny sweet-scented flowers in terminal racemes or panicles; perianth in 4 parts; 4 stamens; 2 species in N.A. *M. canadense* inhabits woods and clearings up to subalpine areas, Lab. to Man., s to. Ga. and Ia.

FETID ADDER'S-TONGUE (SCOLIOPUS) Less than 1'; 2 broad basal leaves; a few-flowered stemless umbel, ill-scented flowers on long stalks. Sepals 3, broad; petals 3, erect, linear; stamens 3; 2 species, in nw U.S. **Slink-pod,** *S. bigelovii,* grows on moist slopes among redwoods, n Coast Ranges, Calif.

MANDARIN (DISPORUM) Downy plants, stems simple or few-branched, leaves sessile; flowers hanging, single or in few-flowered umbels; 5 species in N.A. **Yellow Mandarin,** *D. languinosum,* grows in rich woods, w N.Y., s Ont., s to Ga., Ala., and Tenn.; **Fairy Bells,** *D. hookeri,* on shaded wooded slopes, from B.C. s to cen. Calif., e to Alta., n Ida., and w Mont.

TWISTED-STALK or **MANDARIN** (STREPTOPUS) Plants not downy, similar to *Disporum;* flowers hanging singly or in 2's on bent or twisted stalks; 4 species in the cooler parts of N.A. **White Mandarin,** *S. amplexifolius,* grows in moist woods, Alaska to Lab., s to Calif., e through most of Canada and the U.S. **Rose Mandarin,** *S. roseus,* is found in mt. woods, Alaska s to Oreg., e across s Canada and n U.S. to N.J., s in mts. to Ga.

SOLOMON'S-SEAL (POLYGONATUM) Stems bare below, leafy above; flowers nodding, pedicels jointed; 4 species, mostly e of the Great Plains, 1 in sw U.S. *P. biflorum* grows in dry or moist woods, from Fla. to Tex., n to Conn., s Ont., Ill., Ia., and Neb.

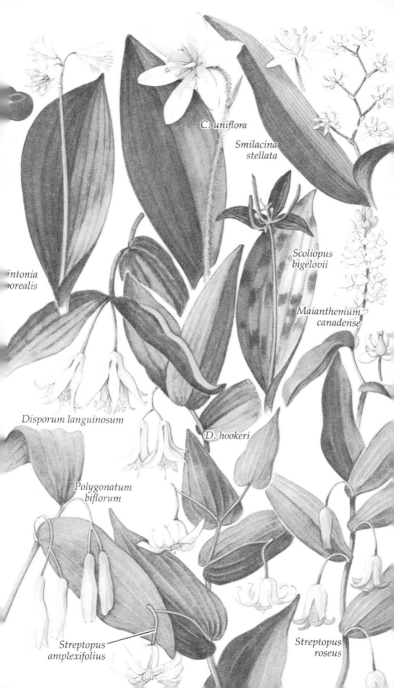

C. uniflora

Smilacina stellata

Clintonia borealis

Scoliopus bigelovii

Maianthemum canadense

Disporum languinosum

D. hookeri

Polygonatum biflorum

Streptopus amplexifolius

Streptopus roseus

RUSH-FEATHERLING (PLEEA) One species, *P. tenuifolia*. Scapes 1–2' tall; leaves grasslike, 6–12" long; ¾" flowers in a 6" spike, perianth parts alike, stamens 9. Rare, in moist open sandy areas, Coastal Plain, se N.C. to Fla.

LILY-OF-THE-VALLEY (CONVALLARIA) Stemless plants with 2–3 leaves; scape tilted, with a 1-sided raceme of sweet-scented flowers; 2 species. *C. majalis* (not shown) is European, escaped in N.A.; it forms dense clumps. **Native Lily-of-the-valley**, *C. montana*, is not colonial; it grows in woods or on slopes, mountains of Va. and W.Va. to n Ga. and e Tenn.

INDIAN CUCUMBER-ROOT (MEDEOLA) One species, *M. virginiana*. Stems to 3' high, simple, with deciduous wool, rising from a white cucumber-flavored tuber; a whorl of 5–9 leaves at the middle, another of 3 much smaller leaves at the top, with a sessile umbel of nodding flowers. Perianth parts alike, recurved; 3 threadlike stigmas. Inhabits rich woods, from Que. to Minn., s to Fla. and La.

TRILLIUM Low plants with a simple stout stem, a whorl of 3 leaves, and a large terminal flower, the flower parts in 3's. About 26 species, in the temperate wooded areas of N.A.

Nodding Trillium, *T. cernuum*, ranges from Nfld. to Wisc., s to Md., Pa., Ohio, Ind., Ill., and Ia., upland to W.Va. and Ga.

Giant Trillium, *T. chloropetalum*, grows in moist woods, w Wash., w of Cascades, and Willamette Valley, Oreg., to cen. Calif.

Stinking Benjamin or **Squaw-root**, *T. erectum*, with ill-scented flowers, likes rich woods, ne N.A., upland to Ga. and Tenn.

Large White Trillium, *T. grandiflorum*, ranges from Ga. to Ark., n to w Me., w N.H., s Que., s Ont., Mich., Wisc., and Minn.

Painted Trillium, *T. undulatum*, of acid woods and swamps, from Que. to e Man., s to n N.J., Pa., W.Va., Mich., Wisc., and Ga.

COLIC-ROOT (ALETRIS) Stemless plants from a thick bitter rhizome; leaves in a basal rosette; the ½" flowers in a spike-like raceme on scapes to 3' tall; perianth tubular, 6-toothed, mealy in texture; 4 species in e N.A. **Miller's-maid** or **Unicorn-root**, *A. farinosa*, grows in dry or moist peat, sand, or gravel, from Fla. to Tex., n to s Ont., and Me.

CAT-BRIER or **GREEN-BRIER** (SMILAX) A genus of prickly woody vines with tendrils; 5 herbaceous species in N.A. **Carrion-flower** or **Jacob's-ladder**, *S. herbacea*, has umbels of 20–100 or more carrion-scented flowers; grows in rich woods and meadows, w N.B. to Man., s to Mo., Va., upland to Ga. and Ala.

*Pleea
tenuifolia*

*Convallaria
montana*

*Medeola
virginiana*

rillium cernuum

T. erectum

T. chloropetalum

T. grandiflorum

*Aletris
farinosa*

T. undulatum

*Smilax
herbacea*

SPANISH-BAYONET or **BEARGRASS** (YUCCA) Leaves spine-tipped, large panicles of showy flowers; 38 species in arid N.A., many with woody trunks. **Blue Yucca,** *Y. baccata*, forms low dense clumps; ranges from sw Tex. to se Calif., n to sw Colo., s Utah, s Nev.

NOLINA Like *Yucca* but leaf margins may be spiny; panicle branches subtended by long bracts; 10 species in s U.S. **Sachuista,** *N. microcarpa*, grows from w Tex. to Ariz.

RED-FLOWERED YUCCA (HESPERALOE) A flowering stem to 8' high; basal leaves to 4' long, 1" wide, with thready edges. One species, *H. parviflora*, grows in the U.S., in cen. Tex.

AMARYLLIS FAMILY (AMARYLLIDACEAE)

Perennials from bulbs, corms, or rhizomes; leaves narrow, entire; flowers on a scape, 6 perianth parts, usually 6 stamens, 3-celled ovary, 3-lobed stigma. Eleven genera in N.A.

CENTURY-PLANT (AGAVE) is a rosette of succulent spiny leaves, flowering once after 8–20 years; 26 species in s U.S. **Utah Agave,** *A. utahensis*, ranges from s Utah to se Calif.

ZEPYHR-LILY (ZEPHYRANTHES) Grasslike leaves from a coated bulb; scape hollow, 1-flowered; flowers funnel-form; 6 species in se N.A. **Atamasco-lily,** *Z. atamasco*, grows in rich woods and damp clearings, from Fla. to Miss., n to Va.

RAIN-LILY (COOPERIA) Like *Zephyranthes* but is night-blooming; the sweet-scented flowers open in the afternoon or evening. Five species, ranging from N.M. to La., n to Kans. *C. drummondii*, the most widespread, covers the entire range.

STAR-GRASS (HYPOXIS) Small herbs with grassy hairy leaves and few-flowered scapes; perianth tubular, hairy outside. Nine species in e and s N.A. **Yellow Star-grass,** *H. hirsuta*, grows in open woods and meadows, Fla. to Tex., n to Man. and Me.

SWAMP-LILY (CRINUM) Straplike basal leaves from a necked bulb; scape solid, to 3' high, topped by an umbel of short-stalked flowers. Four species in se U.S. *C. americanum* grows in wet places on the Coastal Plain, Fla. to Tex.

SPIDER-LILY (HYMENOCALLIS) Like *Crinum* but flowers have a showy cup, or corona, connecting the bases of the filaments; 7 species in se U.S. *H. caroliniana* grows in wet areas from Ga. to Tex., n to Ky., Mo., and Ark.

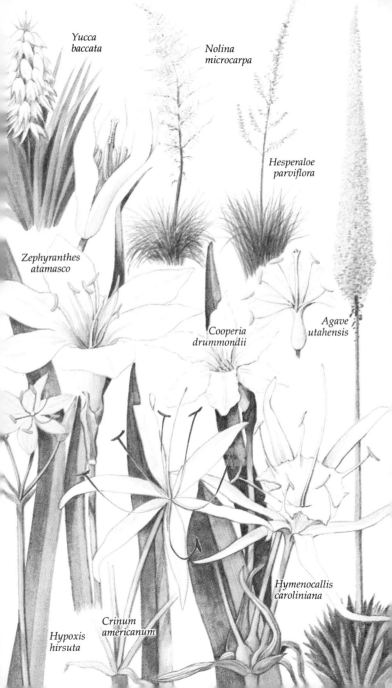

Yucca baccata

Nolina microcarpa

Hesperaloe parviflora

Zephyranthes atamasco

Cooperia drummondii

Agave utahensis

Hymenocallis caroliniana

Crinum americanum

Hypoxis hirsuta

IRIS FAMILY (IRIDACEAE)

Herbs with leafy stems; leaves linear, 2-ranked, folded lengthwise astride the stem. Flower parts in 3's, the sepals petal-like; the style may be simple or 3- or 6-cleft, petal-like in some. Six native and 3 escaped genera in N.A.

BLACKBERRY LILY (BELAMCANDA) is Asian, the plants resemble *Iris*; the stem is widely branched, to 3' tall; many-flowered, each flower lasting a day. One species, *B. chinensis*, is established from Conn. to Kans., s to Ga. and e Tex.

CELESTIAL-LILY (NEMASTYLIS) has cylindrical stems, a few pleated leaves, and a few quick-fading flowers. Perianth parts alike; the style of 3 forked branches, each clasping a stamen base; 4 species in e and s U.S. **Prairie-iris,** *N. geminiflora,* ranges from La. and Tex., n to w Tenn., Mo., and se Kans.

PINEWOODS-LILY (EUSTYLIS) One species, *E. purpurea*, in N.A. Stems wiry, branched, often zigzag, to 30" high; the 3 sepals larger than the petals, with depressed bases, forming a cup in the center of the flower. Grows in e and s Tex., Ark., Okla., and La.

BLUE-EYED GRASS (SISYRINCHIUM) Low slender plants; stems 2-edged or winged; leaves linear to lance-like; flowers yellow, pink, rose-purple, or, rarely, white, with 1 to few in an umbel; perianth parts alike, spreading, sharp-pointed. About 44 species, throughout N.A. *S. angustifolium* ranges from Fla. to Tex., n to s Ont., and Nfld.

IRIS has a simple or compound raceme of showy flowers. The 3 broad sepals often curve downward, the 3 narrower petals, upward. The style divides into 3 flat arching petal-like parts that hide the stamens. About 36 species, throughout N.A.

Lamance Iris, *I. brevicaulis,* grows in moist or wet soil, e Tex. to Ala., n to Kans. and Ohio.

Copper Iris, *I. fulva,* also grows in wet locations, La. to Ala., n to sw Ill. and se Mo.

Rocky Mountain Iris, *I. missouriensis,* likes wet meadows, N.D. to B.C., s to N.M. and s Calif.

Coast Iris or **Long-petaled Iris,** *I. longipetala,* grows in heavy wet soil on open sites, coastal region of cen. Calif.

Tough-leaved Iris, *I. tenax,* varies in color from white to deep purple. Grows in open grassy places, from sw Wash. to sw Oreg., w of the Cascades.

Yellow Iris, *I. pseudacorus,* is European; its rhizome yields a black dye once used for ink. An escape to wet sites from Nfld. to Minn., s to Ga.

Belamcanda
chinensis

Nemastylis
geminiflora

Sisyrinchium
angustifolium

Eustylis
purpurea

Iris
brevicaulis

Iris
missouriensis

Iris
fulva

Iris
tenax

Iris
longipetala

Iris
pseudacorus

BLOODWORT FAMILY (HAEMODORACEAE)

REDROOT (LACHNANTHES) One species, *L. tinctoria*, in the single genus in N.A. Stems to 3' tall from rhizomes with red sap; dingy wool on flowers and upper stem. Grows in wet areas, Fla. to La., n to se Va.; Del. to se Mass.; Queen's Co., N.S.

BURMANNIA FAMILY (BURMANNIACEAE)

A mostly tropical family; 2 genera and 4 species in se N.A.

BURMANNIA Tiny plants; leaves linear or scale-like; flowers 3-winged, in racemes or terminal clusters; 3 species in N.A. *B. biflora* has threadlike 6" stems, scale-like leaves, ¼" flowers; grows in moist woods and bogs, e Tex. to Fla., n to se Va.

NODDING-NIXIE (APTERIA) One species, *A. aphylla*, in N.A. Slender simple or branched stems to 8" with scale-like leaves; flowers ½" long. In moist shady places, from Ga. and Fla. to Tex.

CANNA FAMILY (CANNACEAE)

CANNA is the only genus. Erect plants to 5' tall; stems sheathed by large alternate leaves; zygomorphic flowers in terminal panicles; 2 native species, in se U.S. **Golden Canna,** *C. flaccida*, grows in wet soil of Coastal Plain, se Va. to Tex.

GINGER FAMILY (ZINGIBERACEAE)

BUTTERFLY-LILY (HEDYCHIUM) is Asian; 1 species, *H. coronatum*, has escaped in marshes, s Ga. to s La. Plant 3–6' tall; leaves sessile, 2-ranked, 8–24" long. Flowers are fragrant.

ORCHID FAMILY (ORCHIDACEAE)

Perennials of diverse form and habitat, with simple leaves and 1 to many zygomorphic flowers in a terminal spike or raceme. The perianth has 3 sepals, often petal-like; 3 petals—one, the lip, differs in form, size, and color. The 1 or 2 fertile stamens and the pistil are united into a column in the heart of the flower. In N.A., 52 genera, 25 of them only in s Fla., many of the others represented throughout N.A.

LADY'S-SLIPPER (CYPRIPEDIUM) has plaited leaves sheathing the downy stem; the lip is an inflated pouch; in some, 2 of the sepals are united under the lip; 10 species in N.A.

Yellow Lady's-slipper, *C. calceolus*, likes rich woods, bogs, Nfld. to B.C., s to N.J., Ga., Ohio, Mo., Tex., N.M., Ariz.

Ram's-head, *C. arietinum*, likes damp woods or bogs, sw Que. to Man., s to N.Eng., N.Y., Mich., Wisc., and Minn.

Moccasin-flower, *C. acaule*, grows in dry acid woods or in bogs, Nfld. to n Alta., s to Ga., Ala., Tenn., and Minn.

Mountain Lady's-slipper, *C. montanum*, likes moist open woods, Alaska to cen. Calif., e to Alta., Mont., and Wyo.

Lachnanthes tinctoria

Burmannia biflora

Apteria aphylla

Canna flaccida

Cypripedium calceolus

Cypripedium acaule

Cypripedium montanum

Hedychium coronatum

Cypripedium arietinum

ORCHIS Stemless plants with 1–3 leaves; flowers subtended by bracts in a raceme to 10" high; petals larger than the sepals; the base of the lip elongated into a spur. Two species, in the cooler parts of N.A. **Showy Orchis,** *O. spectabilis*, prefers rich woods, Que. and Ont., s to Ga., Ala., Mo., and ne Kans.

REIN ORCHID (HABENARIA) Erect plants with leafy or bracted unbranched stems; leaf bases sheathe the stem; flowers mosly small, in loose or dense racemes or spikes, the lip entire or 3-lobed, in some fringed or toothed; base of lip spurred. About 35 species in N.A., widespread.

Yellow Fringed Orchid, *H. ciliaris*, to 3' tall; grows in wet places, from Ont. to Fla., w to Ill., Mo., Ark., e and se Tex.

Bog-candle, *H. dilatata*, to 3', has spicy-fragrant flowers. In wet areas, Alaska to Lab., s to Calif., N.M., S.D., Minn., N.J.

Purple Fringed Orchid, *H. fimbriata*, to 3', grows in rich woods and meadows, Nfld. to se Ont., s to N.J., W.Va., Tenn., N.C.

Northern Green Orchid, *H. hyperborea*, to 16"; in bogs and woods, Alaska to Greenland, s to Ariz., N.M., Neb., Pa., N.Eng.

Alaskan Orchid, *H. unalascensis*, 1–2', grows in dry or moist areas, Alaska to Que., s to Baja Calif., Nev., Utah, Colo., and S.D.

Frog Orchid, *H. viridis*, 8–20", grows in diverse habitats, Nfld. to Alaska, s to B.C., Neb., Ill.; mts. to N.M., W.Va., N.C.

ROSE POGONIA or **SNAKE-MOUTH** (POGONIA) Basal petioled leaves; erect stem to 2' tall with 1 leaf halfway up; 1–2 terminal flowers, each subtended by a bract; the lip is bearded. One species, *P. ophioglossoides*, in N.A.; grows in wet places from Nfld. s to Fla., w to Minn., Ill., and Tex.

SPREADING POGONIA (CLEISTES) One species, *C. divaricata*, in N.A. Similar to *Pogonia*; flowers with slender brownish sepals, the lip crested, with a triangular tip. Grows in damp soil, N.J. and Del. to cen. Fla., w to Tenn., Ky., and Tex.

WHORLED POGONIA (ISOTRIA) Naked scapes to 16" tall; a whorl of 5–6 leaves just below the 1–2 flowers. Two species in N.A. *I. verticillata* grows in acid woodlands, from N.Eng. to Fla., w to Mich., Mo., Ark., and Tex.

NODDING POGONIA or **THREE-BIRDS** (TRIPHORA) Delicate stems under 1' tall; leaves alternate, clasping the stem; flowers 2–3, in upper leaf axils. Four species in N.A., 3 restricted to s Fla. *T. trianthophora* grows in humus of hardwood forests, from e Canada to cen. Fla., w to Wisc., Ia., Mo., Ark., and e Tex.

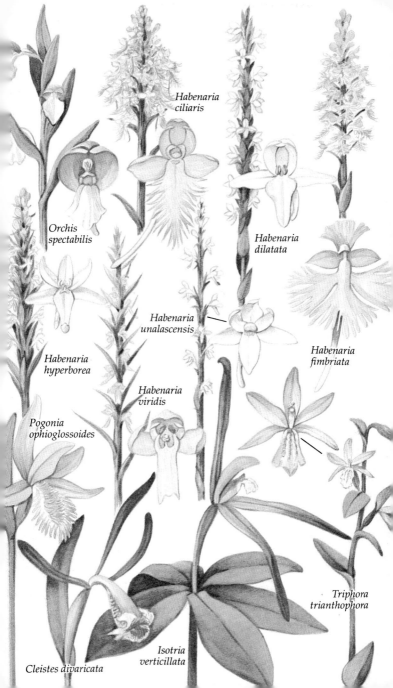

Habenaria ciliaris

Orchis spectabilis

Habenaria dilatata

Habenaria unalascensis

Habenaria fimbriata

Habenaria hyperborea

Habenaria viridis

Pogonia ophioglossoides

Triphora trianthophora

Cleistes divaricata

Isotria verticillata

GRASS-PINK (CALOPOGON) Stem naked, sheathed by 1 basal grass-like leaf; showy flowers in a raceme, the flaring lip bearded; 5 species, in e and se N.A. *C. pulchellus* likes wet soil, ranges from Nfld. to s Fla., w to Minn., Ia., Mo., Okla., and Tex.

SWAMP-PINK (ARETHUSA) One species, *A. bulbosa,* in N.A. Scape to 1' high, sheathed, with single 2" flower; a leaf appears after flowering. Grows in sphagnum and peat, Nfld. to Minn., s to Del., Md., Ohio, n Ind., mts. to S.C., but extremely rare in U.S.

LADIES'-TRESSES (SPIRANTHES) Stem leafy below, with bracts above; flower spike often spiraled; flowers usually white, some marked, tinted, or vividly colored; petals fused with the upper sepal. About 25 species in N.A., widely distributed.

Pearl-twist, *S. tuberosa,* with oval leaves, grows in dry soil; ranges from Ga. to Miss., n to N.J., Ohio, and s Ind.

Scarlet Ladies'-tresses, *S. cinnabarina,* has 1" flowers; grows in the Chisos Mts. in w Tex. (s to Guatemala).

Green-lipped Ladies'-tresses, *S. gracilis,* to 19" high, also has oval, not grasslike, basal leaves. From N.S. and N.B. s to cen. Fla., w to Minn. and Tex.

Nodding Ladies'-tresses or **Screw-auger,** *S. cernua,* is about 16" tall, with ½" flowers; grows in moist areas, N.S. and Que. to s Fla., w to S.D., Okla., Tex.

HELLEBORINE (EPIPACTIS) One or more 2–4' stems with clasping leaves; flowers in a leafy raceme; lip saclike at base; 2 species in N.A. **Giant Helleborine,** *E. gigantea,* grows in wet soil and limestone, from B.C. to Baja Calif., e to the Rocky Mts.

PHANTOM ORCHID (EBUROPHYTON) Stem 8–24" tall, with papery sheathing bracts; plant white, aging to brown. One species, *E. austinae;* grows in coniferous forests, Wash. and Ida. to s Calif.

RATTLESNAKE-PLANTAIN (GOODYERA) Plants a basal rosette of oval leaves and a spike of small flowers; upper sepal and petals unite in a hood over the saclike beaked lip; 4 species in N.A. *G. oblongifolia* grows in dry to damp soil, dense to open forests, Alaska to N.S., s to Me., Minn.; in w U.S. to Mexico.

SHADOW-WITCH (PONTHIEVA) Like *Goodyera* but flowers in a loose raceme, sepals free, petals triangular; 1 species, in se U.S. *P. racemosa* grows in damp woods, from Tex. to Fla., n to se Va.

TWAYBLADE (LISTERA) Stem with a pair of leaves at the middle; flowers green to purplish in a terminal raceme; 7 species in N.A. *L. cordata* grows in mossy places, Alaska to Greenland, s to Calif., Nev., Utah, N.M., Minn., Mich., and N.Y., and in mts. to N.C.

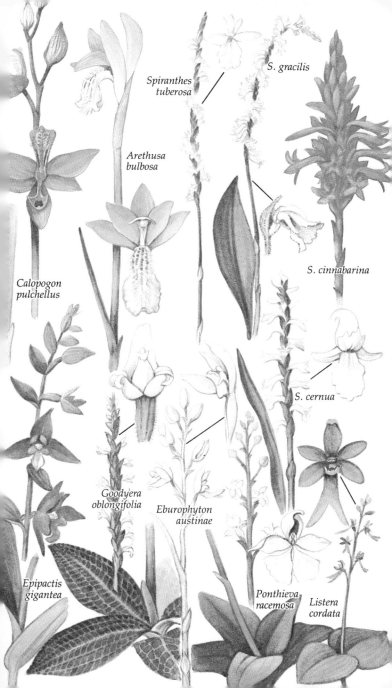

Spiranthes
tuberosa

S. gracilis

Arethusa
bulbosa

S. cinnabarina

Calopogon
pulchellus

S. cernua

Goodyera
oblongifolia

Eburophyton
austinae

Epipactis
gigantea

Ponthieva
racemosa

Listera
cordata

CORAL-ROOT (CORALLORHIZA) Saprophytes, lacking chlorophyll; rhizome coral-like; scape sheathed by bracts; flowers in a raceme, lip base swollen or spurred; 6 species in N.A. **Striped Coral-root,** *C. striata,* to 20", grows in moist areas, Que. and Ont. to Wash., Oreg., and Calif. sw to N.M. and Tex.

CORAL-ROOT (HEXALECTRIS) Like *Corallorhiza* but rhizomes made up of rings, lip base not swollen or spurred; 5 species in e and s U.S. **Crested Coral-root,** *H. spicata,* to 3', ranges from W.Va. and Md. to cen. Fla., w to Ind., sw to N.M.

ADDER'S-MOUTH (MALAXIS) Low plants, stems simple, 1–2 leaves near the middle; tiny flowers in racemes; 8 species in N.A. **White Adder's-mouth,** *M. brachypoda,* in damp soil, Alaska to Lab., s to Minn., Ind., n N.J.; in mts. to Calif., Colo., and Tenn.

TWAYBLADE (LIPARIS) A pair of glossy basal leaves, short scapes, racemes of few to many flowers; 3 species in n and e N.A. **Purple Scutcheon,** *L. lilifolia,* to 1' tall, grows in clearings and woods, from s Me. to Minn., s to Ark., Ala., and Ga.

FAIRY-SLIPPER (CALYPSO) One species, *C. bulbosa.* A single basal leaf appears in fall, withers the next summer; scape to 8" tall, with 1–2 flowers. Grows in cool woods, Lab. to Alaska, s to n Calif., Ariz., Minn., Wisc., Mich., and N.Y.

ERYTHRODES is a tropical genus with 1 species, *E. querceticola,* in se U.S. Slender leafy 1' plants, leaves with short clasping petioles; a spike-like raceme of tiny flowers. Grows in moist woodlands, from Fla. to w La., possibly to e Tex.

CRIPPLED CRANE-FLY (TIPULARIA) One species, *T. discolor,* in N.A.; a chain of corms produces in fall a plaited leaf, purple beneath, and in summer a 16" scape of asymmetric flowers in a raceme: 1 petal overlaps the upper sepal; lip 3-lobed, the base spurred. Grows in hardwood forests, from N.Y. and Pa. to n Fla., w to Ohio, Ind., Ky., Ark., Tex.

EULOPHIA A tuft of grasslike leaves with overlapping bases; a bracted 3' scape rising to one side of the plant; 1" flowers in a raceme, lip saclike at the base. Two species in se U.S. *E. ecristata* occurs in N.C., Fla., La.

BEAKED ORCHID (STENORHYNCHUS) One species, *S. orchioides,* in Fla. Stems to 3' tall, leafless at flowering; 1" flowers, of red, white, or green. Leaves, 1', appear after flowering.

Malaxis
brachypoda

Hexalectris
spicata

Corallorhiza
striata

Liparis
lilifolia

Calypso
bulbosa

Eulophia
ecristata

Erythrodes
querceticola

Tipularia
discolor

Stenorhynchus
orchioides

EPIDENDRUM Leafy epiphyte; stems branching or merely pseudo-bulbs; inflorescence terminal; petals as broad as the sepals or narrower; lip expanded, often deeply lobed; 11 species in se U.S., 10 limited to s Fla. **Green-fly Orchid,** *E. conopseum,* grows on many kinds of trees, from S.C. to Fla. and La.

LIZARD'S-TAIL FAMILY (SAURURACEAE)

Perennials of wet areas, with jointed stems, alternate heart-shaped leaves, and tiny flowers in a spike. Two genera in N.A.

YERBA MANSA (ANEMOPSIS) One species, *A. californica.* Colonial plants 1' tall; leaves mostly basal, stem leaves subtended by a sheathing bract. Spike to 1½" long, a whorl of petal-like bracts below; in alkaline or salty soil, ne Oreg. to Baja Calif., e to cen. Colo., w Tex.

LIZARD'S-TAIL (SAURURUS) Plants colonial, to 3' tall, stem simple or branched, leafy above, bare below; spike to 1' long, ½" thick, the tip nodding. One species, *S. cernuus,* in N.A.; in swamps and shallow water, ranging from sw Que. and s Ont. to s Fla., w to Minn., Ill., Mo., Kans., and Tex.

BIRTHWORT FAMILY (ARISTOLOCHIACEAE)

Low plants or vines, with alternate petioled leaves; flower parts in 3's; sepals petal-like, often bizarre; petals rudimentary, or none; stamens 6–36; ovary 4- to 6-celled. Two genera in N.A.

WILD GINGER (ASARUM) Stemless plants with aromatic rhizomes; heart- or kidney-shaped leaves on long petioles; solitary 3-lobed flowers near the ground, 12 stamens; 14 species in N.A., all woodland plants. *A. canadense* ranges from Que. to N.C., w to se Man. and e Kans.; *A. caudatum,* from B.C., s (w of the Cascades) to Sta. Cruz Mts., Calif., e to w Mont. and ne Oreg.

BIRTHWORT (ARISTOLOCHIA) Upright or twining plants; flowers lateral or in the leaf axils; sepals united in an inflated and constricted tube; 6 stamens; 13 species in N.A.

California Pipe-vine, *A. californica,* grows on stream banks and lake borders, n Coast Ranges and n Sierra Nevada, Calif.

Woolly Dutchman's-pipe, *A. tomentosa,* grows in woodlands, N.C. to sw Ind. and se Kans., s to Fla. and e Tex.

Dutchman's-pipe, *A. durior,* is a high-twining vine of woods and stream banks, sw Pa. and W.Va., s upland to Ga. and Ala.; escaped e to N.J., N.Eng.

Virginia Snakeroot, *A. serpentaria,* has slender erect 2' stems. Inhabits rich woods, from se N.Y. and sw Conn. to Fla., w to se Kans. and Tex.

Epidendrum conopseum

Saururus cernuus

Anemopsis californica

Asarum canadense

Asarum caudatum

Aristolochia californica

Aristolochia tomentosa

Aristolochia serpentaria

Aristolochia durior

BUCKWHEAT FAMILY (POLYGONACEAE)

Plants with jointed stems and simple leaves, most with stipules sheathing the stem. Flowers tiny, often in an involucre consisting of a little cup or tube of fused bracts; sepals 3–6, petals absent, stamens 3–9, 1 pistil with 2–4 stigmas. There are 16 genera with herbaceous species in N.A., many weedy, some with showy masses of flowers.

SMARTWEED or **KNOTWEED** (POLYGONUM) Stems erect or climbing, with swollen joints and lance- or arrowlike alternate leaves. Flowers single or in heads or spikes; more than 70 species, mostly weedy, in the U.S. and s Canada. **Pinkweed,** *P. pensylvanicum,* is common in e N.A., w to Utah and Tex.; **Lady's-thumb,** *P. persicaria,* is ubiquitous; both grow to over 3′ in wet or disturbed soil. **Princess-feather,** *P. orientale,* to 9′, is an Asian escape found e of the Rocky Mts.

JOINTWEED (POLYGONELLA) Freely branched stems; narrow alternate leaves, jointed at the base; pink, white, or purple flowers on jointed pedicels in a raceme; 5 sepals, 8 stamens; 8 species in e and s N.A. *P. articulata* grows in dry sand, Me. to Minn., s to ne N.C., n Ind., Wisc., and Ia.

SPINE-FLOWER (CHORIZANTHE) Small much-branched brittle plants; leaves simple, mostly basal, lacking stipules; stems with bracts; flowers in cymes, hidden by involucres with 3, 5, or 6 spine-tipped teeth; 36 species in arid w N.A., mostly in Calif. *C. fimbriata* and *C. membranacea* show the range of form.

WILD BUCKWHEAT (ERIOGONUM) About 180 species, mostly of arid w N.A. Shrubby to almost stemless plants with alternate or whorled leaves, lacking stipules; both stems and leaves more or less woolly. Most are many-flowered, the flowers surrounded but not hidden by a 3- to 10-lobed or toothed involucre. The flowers have 6 sepals and 9 stamens.

Skeleton-weed, *E. deflexum,* is extremely drought-resistant; abundant, from se Oreg. to Baja Calif., e to Ida. and Ariz.

E. pyrolaefolium, a low cushionlike alpine plant, in the Cascades, n Calif. to Wash., e to Ida. and Mont.

Desert-trumpet, Bladder-stem, or **Indian Pipe-weed,** *E. inflatum,* has very small involucres; Utah and N.M. to s Calif.

E. caespitosum has 4″ flowering stems tipped by 1 involucre with many flowers; se Oreg. to n and se Calif., e to Mont. and Colo.

Tibinagua, *E. nudum,* to 40″ high, grows from near sea level to subalpine regions, from s Wash. to s Calif.

Sulfur-flower, *E. umbellatum,* with flower stems to 16″ tall; ranges from B.C. to sw Oreg. and se Calif., e to Mont. and Colo.

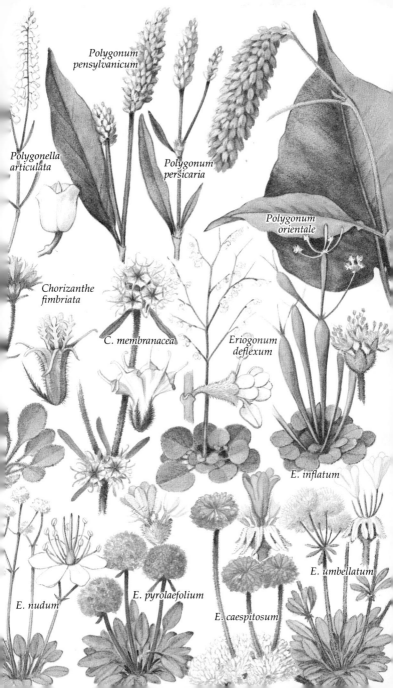

Polygonum pensylvanicum

Polygonella articulata

Polygonum persicaria

Polygonum orientale

Chorizanthe fimbriata

C. membranacea

Eriogonum deflexum

E. inflatum

E. nudum

E. pyrolaefolium

E. caespitosum

E. umbellatum

SANDALWOOD FAMILY (SANTALACEAE)

BASTARD TOAD-FLAX (COMANDRA) A root parasite with alternate leaves, axillary or terminal flowers. Calyx petal-like, 5-lobed; petals lacking; 5 stamens; 1 pistil; 2 N.A. species. *C. livida*, 4–12″ tall, has flowers in 3's, triangular calyx-lobes; ranges from Alaska to Lab., s to n U.S. *C. umbellata* has flowers in clusters; grows in much of N.A.

AMARANTH FAMILY (AMARANTHACEAE)

Mostly weeds; flowers tiny, solitary or clustered, subtended by 3 dry overlapping, sometimes brightly colored bracts.

SILVERHEAD (PHILOXERUS) One species, *P. vermicularis*, in N.A. Stems branched, 4″ to 6′ long, prostrate, some erect to 20″; leaves opposite, fleshy; ½″ flower heads. Coastal areas, Fla. to Tex.

GLOBE-AMARANTH or **BALL-CLOVER** (GOMPHRENA) Small plants with leaves opposite, nodes swollen, flowers in heads; 8 species in N.A. *G. caespitosa*, to 6″ tall, is woolly; ranges from w Tex. to Ariz.

COTTON-WEED (FROELICHIA) Like *Gomphrena* but larger; flowers in spikes, perianth a 5-lobed woolly tube; 6 species in warmer N.A. *F. gracilis*, to 2′, grows in gravel and sand, Ia. to Colo., s to Ariz. and Tex.; locally e to N.Y., N.J., and Va.

FOUR-O'CLOCK FAMILY (NYCTAGINACEAE)

Stems forked or branched in 3's; leaves mostly opposite; flowers subtended by bracts or involucres; calyx tubular, 5-lobed; petals lacking; stamens 1–9; 1 pistil; 15 herbaceous genera in N.A.

HERMIDIUM One species, *H. alipes*, to 1′ tall with thick leaves; 4–6 flowers in terminal clusters, surrounded by leafy bracts; ranges from Nev. and s Calif. to Utah.

MOONPOD (SELINOCARPUS) Stem downy, much-forked; leaves thick; flowers axillary, 2–3 narrow bracts below; fruit 3- to 5-winged; 5 species in sw U.S. **Spreading Moonpod,** *S. diffusus*, to 1′ tall, grows in dry soil, Tex. w to s Utah and se Calif.

MOONPOD (AMMOCODON) Like *Selinocarpus* but inflorescence much-branched; 1 species, *A. chenopoioides*, ranges from w Tex. to Ariz.

SPIDERLING (BOERHAAVIA) Forked stems, ½″-wide flowers in racemes or panicles, subtended by tiny bracts; about 20 species in s and sw U.S. *B. coccinea* ranges from Fla. to se Calif.; *B. coulteri* is abundant in Ariz. and s Calif.

C. umbellata

Philoxerus
vermicularis

Comandra
livida

Gomphrena
caespitosa

Froelichia
gracilis

Hermidium
alipes

Selinocarpus
diffusus

mocodon
iopoioides

Boerhaavia
coccinea

B. coulteri

TRUMPETS (ACLEISANTHES) Downy plants with forked branches; thick leaves; flowers axillary or terminal, each with 1–3 small basal bracts; calyx tube very long; 2–5 unequal stamens; 6 species in sw U.S. **Angel Trumpets,** *A. longiflora,* has 4–7″ fragrant nocturnal flowers. Ranges from s and w Tex. to s Calif.

UMBRELLA-WORT (ALLIONIA) Prostrate downy plants with forked branches; flowers axillary in 3's, 1 bract under each group. Calyx tube short, oblique, 4–5 lobed; stamens 4–7; 7 species in N.A., mostly in SW. **Hierba de la Hormiga,** *A. incarnata,* with 6–40″ stems, grows from se Calif. to s Colo., s to Tex.

SAND VERBENA (ABRONIA) Sand-loving plants with sticky hairs; flowers in heads, each head subtended by 5 bracts; calyx tube long, 5-lobed; usually 5 stamens; 23 species in w N.A. **Snowball,** *A. fragrans,* ranges from Ida. to S.D., s to Mexico and Tex. *A. micrantha* grows from e Mont. and N.D., s and w to Nev., n Ariz., and n Tex. **Red Sand-verbena,** *A. maritima,* is on ocean beaches from San Luis Obispo Co., Calif., to Mexico.

FOUR-O'CLOCK (MIRABILIS) Erect or sprawling weedy plants with showy flowers in axillary and/or terminal saucerlike involucres; calyx tube 5-lobed; stamens 3–6. About 35 species in drier w N.A. **Scarlet Four-o'clock,** *M. coccinea,* grows in w Tex., sw N.M., and se Ariz.; **Wishbone Bush,** *M. bigelovii,* in the Colorado and Mojave deserts; **Wild Four-o'clock,** *M. nyctaginea,* from Mont. to Mexico, e to Wisc. and Ala.

WARTCLUB (COMMICARPUS) Sprawling plants with branched vine-like stems to 10′ long; flowers in long-stalked umbels. One species, *C. scandens,* in N.A.; ranges from s Tex. to se Ariz.

RINGSTEM (ANULOCAULIS) Gypsum-loving erect branched plants; a sticky ring on the internodes; flowers with basal bracts, in umbels or racemes; 4 species in sw U.S. *A. leiosolenus,* to 40″ high, grows from w Tex. to s Nev. and cen. Ariz.

CYPHOMERIS Upright slender branches, a sticky area at middle of each upper internode; intense red flowers in long spike-like terminal or axillary racemes; 2 species in sw U.S. *C. gypsophiloides* grows in w Tex. and s N.M.

SCARLET MUSK-FLOWER (NYCTAGINIA) One species, *N. capitata;* base of plant freely branched; stems and leaves with sticky hairs when young; branches 4–16″ long; flowers 8–15 per involucre, 5-lobed; stamens 5–8. Coastal Tex. to se N.M.

*Acleisanthes
longiflora*

*Allionia
incarnata*

*Abronia
fragrans*

*Abronia
micrantha*

*Mirabilis
coccinea*

M. bigelovii

*Abronia
maritima*

*Cyphomeris
gypsophiloides*

M. nyctaginea

*Anulocaulis
leiosolenus*

*Nyctaginia
capitata*

*Commicarpus
scandens*

PURSLANE FAMILY (PORTULACACEAE)

Succulents with simple leaves; flowers single or variously clustered; sepals 2–8, mostly 2; petals 2–15, mostly 5; stamens often equal to petals; 1 pistil. Eight genera, mostly in w N.A.

FLAME-FLOWER (TALINUM) Stems short or tall; leaves thick, alternate to opposite, flat or cylindrical; flowers axillary or in cymes; petals 5 or more; stamens few or many; 16 species in sw U.S. *T. auranticum* grows from Tex. to Ariz.

CALANDRINIA Alternate leaves; flowers in racemes; petals 3–7, mostly 5; stamens 3–14; 4 species in w N.A. **Red-maids,** *C. ciliata,* ranges from sw B.C. to s Calif. and Ariz.

SPRING-BEAUTY (CLAYTONIA) has 1 to many basal leaves, simple flower stems, a pair of leaves below the racemes; 5 petals, 5 stamens; 13 species in N.A., mostly n. *C. virginica* grows from Minn. to Tex., e to Que., sw N.Eng., and Ga.

MONTIA Like *Claytonia* but has 2–5 petals, 3–5 stamens; some have several alternate leaves on the flower stem. About 18 species in N.A. *M. spathulata* ranges from B.C. to s Calif.

PUSSY-PAWS (SPRAGUEA) Tiny flowers in dense heads rising from a leafy rosette; 1 species in w N.A. *S. umbellata* grows from B.C. to Baja Calif., e to Mont. and Utah.

CALYPTRIDIUM Small sprawling plants, leaves mostly basal, tiny flowers in S-shaped clusters; 7 species in w N.A. *C. roseum* grows in dry soil, from cen. Oreg. to Calif., e to Ida. and Utah.

LEWISIA Many basal leaves, 1 or more leafy or bract-bearing scapes. 1 to many flowers in corymbs or cymes; petals 5–18, stamens 4–50. Fifteen species, in w N.A.

Bitter-root, *L. rediviva,* mostly in dry soil, B.C. to s Calif., e to Mont., Colo., and n Ariz.

L. brachycalyx grows in marshy areas in the mountains, s Calif. to N.M., n to s Utah.

Dwarf Lewisia, *L. pygmaea,* grows to above timberline, Wash. to Mont., s to N.M. and s Calif.

Three-leaved Lewisia, *L. triphylla,* is common from Wash. to s Sierra Nevada, e to Rocky Mts.

PURSLANE (PORTULACA) Succulent with alternate, opposite, or whorled flat to cylindrical leaves; flowers of 4–5 petals, 6 to many stamens; 11 species in N.A. **"Pusley,"** *P. oleracea,* from Europe, and South American **Rose-moss,** *P. grandiflora,* are now widespread in the U.S. and s Canada. *P. mundula* is native; it grows from Mo. to Ariz.

Calandrinia ciliata

Talinum auranticum

detail of leaf

Claytonia virginica

petal

Spraguea umbellata

Calyptridium roseum

...ntia ...lata

L. pygmaea

L. brachycalyx

...visia ...viva

L. triphylla

P. grandiflora

P. mundula

Portulaca oleracea

CARPET-WEED FAMILY (AIZOACEAE)

Succulents with alternate to whorled leaves, flowers single in axils o in axillary or terminal clusters. Sepals 5–8, usually fused as a tube petals lacking in most genera; stamens 2 to many, sometimes sterile petal-like; 1 pistil of 3–20 cells, each with its own style. Seven genera i N.A., some weedy.

SEA-PURSLANE (SESUVIUM) Sprawling plants with opposite fleshy leaves, solitary flowers; calyx tubular, 5-lobed; petals absent; stamens 1 to many; ovary with 2–5 cells; 5 species in warmer N.A. *S. portulacas trum* forms clumps to 6' wide on beaches, Tex. to Fla., n to N.C.; *S verrucosum*, with 3' stems dotted with crystalline globules, grows in moist saline or alkaline soil, Mo. and Ark. to Tex., N.M., Ariz., and Calif.

MESEMBRYANTHEMUM Reclining stems upturned at the tips; opposite 3-angled fleshy leaves united at the base; large solitary flowers with many petals and stamens, 10–16 feathery stigmas; 9 species in Pac. N.A., some probably introduced by natural means in pre-Colum bian times. **Sea Fig,** *M. chilense*, is coastal, s Oreg. to Baja Calif. **Ice plant,** *M. crystallinum*, grows locally throughout s Calif. **Hottentot Fig,** *M. edule*, is African, now naturalized in cen. and s Calif.

PINK FAMILY (CARYOPHYLLACEAE)

Herbs with swollen joints and whorled or opposite simple leaves, usually united at the base. Flowers have 4–5 sepals, often united in a tube; 4–5 petals (rarely fewer or none); stamens as many or twice as many as sepals; 1 pistil with 2–5 styles, sometimes united; 28 genera in N.A.; some are aggressive weeds.

CHICKWEED and **STARWORT** (STELLARIA) Trailing, matted, or up-right plants; flowers with 4–5 distinct sepals, 4–5 white forked petals (none in some), 10 stamens or less, 3 styles (rarely 4–5). About 30 species in N.A., many weedy. **Common Chickweed,** *S. media*, is Eurasian; **Common Stitchwort,** *S. graminea*, is European; both are now widespread in N.A.

MOUSE-EAR CHICKWEED (CERASTIUM) Like *Stellaria* but hairy; some sticky; about 25 species in N.A. *C. arvense* grows from Alaska to Lab., s over much of the U.S., not in the SE.

PEARLWORT (SAGINA) Small matted plants; 10 species in cooler N.A. *S. nodosa* grows in damp soil from Nfld. and Lab. to Minn., s on the coast to ne Mass.; **Bird's-eye,** *S. procumbens*, an arctic plant, ranges s to n Calif., e to Md. and Del.

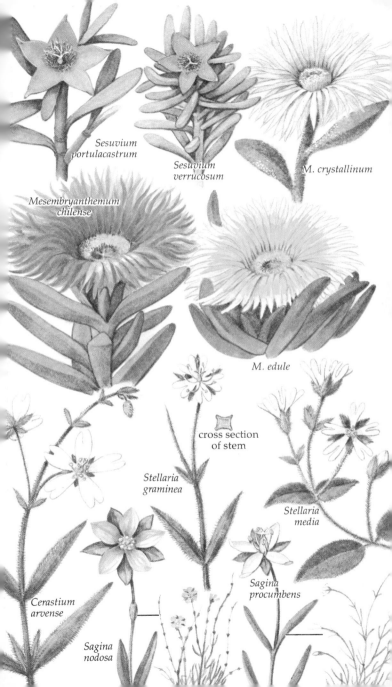

Sesuvium
portulacastrum

Sesuvium
verrucosum

M. crystallinum

Mesembryanthemum
chilense

M. edule

cross section
of stem

Stellaria
graminea

Stellaria
media

Cerastium
arvense

Sagina
nodosa

Sagina
procumbens

SANDWORT (ARENARIA) Low, often tufted plants; leaves sessile; flowers small, often white, with 5 distinct sepals, 5 petals (absent in a few), sometimes notched or forked; styles 2–5, usually 3. Perhaps 50 species in N.A., mostly in sandy soil. **Grove Sandwort,** *A. lateriflora,* is circumboreal, s to Calif., in Rocky Mts. to N.M., in the e to Mo. and Md.; *A. lanuginosa* grows in woods, s Calif. and Utah to Fla., n to se Va.

SAND-SPURREY (SPERGULARIA) Low plants; leaves threadlike, in pairs or whorled, with scaly stipules; flowers pink or white, in bracted terminal cymes, of 5 sepals, 5 petals (none in some), unnotched, 2–10 stamens, 3 styles; 12 species widely distributed in N.A., mostly in saline or alkaline soil. **Purple Sand-spurrey,** *S. rubra,* is common in w U.S.; also from Minn. to Nfld., s to Va., rarely to Ala.

SPURREY (SPERGULA) Like *Spergularia* but the flowers have 5–10 stamens, 5 styles. European; 2 species naturalized in N.A. **Corn-spurrey,** *S. arvensis,* to 18″ tall, is a common weed from Alaska to Nfld., s to Calif., Tex., Mo., and Va.

CATCHFLY, CAMPION, or **WILD PINK** (SILENE) Stems single or clustered; leaves in pairs or whorled; flowers solitary or in cymes. Sepals united in a 5-lobed bell or tube; 5 petals with round, forked, or toothed ends, and with claws or teeth at the base of the blade; 10 stamens; 3–5 styles, usually 3. About 50 species in N.A., widespread.

Fire-pink, *S. virginica,* has slender 8–24″ weak stems, with 2–6 pairs of leaves; in open woods, clearings, s Ont. to Minn., s to Okla. and Ga.

Moss-campion, *S. acaulis,* a dwarf, forms dense mats; flowers solitary, terminal. In the Arctic, s to Que. and N.H.; in mts. to Nev., Ariz., N.M.

Sleepy Catchfly, *S. antirrhina,* has stems to 32″ tall, branched as in a panicle, dark glutinous bands below the joints. Grows throughout temperate N.A.

Sweet-william Catchfly or **None-so-pretty,** *S. armeria,* is Eurasian; it has escaped from cultivation from Que. to Va., w to Minn. and Ia., and in Pac. NW.

Bladder-campion or **Maiden's-tears,** *S. cucubalis,* from Eurasia; now naturalized, from Nfld. to B.C., s to s Calif., Colo., Kans., Mo., Tenn., and Va.

Forked Catchfly, *S. gallica,* is European, now in the Pac. states and Ariz.; also N.S. to N.J., w to Mich. and Mo., sw to the e third of Tex.

Night-flowering Catchfly or **Sticky Cockle,** *S. noctiflora,* to 3′ high, with sticky hairs and fragrant flowers; a European escape now in most of N.A.

Starry Campion or **Widow's-frill,** *S. stellata,* is a 3′ native of woods and clearings; grows from Mass. to Minn., s to Ga., Ala., Ark., Okla., and e Tex.

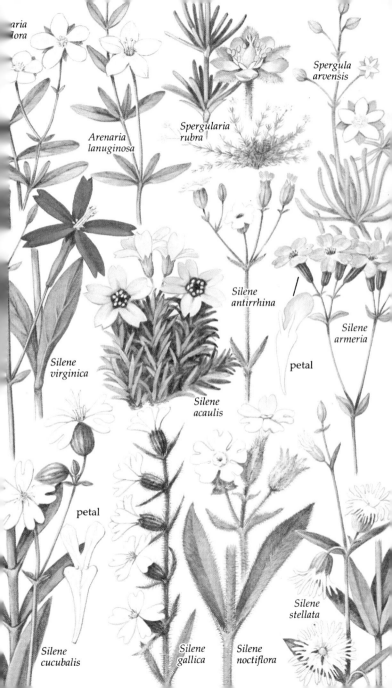

*aria
lora*

*Arenaria
lanuginosa*

*Spergularia
rubra*

*Spergula
arvensis*

*Silene
antirrhina*

*Silene
armeria*

petal

*Silene
virginica*

*Silene
acaulis*

petal

*Silene
cucubalis*

*Silene
gallica*

*Silene
noctiflora*

*Silene
stellata*

CAMPION (LYCHNIS) Like *Silene* (p. 66) but usually with 5 styles, rarely 4; 15 species in arctic and temperate N.A.

Mullein-pink or **Dusty-miller,** *L. coronaria,* is densely woolly-white, with thready twisted calyx teeth; Me. to s Ont., s to Del. and Ind., also Pac. NW.

Red Campion, *L. dioica,* an open-branched leafy plant with triangular calyx teeth; ranges from Nfld. to Del., w to Ont. and Mo., in Pac. NW, w of Cascades.

Evening-lychnis, *L. alba,* with fragrant nocturnal flowers, is easily mistaken for *Silene noctiflora* (p. 66); B.C. to Que., s to Calif. and Utah, e to N.C.

Ragged-robin or **Cuckoo-flower,** *L. flos-cuculi,* has sticky hairs on the upper stem and leaves; deeply 4-cleft petals; from Que. to N.Y., s to N.S., N.Eng., Pa.

CORN-COCKLE (AGROSTEMMA) A European genus of 2 species; one, *A. githago,* is naturalized in much of N.A. Plants to 3' tall, silky with fine white hairs. Flowers usually several, in open terminal cymes; calyx tube with 5 toothlike lobes to 1½"; 5 shorter simple petals; 10 stamens; 5 styles.

COW-COCKLE (VACCARIA) Plants to 32" tall, coated by "bloom" (as on grapes); leaves paired; flowers in an open flat-topped cyme. Calyx tubular, 5-angled up to the lobes; 5 petals with broad basal claws; 10 stamens; 2 styles, rarely 3. European; 1 species, *V. segetalis,* is common in most of temperate N.A.

SOAPWORT or **BOUNCING-BET** (SAPONARIA) Like *Vaccaria,* but calyx tube smooth, unangled. European; 1 species, *S. officinalis,* formerly cultivated, is now widely established in N.A.; leafy plants that form large clumps to 3' tall, with thick sap that lathers in water.

PINK (DIANTHUS) Stems stiff and erect, leaves grasslike, flowers terminal, solitary or in cymes. Calyx tube narrow, 1–5 pairs of overlapped bracts at its base; petals 5; stamens 10; styles 2. Eurasian; several are escapes in N.A.

Deptford Pink or **Grass Pink,** *D. armeria,* is in s Que. and Ont., s to L.I., Ga., Ky., and Mo.; also Wash., Ida., and Mont.

Childing Pink, *D. prolifer,* occurs locally from s N.Y. to Del., Va., Ky., and Ohio; most of e Tex.; Sacramento Valley, Calif.

Sweet William, *D. barbatus,* has many color forms, to dark red and purple; Que. to N.D., s to Del.; w Wash. to n Calif.

Maiden Pink, *D. deltoides,* with 12" flower stems, forms low mats; grows in Wash., w Mont.; also N.Eng. to N.J. and Ill.

ACHYRONYCHIA, with 1 species in w Ariz. and s Calif., *A. cooperi.* Stems 1–6" long, paired leaves, plants form mats on desert floor; flowers tiny, of 5 white sepals, 10–15 stamens.

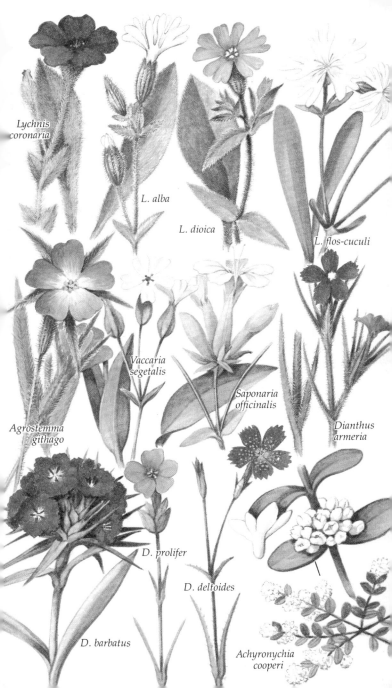

Lychnis coronaria

L. alba

L. dioica

L. flos-cuculi

Vaccaria segetalis

Saponaria officinalis

Dianthus armeria

Agrostemma githago

D. prolifer

D. deltoides

D. barbatus

Achyronychia cooperi

WATER-LILY FAMILY (NYMPHAEACEAE)

Aquatic perennials. Flowers solitary; 3 to many sepals, petals, and stamens; 1 to several pistils; 5 genera in N.A.

WATER-SHIELD or **PURPLE WEN-DOCK** (BRASENIA) One species, *B. schreberi;* sepals and petals 3–4 each; stamens 18–36; pistils 4–18, separate. Ranges from B.C. to P.E.I., s over most of the U.S.

COW-LILY or **SPATTER-DOCK** (NUPHAR) Flowers of 5–12 showy sepals, inner ones yellow or reddish; 10–20 small petals; many stamens; 1 pistil; 13 species, in much of N.A. *N. advena* is in e N.A.

WATER-LILY (NYMPHAEA) Flowers of 4 sepals, many petals, grading into many stamens; 1 pistil, 10–30 stigmas; 5 species in N.A. *N. odorata* is in e N.A.; *N. mexicana*, in Fla. and Tex.

LOTUS (NELUMBO) Sepals and petals 20 or more, nearly alike, outermost greenish; 2 species. **Yellow Lotus,** *N. lutea,* is native to e N.A.

BARBERRY FAMILY (BERBERIDACEAE)

Leaves alternate, simple or compound; flowers solitary or in racemes; flower parts often in 6's, 1 pistil; 6 herbaceous genera in N.A.

VANILLA-LEAF (ACHLYS) Stemless; leaves of 3 or more leaflets; scapes with a spike of tiny flowers; 2 species, in wooded w N.A. **Deer-foot,** *A. triphylla,* grows from B.C. to nw Calif.

INSIDE-OUT FLOWER (VANCOUVERIA) Flowers of 6–9 bracts; 6 sepals, petals, stamens; stigma a cup; 3 species, in woods, coastal w N.A. *V. hexandra* ranges from sw Wash. to nw Calif.

BLUE COHOSH (CAULOPHYLLUM) Stem 1–4′ tall; 1 huge compound leaf; flower parts in 6's, a fat pistil. One species, *C. thalictroides,* in ne N.A., grows in mts. of Tenn., S.C., and Mo.

UMBRELLA-LEAF (DIPHYLLEIA) Stem 2–3′; leaves 2-cleft; flower parts in 6's. One species, *D. cymosa,* in N.A., from Va. to Ga.

TWINLEAF (JEFFERSONIA) Leaves of 2 leaflets; flowers usually of 4 sepals, 8 petals, and 8 stamens. One species, *J. diphylla,* in N.A.; in woods, ne Ia. to Wisc., s Ont. and N.Y., s to Md. and Ala.

MAY-APPLE or **MANDRAKE** (PODOPHYLLUM) Stem tip with a pair of leaves, a single flower at the fork; 6 sepals, 6–9 petals, 12–18 stamens. One species, *P. peltatum,* in e N.A.

Nymphaea odorata

Nymphaea mexicana

Brasenia schreberi

Nelumbo lutea

Nuphar advena

Achlys triphylla

Vancouveria hexandra

Caulophyllum thalictroides

Diphylleia cymosa

Jeffersonia diphylla

Podophyllum peltatum

BUTTERCUP FAMILY (RANUNCULACEAE)

Leaves usually alternate, simple or compound; flowers regular or zygo-morphic, the parts free; sepals 3–15, often petal-like, shed or retained; petals absent or 2–15; stamens few to many; pistils 1 to many, simple; 23 genera in N.A., some narcotic and toxic.

PEONY (PAEONIA) One native species, **Western Peony,** *P. brownii;* 12–24" tall; leaves compound; flowers single; 5 sepals, 5 petals, many stamens, 2–5 pistils. Ranges from B.C. to s Calif.; e to Wyo., Utah.

MARSH-MARIGOLD (CALTHA) Low plants of wet soil; leaves heart-shaped; flowers 1–3 per stalk, of 5–12 petal-like sepals, no petals, many stamens, 5–10 or more pistils. **Cowslip,** *C. palustris,* grows from Alaska to Lab., s to S.C., Ia., and Neb.; **White Marsh-marigold,** *C. biflora,* in mts., Alaska to Calif. and Colo.; **Elk's-lip,** *C. leptosepala,* in mts. in most of w N.A.

GLOBE-FLOWER (TROLLIUS) Like *Caltha* but leaves palmately lobed to compound. One N.A. species, *T. laxus,* from B.C. and Wash. e to Conn., s in Rocky Mts. to Colo.; rare in e U.S.

FALSE RUE-ANEMONE (ISOPYRUM) Compound leaves; flowers of 5–9 showy deciduous sepals, no petals, 10–40 stamens, 2–20 pistils; 5 N.A. species, all similar. *I. biternatum* grows in e N.A.; the others in the Pac. states.

GOLD-THREAD (COPTIS) Low plants; leaves compound, evergreen; flowers of 5–8 showy deciduous sepals, 5–7 petals, 12–25 stamens, 3–10 pistils on thin stalks; 4 N.A. species. *C. trifoliata* is boreal, s to ne U.S., in mts. to N.C.; in w to B.C.; *C. laciniata* ranges from sw Wash. to nw Calif.

COLUMBINE (AQUILEGIA) Showy flowers of 5 colored sepals, 5 spurred petals, many stamens, 5–10 pistils; 23 N.A. species.

"Meetinghouses," *A. canadensis,* 6"–3', has rare yellow- and white-flowered forms. Grows in ne N.A., s to Tex.; in mts. to Ga., Ala.

Rocky Mountain Columbine, *A. coerulea,* ranges widely at upper elevations in the U.S. Rocky Mts., sw Mont. to n Ariz. and n N.M.

Northwest Crimson Columbine, *A. formosa,* a woodland plant, grows from Alaska to Baja Calif., and e to Alta., Mont., and Utah.

A. chrysantha, 16"-4' tall, has 3" spurs on the petals. Among boulders and in canyons, n Ariz., N.M., Colo., and w Tex.

A. jonesii is alpine, grows only on limestone; s Alta., s along and in mountains just e of Continental Divide to nw Wyo.

Caltha biflora

Caltha palustris

Paeonia brownii

Caltha leptosepala

Trollius laxus

Isopyrum biternatum

Coptis trifoliata

Coptis laciniata

Aquilegia canadensis

A. jonesii

A. coerulea

A. chrysantha

A. formosa

BUGBANE (CIMICIFUGA) Woodland plants 3–6' tall; flowers in compound racemes, of 4–5 sepals, no petals, many stamens, the outermost often forked and petal-like; 1–5 pistils; 5 species in e or w N.A. *C. racemosa* grows in e N.A.

LARKSPUR (DELPHINIUM) Erect plants, leaves divided, flowers zygomorphic in terminal racemes; 5 sepals, the uppermost spurred; 4 petals (rarely 2 fused as 1), the upper 2 with spurs inside the calyx spur, the lower 2 broad and clawed; many stamens; 3 pistils, or fused as 1; 67 species in N.A.

Rocket Larkspur, *D. ajacis,* is a European escape, now in much of the U.S. and s Canada.

Red Larkspur, *D. nudicaule,* grows in open woods in the mountains, s Oreg. to s Calif.

Dwarf Larkspur, *D. tricorne,* ranges from Pa. to Minn. and Neb., s to Ga., Ala., Ark., and Okla.

D. nuttallianum has hairy flowers; sw B.C. to Neb., N.M., and Ariz.; also B.C. to n Calif.

MONKSHOOD (ACONITUM) Weak-stemmed 3' plants; flowers zygomorphic, in terminal racemes; sepals 6, upper one a helmet, lateral 2 oval, lower 2 narrower; usually 2 petals, spurred, hidden in the helmet; pistils 3–5; 8 species in N.A. *A. columbianum* grows along mt. streams, Alaska to Calif., in the Rocky Mts. to N.M.; *A. uncinatum,* in moist soil, Md. to Ind., s in mts. to Ga. and Ala.

ANEMONE Erect plants; leaves divided; flowers solitary, or in umbels subtended by leafy involucres; sepals 4–20, petal-like; petals absent; many stamens and pistils. About 25 species in N.A.

Meadow Anemone, *A. canadensis,* grows e of the Rocky Mts., Alta. to N.M., e to se Que., W.Va., N.J.

Western Pasque-flower, *A. occidentalis,* grows in mts., n B.C. to cen. Calif., e to Mont.

Thimbleweed, *A. cylindrica,* in Rocky Mts., B.C. to Ariz. (not in Ida.), e to Me. and N.J.

Pasque-flower, *A. patens,* of nw N.A., ranges se to Wash., Utah, N.M., Tex., Mo., Ill., and Mich.

RUE-ANEMONE (ANEMONELLA) Flowers in umbels; 5–10 showy sepals, no petals, many stamens, 4–15 pistils. One species, *A. thalictroides,* grows in woods, from Minn. to Me., s to Okla. and nw Fla.

PHEASANT'S-EYE (ADONIS) Stems erect, 8–24"; leaves dissected; flowers single, of 5 sepals, 5–20 petals, many stamens and pistils. Eurasian; *A. annua* is an escape in e N.A., w to e Tex.

MOUSE-TAIL (MYOSURUS) Low tufted plants; flowers single, of 5 spurred sepals, 5 petals, 5–20 stamens, 10–500 pistils on a spike-like receptacle; 5 species in N.A. *M. cupulatus* grows in the SW; *M. minimus,* throughout most of the U.S. and s Canada.

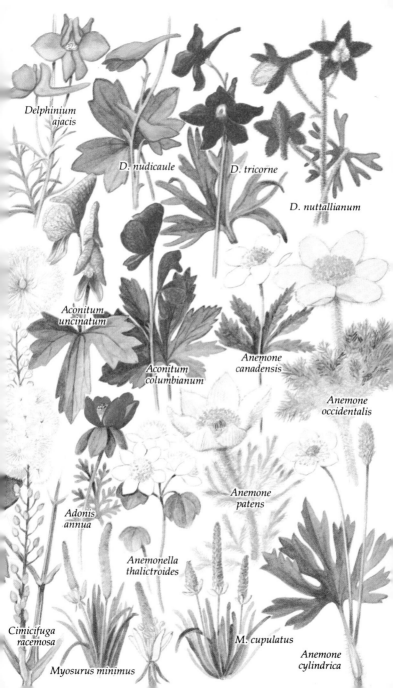

Delphinium ajacis

D. nudicaule

D. tricorne

D. nuttallianum

Aconitum uncinatum

Aconitum columbianum

Anemone canadensis

Anemone occidentalis

Anemone patens

Adonis annua

Anemonella thalictroides

Cimicifuga racemosa

M. cupulatus

Myosurus minimus

Anemone cylindrica

CLEMATIS Erect herbs or vines; leaves opposite, simple or compound; flowers solitary or in panicles, usually of 4 sepals, often fused in a bell; tiny petals or none, transitional into the many stamens; many pistils in a head. About 35 species in N.A.

Blue Jasmine or **Curl-flower,** *C. crispa,* a vine with 2–5 pairs of leaflets, grows in wet sites, Fla. to Tex., n to Va. and Mo.

Virgin's-bower, *C. lasiantha,* with spreading sepals, climbs over chaparral, from n Calif. to n Baja Calif.

Sugar Bowls or **Hairy Leather-flower,** *C. hirsutissima,* 8″–2′ tall, grows in plains and ponderosa pine forests, Pac. NW to Wyo.

Leather-flower, *C. pitcheri,* is a free climber in woods and low moist places, Ind. to Ia. and se Neb., s to w Tenn. and Tex.

BUTTERCUP and **CROWFOOT** (RANUNCULUS) Aquatic and land plants; stem erect to reclined; leaves alternate, simple to compound; petiole dilated, base stipule-like. Flowers solitary or in corymbs; sepals 3–6, often 5; usually 5 petals but varies from none to 3, 6–10 or more, yellow, rarely white, short- to long-clawed; stamens 5 to many; pistils 5 to many in a head. About 81 species in N.A. The European **Common Buttercup,** *R. acris,* is common from Alaska to Nfld. and the n half of the U.S. **Seaside Crowfoot,** *R. cymbalaria,* grows in salty or brackish mud throughout N.A. except the SE. **Prairie Buttercup,** *R. fascicularis,* grows in e N.A.

FALSE BUGBANE or **TASSEL-RUE** (TRAUTVETTERIA) Erect plants 20″–5′ tall; leaves alternate, of 5–11 dissected lobes; flowers in terminal corymbs, of 4 concave petal-like sepals, no petals, many stamens and pistils; 2 N.A. species. *T. caroliniensis* inhabits moist woods, prairies, stream banks, from sw Pa. to Mo. and nw Fla., and from B.C. s in mts. to cen. Calif., e in B.C. and n Wash. to the Rocky Mts., s to N.M.; also in ne Oreg.

MEADOW-RUE (THALICTRUM) Erect plants with compound leaves, flowers in panicles or racemes, of 4–5 sepals, no petals, 8 to many stamens, 2–15 pistils, often 4–9; 21 species in N.A., mostly woodland and mountain plants. **Purple Meadow-rue,** *T. dasycarpum,* 2–7′ tall, grows in meadows and damp woods, e B.C. to Ont., s to Ariz., N.M., Tex., La., Ill., and Ohio. **Quicksilver-weed,** *T. dioicum,* ranges from N.D. to Me., s to Mo., Ala., and Ga. **Western Meadow-rue,** *T. occidentale,* grows in alpine thickets from B.C. to n Calif., e to Alta. and Colo.

LIVERWORT (HEPATICA) Stemless herbs of dry woods, with 3-lobed leaves and solitary flowers on hairy scapes, each with an involucre, petal-like sepals, no petals; 3 species, in e N.A. *H. americana* grows from Man. to N.S., s to Mo., Ala., and n Fla.

C. hirsutissima

Clematis crispa

C. lasiantha

C. pitcheri

Ranunculus acris

R. cymbalaria

Trautvetteria
caroliniensis

R. fascicularis

Thalictrum
dasycarpum

Thalictrum
occidentale

Thalictrum dioicum

Hepatica americana

POPPY FAMILY (PAPAVERACEAE)

Sap usually milky or colored; flowers terminal, a leaf or bract underneath; sepals 2–3; petals 4–12, often crumpled in the bud; many stamens; usually 1 pistil; 14 genera in N.A.

BLOODROOT (SANGUINARIA) One species, *S. canadensis*, a stemless woodland plant with red-orange sap in the rhizome; solitary flowers of 2 sepals, 8–12 petals, about 24 stamens, a 2-grooved stigma; ranges from e Que. to Man., s to Tex. and n Fla.

CELANDINE-POPPY or **WOOD-POPPY** (STYLOPHORUM) One N.A. species, *S. diphyllum.* Stem with a pair of pinnately divided leaves; yellow sap; flowers 2″ wide, of 2 hairy sepals, 4 petals, 3–4 stigmas; grows in woods, Wisc. to w Pa., s to Mo. and sw Va.

CELANDINE (CHELIDONIUM) Similar to *Stylophorum* but with alternate leaves, flowers 1″ wide or less. Eurasian; one species, *C. majus,* is naturalized from Que. and Ont., s to Ga. and Mo.

HORN-POPPY or **SEA-POPPY** (GLAUCIUM) Leaves alternate, clasping; sap yellow; flowers solitary, 2″ wide. European; *G. flavum* grows on sandy shores, Mass. to Mich., s to Va.; also in Pac. states.

POPPY (PAPAVER) Plants with alternate leaves, milky or colored sap, flowers of 2–3 deciduous sepals, mostly 4 petals, a short fat pistil, 4–20 stigmas fused in a flat disk; 16 species in N.A. **Corn-poppy,** *P. rhoeas,* is European; locally escaped from the Pac. NW to N.S., s over much of the U.S.

PRICKLY POPPY (ARGEMONE) Bristly plants with yellow to orange latex; leaves sessile, with prickly teeth; flowers of 2–3 deciduous sepals, 4–6 petals, 1 prickly pistil, 3–6 stigmas; 15 N.A. species, most in the SW. **White Prickly Poppy,** *A. albiflora,* grows in the SE; **Devil's-fig,** *A. mexicana,* in e U.S., w to Tex.

GOLD POPPY (ESCHSCHOLZIA) Plants with finely dissected leaves and clear sap; flowers of 2 deciduous sepals, mostly 4 petals and 4 erect stigmas. About 10 species, in w N.A. **California Poppy,** *E. californica,* grows from V.I. to s Calif. **Mexican Gold Poppy,** *E. mexicana,* ranges from w Tex. to s Utah and se Calif.

DESERT POPPY (ARCTOMECON) Plant a rosette of long-haired leaves with toothed or lobed tips; 3″ flowers on 12″ naked stems, of 2–3 sepals, 4–6 petals, numerous stamens; 3 species, in sw U.S. **Bear Poppy,** *A. merriamii,* grows at the e edge of Inyo Co., Calif., and in adjacent s Nev.

nguinaria canadensis

Stylophorum diphyllum

Chelidonium majus

Glaucium flavum

Papaver rhoeas

Argemone albiflora

Eschscholzia californica

E. mexicana

Arctomecon merriamii

Argemone mexicana

MANTILIJA POPPY (ROMNEYA) Stems to 7'; leaves divided; clea sap; flowers clustered, 6–8", of 3 sepals, 6 petals; 7–12 stigmas. On species, *R. coulteri*, grows in s Calif.; var. *trichocalyx* is spiny.

CREAM-CUPS (PLATYSTEMON) Hairy plants; leaves narrow, oppo site or whorled; stem 4–12", flowers single, 1–2", of 3 sepals, 6 petal many pistils. One species, *P. californicus*, grows in s Calif.

WIND POPPY (STYLOMECON) Stems 1–2' tall; sap yellow; leave lobed; 1–2" single flowers of 2 sepals, 4 petals; stigma unlobed. On species, *S. heterophylla*, ranges from Lake Co., Calif., to Baja Calif.

MECONELLA Low plants with paired leaves; small single flowers mostly of 3 sepals, 6 petals, 3–6 stamens, a 3-lobed stigma; 3 species, B.C. to Calif. *M. oregana* is in Oreg.; rare to B.C.

CANBYA Tiny plants, forming 1" cushions. Flowers single, of 3 sepals 6 petals, 6–15 stamens, 3 stigmas; 2 species, in w U.S. *C. candida* grow in the Mojave Desert, s Calif.

FUMITORY FAMILY (FUMARIACEAE)

Leaves dissected, alternate or a rosette; flowers zygomorphic, of 2 tin sepals, 2 pairs of petals, a spur or hood on one or both of the outer pair 6 stamens, 1 pistil; 4 genera in N.A.

CORYDALIS Flowers in clusters; both outer petals hooded, upper petal spurred; 13 species in N.A. *C. aurea* grows in most of N.A. excep the SE; *C. caseana* ranges from ne Oreg. to Colo. and n Calif.

MOUNTAIN-FRINGE (ADLUMIA) One species, *A. fungosa*, a climbing woodland plant with compound leaves; flowers heart-shaped, in panicles; grows in se Canada and ne U.S., s in mts. to N.C. and Tenn.

DICENTRA Flowers single or clustered; petals cohering to form a heart-shaped or 2-spurred flower; 9 N.A. species.

Dutchman's-breeches, *D. cucullaria*, of woods or gravel banks, ranges from e N.D. to Kans., e to the Atl.; and along the Columbia R. in Wash., Ida., and Oreg.

Squirrel-corn, *D. canadensis*, grows in rich woods from sw Que. to Minn., s to N.Eng., N.C., Mo.

Golden Ear-drops, *D. chrysantha*, grows in dry gravelly hillsides or in arroyos, from cen. Calif. to n Baja Calif.

Bleeding-Heart, *D. formosa*, is in moist woods, w B.C. to cen. Calif., from the coast to middle heights, Cascades; Coast Ranges.

Steer's-head, *D. uniflora*, is on low to subalpine mt. slopes, from Wash. to Sierra Nevada, Calif., e to Ida., Wyo., and Utah.

Romneya
coulteri

Stylomecon
heterophylla

Platystemon
californicus

Corydalis
aurea

Canbya
candida

Meconella
oregana

Corydalis
caseana

Adlumia
fungosa

D.
canadensis

D.
formosa

Dicentra
cucullaria

D. chrysantha

D.
uniflora

MUSTARD FAMILY (CRUCIFERAE)

Plants with watery pungent juice; leaves alternate, simple, lobed, or pinnately divided; flowers in corymbs or racemes, 4 sepals and 4 petals spread to form a cross, 6 stamens, 2 shorter than the others, 1 pistil. At least 85 native and/or naturalized genera in N.A.; many species are unattractive weeds.

WHITLOW-GRASS (DRABA) Low plants with simple or toothed leaves and simple, branched, or stellate hairs. Flowers in racemes; sepals erect or spread at the tip; petals clawed, the tips rounded to forked. About 90 species in N.A. *D. cuneifolia* grows in dry or sandy soil, s Wash. and w Ida. to Baja Calif., e to Ky. and Fla.; *D. incerta* is alpine and subalpine, B.C. and Alta. to Wash., Ida., Mont., and Wyo.

DRYOPETALON One species, *D. runcinatum*, in sw U.S., in mountains from w Tex. to Ariz. Plant of 1 to several 8–30″ stems, leaves deeply lobed to pinnately divided, lower leaves with dense simple hairs; flowers in a crowded raceme, petals 5- to 9-lobed.

BERTEROA Leafy branched plants to 3′ high; leaves simple, lance-like, with stellate hairs. Flowers in racemes; petals 2-lobed, tips round. European; 2 species in N.A. **Hoary Alyssum,** *B. incana*, grows in fields, from B.C. to N.S., s to Ida., Mo., and N.J.

SWEET ALYSSUM (LOBULARIA) Plants to 1′ tall, branched and spreading from the base; simple narrow leaves; hairs forked, lying flat; petal tips round. *L. maritima*, with honey-scented flowers, is a European escape, N.Eng. to Pac. NW, s over much of the U.S.

ALYSSUM Similar to *Lobularia* but hairs stellate; tiny yellow or white flowers in long racemes; 4 Eurasian escapes in N.A. *A. alyssoides* grows in dry soil, Que. to B.C., s in much of U.S.

BLADDER-POD (LESQUERELLA) Low branched plants with simple or toothed leaves, hoary from hairs or scales; showy flowers in racemes; base of outer 2 sepals inflated, petals unlobed; round or oval fruits "pop" if stepped on. About 54 N.A. species, mostly western. *L. gordonii* ranges from w Tex. and w Okla. to Ariz.; *L. ludoviciana* from Alta. to Man., s to Utah, Neb., Minn., and Ill.; both grow in sand and gravel.

DOUBLE BLADDER-POD (PHYSARIA) Much like *Lesquerella* but sepal bases seldom inflated, the tips often hooded; fruit 2–lobed. About 14 species, of w N.A. *P. didymocarpa* grows in gravelly soil, ne Wash. to Sask., s to s Calif. and N.M.

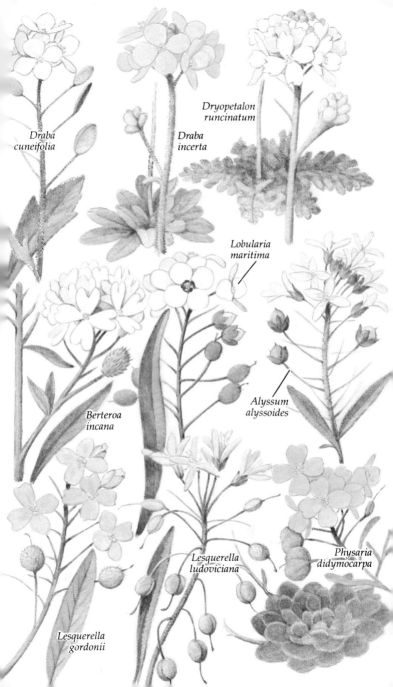

Draba cuneifolia

Draba incerta

Dryopetalon runcinatum

Lobularia maritima

Berteroa incana

Alyssum alyssoides

Lesquerella ludoviciana

Physaria didymocarpa

Lesquerella gordonii

PENNY-CRESS (THLASPI) Hairless plants; leaves entire to toothed or lobed, stem leaves clasping; flowers in racemes, sepals erect, bases no inflated, petal tips round; 6 species in N.A. **Wild Candy-tuft,** *T. mor tanum,* grows from lower valleys to mountain slopes, B.C. to n Calif., to Rocky Mts., s from Alta. to N.M.

PEPPER-GRASS (LEPIDIUM) Plants hairless or with simple hairs leaves entire to finely divided, sometimes clasping; tiny flowers in racemes, petals white to yellow, in some none; stamens 2, 4, or 6. Many species in N.A., mostly weeds. *L. flavum* grows in s Calif. and Nev.; *L. thurberi* from N.M. to s Calif.

SEA-ROCKET (CAKILE) Fleshy plants; stems 1-2' tall, base often re clining; leaves simple to pinnate; tiny flowers in racemes, petals rounded fruits 2-jointed, the upper joint larger; 5 species in N.A. *C. edentule* grows on beaches of the Great Lakes, and the seacoast, s Lab. to S.C. and B.C. to s Calif.

RADISH (RAPHANUS) Leaves with large terminal lobes, small side lobes, sparsely hairy, hair bases swollen; showy racemes of flowers sepals erect, tips hooded; petals clawed, tips round; European. **Jointed Charlock,** *R. raphanistrum,* is a local weed from Wash. to Nfld., s over the n half of the U.S.

MUSTARD (BRASSICA) Similar to *Raphanus* but leaves clasping in some, flowers white or yellow; 10 naturalized species from Eurasia. **Black Mustard,** *B. nigra,* is ubiquitous in N.A.

ROCKET (DIPLOTAXIS) Very similar to *Brassica;* flowers white, yellow, or purplish; Eurasian; 3 species in N.A. **Wall Rocket,** *D. muralis,* is local, se Canada to Tex. and on Pac. coast.

GARDEN-ROCKET (ERUCA) One species, *E. sativa,* a coarse erect hairy plant with pinnately divided leaves and showy flowers in ra cemes; a European escape, now in e N.A., w to N.D., Tex., Ariz., cen. and s Calif.; rare in the NW.

GARLIC-MUSTARD (ALLIARIA) Stem erect, 1-3' tall, simple below the raceme; leaves kidney-shaped to triangular, toothed, on slender petioles; petals rounded. Plant garlic-scented; Eurasian. *A. officinalis* is local in e N.A. and near Portland, Oreg.

MOUSE-EAR CRESS (ARABIDOPSIS) Stem simple or branched, 4-16" tall, leaves entire to toothed, sometimes clasping; hairless or with simple, forked, or branched hairs; 2 species in N.A. One species, *A. thaliana,* is Eurasian, now widespread in N.A.

Lepidium
flavum

L. thurberi

Thlaspi
montanum

Brassica
nigra

Raphanus
raphanistrum

Cakile
edentula

Alliaria
officinalis

Diplotaxis
muralis

Arabidopsis
thaliana

Eruca
sativa

ROCK-CRESS (ARABIS) Stems erect, stiff, simple or branched, smooth to hairy; leaves seldom divided, basal ones with petioles, stem leaves clasping in some; flowers in racemes; sepals erect, in some hairy; petals unnotched, white to red or purple. About 70 species in N.A., of alpine to desert habitats. *A. lyallii* is in mountains, B.C. to Calif., e to Alta., Wyo., and Utah; *A. lyrata* grows on mt. cliffs or in damp woods, Alaska to Vt., s to Wash., Mont., Mo., Tenn., N.C., and Ga.

DAME'S VIOLET (HESPERIS) is European; 1 species, **Damask Violet** or **Mother-of-the-evening,** *H. matronalis,* is an escape in s Canada and n U.S.; stems 2–4' high with simple or forked hairs, toothed leaves, fragrant flowers in corymb-like racemes.

WALLFLOWER (ERYSIMUM) Plants with 2- to 4-parted hairs, the 2-parted ones aligned with the axis they grow on; stems simple or branched; leaves entire to toothed. Racemes crowded; petals clawed, tips round. About 25 species in N.A. **Western Wallflower** or **Prairie-rocket,** *E. asperum,* grows in much of w N.A.

YELLOW-CRESS (RORIPPA) Aquatic or wetland plants, stems often branched, leaves simple to pinnate, hairless or with simple hairs; racemes of small flowers, sepals spreading, petals small or none. About 20 species in N.A. *R. islandica,* 4"–4' tall, is common throughout N.A. **Spreading Yellow-cress,** *R. sinuata,* grows from Wash. to Calif., e to Sask., Ill., Ariz., and Tex.

ARMORACIA One native species, **Lake-cress,** *A. aquatica,* of quiet water; finely divided basal leaves, upper ones divided, toothed, or entire; flowers in loose racemes; ranges from se Canada to Fla. and La.

WINTER-CRESS (BARBAREA) Erect stiff angled stems; basal leaves green all winter; upper leaves clasping; flowers yellow; 3 species in N.A., all similar. *B. orthoceras* grows in moist soil throughout N.A. except the SE.

PURPLE ROCKET (IODANTHUS) One species, *I. pinnatifidus,* in N.A. Basal leaves round or heart-shaped, upper ones toothed, triangular, clasping; sepals erect, purplish; petals white to pale lilac. In alluvium and rich woods, Minn. to Pa., s to Ala. and Tex.

PRINCE'S-PLUME (STANLEYA) Hairless to woolly plants; leaves simple to pinnate, long-petioled to clasping; flowers in tall erect racemes; 6 species, of w N.A., in dry or desert soil containing selenium. *S. pinnata* has the widest range, from se Oreg. to s Calif., e to the Dakotas, w Kans., sw Tex., and N.M.

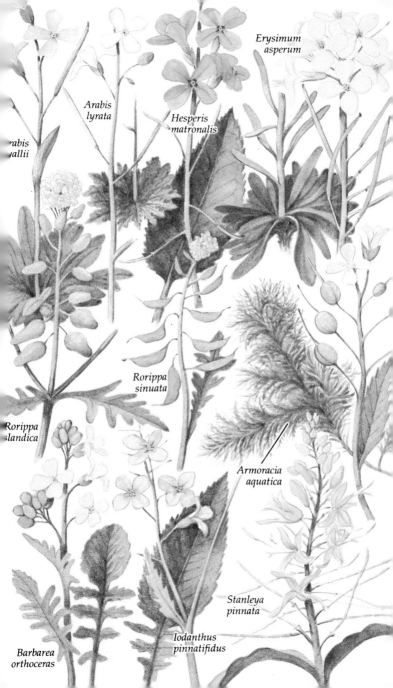

Erysimum asperum

Arabis lyrata

Hesperis matronalis

Arabis drallii

Rorippa sinuata

Rorippa islandica

Armoracia aquatica

Stanleya pinnata

Iodanthus pinnatifidus

Barbarea orthoceras

THELYPODIUM is much like *Stanleya* (p. 86) but is at most only sparsely hairy; racemes often corymb-like, petals white to purple; 21 species in arid w N.A. *T. wrightii* grows on canyon walls and lower mt. slopes, Okla. and Tex. to Utah and Ariz.

TWIST-FLOWER (STREPTANTHUS) Erect hairless plants 1–3′ tall, often lacking basal leaves; stems simple or branched, leaves usually clasping. Calyx urn-shaped, only opening at the tip; petals showy or dull; 30 species in w and sw U.S. **Shield-leaf,** *S. tortuosus*, grows in mts., s Oreg. to s Calif. and Nev.

WILD CABBAGE (CAULANTHUS) Coarse plants 1–4′ tall, stems often hollow or inflated; flowers with a closed urnlike calyx, petals clawed at base, blade curled; stamens all alike; 14 species of w N.A. **Squaw Cabbage,** *C. crassicaulis*, grows in deserts and lower mts., from se Oreg. to se Calif., e to Wyo. and Ariz.

CHORISPORA is Asian; 1 species, *C. tenella*, is now established from w Wash. to Mass., s to n Calif. and in much of arid w U.S. Plants to 20″ high with sparse glandular hairs; basal branches reclining; leaves with wavy toothed edges, most with petioles. Flowers showy, petals with erect claws, round tips.

SELENIA Low hairless plants with a rosette of pinnately dissected leaves, some stemless species; scented flowers in leafy-bracted racemes or from the leaf axils of the rosette, yellow; sepals have crests or appendages outside the tip; 4 species in sw U.S. *S dissecta* inhabits low places, w Tex. and N.M.

LEAVENWORTHIA Similar to *Selenia* but the sepals lack crests or appendages; 7 species, in cen. and se U.S. *L. uniflora* grows in rocky woods, glades, and on limestone, from Ala. to Ark., n to s Ohio, s Ind., and Mo.

SPECTACLE-POD (DITHYREA) Densely hairy plants to 2′ tall with forked or branched hairs; numerous stem leaves; flowers with hairy sepals; fruits "spectacle-shaped"; 2 species in sw U.S. *D. wislizenii* grows in sandy soil, from Tex. and Okla. to Nev.

BITTER-CRESS (CARDAMINE) Smooth to hairy plants (hairs never stellate) with tuberous to elongate rhizomes; leaves simple to pinnate, basal leaves often differing from stem leaves; flowers in racemes, some bracted; outer sepal bases inflated; petals usually clawed, tips round. About 45 species in N.A., in moist sites. **Spring-cress,** *C. bulbosa*, occurs in se Canada and e U.S., as do **Toothwort,** *C. diphylla*, and *C. douglasii*.

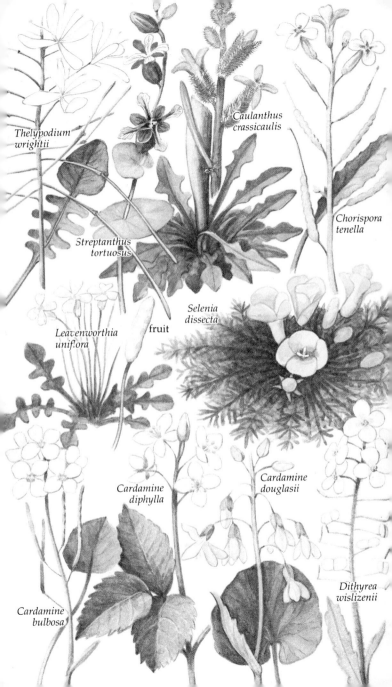

Thelypodium wrightii

Caulanthus crassicaulis

Streptanthus tortuosus

Chorispora tenella

Selenia dissecta

Leavenworthia uniflora

fruit

Cardamine diphylla

Cardamine douglasii

Cardamine bulbosa

Dithyrea wislizenii

LUNARIA A European genus of 2 species, grown for the lustrous septa in its flat oval pods, used in dry bouquets. **Honesty,** *L. annua,* a hairy plant 2–3' tall, with opposite and alternate toothed leaves, 1½" flowers; an escape, Pac. NW and e U.S.

STOCK (MATTHIOLA) Plants covered by dense gray felt of stellate hairs; leaves entire or pinnately lobed; 2" flowers, inner sepal bases inflated, petals long-clawed. European; 2 species escaped in sw U.S. *M. incana* grows in coastal s Calif.

NERISYRENIA Perennials; few to many herbaceous stems from a woody caudex, each branch ending in a raceme. Leaves thickish, entire to toothed; sepals hairy, spreading; petal tips round; 2 species in w Tex. and N.M. The 4"–2' stems and the leaves of *N. camporum* are white from fine dense hair.

PHOENICAULIS Perennial, with leaves in clumped rosettes from a branched caudex, gray from coarse to fine cross-shaped or branched hairs. Flowering stems 1–8" tall, smooth, bracted; sepal bases a little swollen, petals long-clawed. One species, *P. cheiranthoides,* ranges from cen. Wash. to cen. Calif., e to Ida. and Nev.

RUSH-MUSTARD (SCHOENOCRAMBE) Perennials with rhizomes; stems to 30" high, erect to reclining, smooth to hairy; leaves narrow; yellow flowers in bractless racemes; sepal bases slightly swollen; 1 species, of w U.S. *S. linifolia* has caudex, hairless but coverd by waxy "bloom"; grows from B.C. to Nev., e to Mont. and N.M.

SMELOWSKIA Hoary cushionlike alpine and subalpine plants with a branched caudex covered by old matted leaves; flowers in corymbs that elongate to racemes as the pods set; 5 species in w N.A. *S. calycina* ranges s to Wash., Nev., Utah, and Colo.

KEELPOD (SYNTHLIPSIS) One species, *S. greggii,* in w Tex. Plant with many weak sprawling 8–28" stems from a caudex; leaves nearly entire to deeply toothed; densely hairy, including the sepals and keeled pods. Grows in sand, gravel, or limestone.

TROPIDOCARPUM has 4–12" erect to reclining stems, downy with fine hairs, pinnately divided leaves, racemes of small yellow flowers in the axils of leaflike bracts; 2 species, in Calif. *T. gracile* grows in grassy sites, from n Calif. to Baja Calif.

WAREA Stems slender, 1–5' tall, with small entire leaves; flowers crowded in heads at the stem tip; 4 species, of the se Coastal Plain. *W. sessilifolia,* 1–2', grows in Fla.

unaria
annua

cross
section
of fruit

Nerisyrenia
camporum

Matthiola
incana

Schoenocrambe
linifolia

Phoenicaulis
cheiranthoides

Smelowskia
calycina

Synthlipsis
greggii

Tropidocarpum
gracile

fruit

Warea
sessilifolia

CAPER FAMILY (CAPPARIDACEAE)

Plants with a rank odor; leaves alternate, palmately compound, of 1–1 leaflets; flowers axillary and single or in axillary or terminal racemes zygomorphic, of 4 sepals, 4 petals forming a cross, 4–27 or more sta mens, 1 pistil; 5 herbaceous genera in N.A.

SPINY CAPER (OXYSTYLIS) One species, *O. lutea,* in se Calif. and sv Nev. Leaves of 3 leaflets; axillary flowers in dense clusters; 4 stamens long styles that become spiny as the pods ripen.

SPIDER-FLOWER (CLEOME) Erect plants, often spiny, some with glandular hairs; 1–11 entire to toothed leaflets; flowers single and axillary or in terminal racemes; 6 stamens; 12 species in N.A. **Stinking Clover,** *C. serrulata,* is found throughout sw Canada and w U.S., loca e of Ill.; **Yellow Bee-plant,** *C. lutea,* grows in sandy soil, e Wash. to Calif., e to Mont., Neb., and N.M.

STINKWEED (CLEOMELLA) Much like *Cleome* but not spiny or glan dular and has 3 entire leaflets with short sharp tips; 11 species, all with yellow flowers, in arid w U.S. **Mojave Stinkweed,** *C. obtusifolia,* grow: in cen. and s Calif., sw Nev.

JACKASS CLOVER (WISLIZENIA) One highly variable species, *W refracta,* easily confused with *Cleomella,* but the leaflets have round tips Grows in semidesert, from w Tex. to Nev. and Baja Calif.

CLAMMY-WEED (POLANISIA) Evil-scented plants with sticky hairs 3 leaflets; flowers in bracted racemes; petals have slender claws, the tips notched; stamens 6 to many; 8 N.A. species. *P. trachysperma* grows in sand or gravel, from se Oreg. and ne Calif. to Minn., s to Ariz. and Tex.; *P. jamesii* prefers sand, ranges from Colo. to Ill., s to La. and w Tex.

MIGNONETTE FAMILY (RESEDACEAE)

Plants with alternate simple to pinnately divided leaves, terminal spikes of irregular flowers of 4–8 sepals, 2–8 variously lobed petals, 3–50 stamens, a 2- to 6-lobed pistil; 2 genera.

OLIGOMERIS One species, *O. linifolia,* ranges from Tex. to s Calif. Stem to 1', erect, branched at the base; clustered narrow leaves; 6" spikes of tiny flowers with 4 sepals, 2 petals, and 3 stamens.

MIGNONETTE (RESEDA) To 3' tall; flowers of 4–6 sepals, 4–7 petals, 10–40 stamens. European; 4 species are escapes in N.A. **White Mignonette,** *R. alba,* grows along the Pac. coast; **Yellow Mignonette,** *R. lutea,* from N.Eng. to Md. and Ia., and in the Pac. states.

*Oxystylis
lutea*

*Cleome
serrulata*

*Cleome
lutea*

*Cleomella
obtusifolia*

*Polanisia
trachysperma*

fruit

*Wislizenia
refracta*

*Reseda
alba*

P. jamesii

*Oligomeris
linifolia*

fruit

fruit

R. lutea

PITCHER-PLANT FAMILY (SARRACENIACEAE)

Perennial insectivorous bog plants with hollow leaves partially filled with liquid, winged on one side, with an expanded hood. Insects are lured to fluid inside, trapped, and digested as a nitrogen source. Flowers solitary on scapes, 3 bracts below the 5 petal-like sepals; 5 petals; many stamens; a 5-lobed umbrella-like stigma; 2 genera in N.A.

COBRA-PLANT (DARLINGTONIA) Strongly hooded, to 20″ tall, ending in a forked appendage; flowers 4″ wide. One species, *D. californica,* grows in coastal bogs and along inland streams, cen. Oreg. to n Calif.; introduced near Seattle, Wash.

PITCHER-PLANT or **TRUMPET** (SARRACENIA) Generic characters the same as for the family; 8 species in N.A., all but 1 restricted to se U.S. They cross easily, hence there are many hybrids.

Hooded Pitcher-plant, *S. minor,* has erect dotted strongly hooded 6–12″ leaves; large odorless flowers; grows in bogs, wet pinelands, Coastal Plain, Fla. to N.C.

Sweet Pitcher-plant, *S. rubra,* has 4–16″ erect leaves, the hood arched when young; its flowers have the odor of violets. In bogs, pinelands, w Fla. to s N.C.

Sidesaddle-flower or **Indian Cup,** *S. purpurea,* the national flower of Nfld., has pitcher-shaped leaves 4–12″ long, often reclined, the hood erect and open; flowers 2″ wide. Grows in sphagnum and peat, Lab. to Mackenz., s to La. and Fla.

Trumpets or **Huntsman's-horn,** *S. flava,* has erect trumpetlike yellow-green leaves 1–3′ tall, the hood erect or arching over the open mouth. The flowers have a strong musky "feline" odor. Grows in wet pinelands, from n. Fla. to Ala. and se Va.

SUNDEW FAMILY (DROSERACEAE)

Low plants of swampy places, with a basal rosette of glandular-hairy insectivorous leaves; flowers in racemes, of 4–5 sepals and petals, 4–20 stamens, 3–5 styles, often forked, and then with 6–10 stigmas. There are 2 genera in N.A.

SUNDEW (DROSERA) Leaves with glandular hairs that exude glittering drops of clear sticky fluid; flowers white to red, in 1-sided racemes, usually of 5 sepals, petals, and stamens; 3–5 deeply forked styles; 8 N.A. species, several widespread. *D. rotundifolia* and *D. linearis* illustrate the range of form.

VENUS' FLY-TRAP (DIONAEA) One species, *D. muscipula,* of coastal N.C. and S.C. Leaves 2–6″ long with winged petioles, the 2-lobed spiny-edged blade attracts, closes on, and digests insects; 1″ flowers in corymbs, on scapes 4–16″ high.

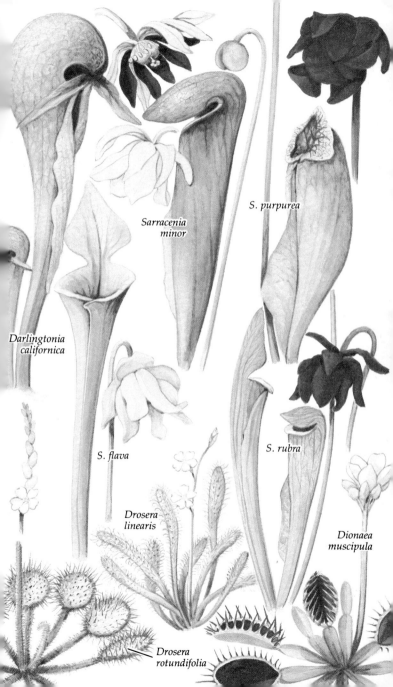

Darlingtonia
californica

Sarracenia
minor

S. purpurea

S. flava

S. rubra

Drosera
linearis

Dionaea
muscipula

Drosera
rotundifolia

STONECROP FAMILY (CRASSULACEAE)

Succulents with alternate, opposite, or whorled simple fleshy leaves; flowers usually in axillary or terminal cymes; flower parts in 4's or 5' (including pistils); stamens equal to or twice as many as petals.

PIGMYWEED (TILLAEA) Tiny delicate plants with threadlike stem and opposite fleshy leaves, forming 4–6" tufts or mats on pool-edge and fresh or tidal mud; flowers axillary, solitary or clustered; 2 N.A. species. *T. aquatica* grows in most of N.A.

STONECROP (SEDUM) Leaves entire to fine-toothed, cylindrical to flat, alternate, opposite, or whorled; flowers in broad to 1-sided terminal cymes; sepal bases united; petals free or united to halfway up; 8–10 stamens; pistils free or fused at base. About 46 species in N.A.

Rose-flowered Sedum, *S. laxum,* has mat-forming rosettes of 1" flattened leaves; 8–16" flowering stems, flower parts in 5's; grows in sw Oreg. and nw Calif.

Yellow Stonecrop, *S. nuttallianum,* a tufted plant 1–3" high, has cylindrical alternate leaves, flowers in a 2- to 5-forked cyme; sw Mo. to cen. Tex.

Rock-moss or **Widow's-cross,** *S. pulchellum,* has 4–12" branches crowded with cylindrical leaves, a 4- to 7-forked cyme that spreads at flowering; se U.S., w to Kans.

Live-forever or **Frog-plant,** *S. purpureum,* is an aggressive European escape, Nfld. to Wisc., s to Md. and Ind.; stems 8–30" with coarsely toothed leaves.

Roseroot, *S. rosea,* has a thick rhizome, rose-scented if cut; stem 1–16" high, spiraled or whorled leaves. Arctic N.A., s in mts. to Calif., Colo., and Pa.

S. stenopetalum has narrow alternate keeled leaves, 8" flowering stems, sometimes produces bulblets on the cymes. Ranges from B.C. to Calif., e to w Mont.

ECHEVERIA Leaves in a rosette, flower stems axillary, leafy; flowers in cymes or panicles, of 5 sepals, 5 partly fused petals with spread tips, 5 stamens, 5 partly fused pistils; possibly 35 species in w U.S.

E. edulis has cylindrical leaves to 6" long; 6–20" flowering stems; grows on dry hillsides, s Calif.

E. pulverulenta forms a 20" rosette; its 8–16" flowering stems are dense with clasping leaves; s Calif., Nev., and w Ariz.

E. cymosa is variable; flowers red or yellow, on an 8" stem; mts. of s Calif. and Sierra Nevada.

Desert Savior, *E. lanceolata,* has 2' green or red flowering stems; green or orange petals; s Calif.

Bluff Lettuce, *E. farinosa,* is on coastal cliffs, cen. Calif. to Oreg.; its leaves are covered by white "meal"; rosettes to 5" wide.

Tillaea aquatica

S. nuttallianum

S. pulchellum

Sedum laxum

S. purpureum

S. stenopetalum

S. rosea

Echeveria edulis

E. pulverulenta

E. lanceolata

E. cymosa

E. farinosa

SAXIFRAGE FAMILY (SAXIFRAGACEAE)

Leaves mostly basal, opposite or alternate on stem; flower parts mostly in 4's or 5's, stamens 5–10, pistils often fewer than petals, free or fused; 25 herbaceous genera in N.A.

DITCH-STONECROP (PENTHORUM) One species, *P. sedoides*, an erect or sprawling bushy plant to 30" high, leaves alternate, toothed; flowers in a cyme of S-shaped branches, 5–7 sepals, no petals, 10 stamens, 5–7 pistils with fused bases; grows in moist sites, e N.A.

WHIPPLEA One species, *W. modesta*; its woody horizontal stem sends up 3" shoots with opposite leaves and terminal heads of flowers, 5–6 sepals and petals, 10–12 stamens, 4–5 styles; grows in Coast Ranges of Calif., n to nw Wash.

FALSE GOAT'S-BEARD (ASTILBE) One native species, *A. biternata*, 3–6' tall, with compound leaves, cut-lobed and toothed leaflets; flowers on spikes in a compound panicle, 4–5 sepals, 3–5 petals (tiny or none in female flowers), 10 stamens, 2–3 styles. Grows in mountain woods, from Va. and W.Va. to Ga. and Tenn.

SULLIVANTIA Low spreading plants of wet rock cliffs; leaves cut-toothed, slightly lobed; flowers in a cyme on a nearly leafless 4–13' stem, 5-lobed calyx, 5 petals, 5 stamens, 2 stigmas; 4 species, 2 in nw and 2 in ne N.A. *S. sullivantii* grows in s Ohio, n Ky., and se Ind.

BOYKINIA Leaves round, palmately lobed and toothed, on long petioles; white flowers in cymes, 5-lobed tubular calyx, 5 petals, 5 stamens, 2 styles; 6 species, of moist mountain sites. **Brook-saxifrage,** *B. aconitifolia*, is in the s Appalachian Mts.; **Brook-foam,** *B. elata*, in mountains from B.C. to s Calif.

SAXIFRAGE (SAXIFRAGA) Plants of mountains and rocky places with clustered basal leaves; flowers solitary or in racemes, cymes, or panicles, the calyx 5-lobed, 5 petals, 10 stamens, 2 styles. About 70 N.A. species, chiefly of cool and cold regions.

Tufted Saxifrage, *S. cespitosa*, has glandular 8" flowering stems with 1–5 leaves; Arctic, s to Que.; Oreg.; in Rocky Mts. to Ariz.

Mountain-lettuce, *S. micranthidifolia*, has panicles on 1–3' scapes; leaves with 24–80 sharp teeth; grows in Appalachian Mts.

Purple Mountain-saxifrage, *S. oppositifolia*, is a matted plant with bristly 4-ranked leaves; in Arctic, s to Que.; high w mts.

S. flagellaris, 3–6", has spine-tipped glandular leaves, whip-like runners; flowers often single; in Arctic, s to Ariz., N.M.

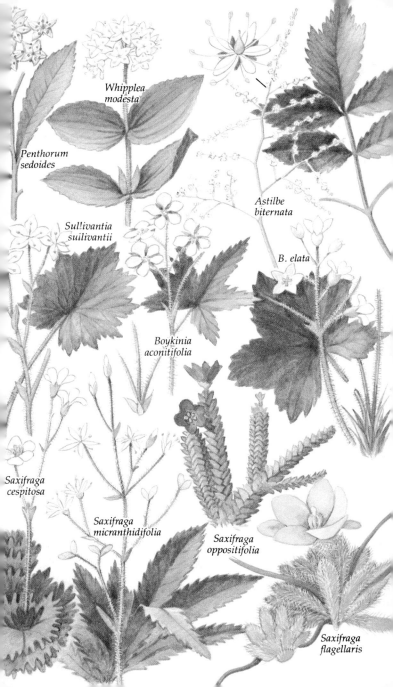

Whipplea
modesta

Penthorum
sedoides

Astilbe
biternata

Sullivantia
sullivantii

B. elata

Boykinia
aconitifolia

Saxifraga
cespitosa

Saxifraga
micranthidifolia

Saxifraga
oppositifolia

Saxifraga
flagellaris

UMBRELLA-PLANT (PELTIPHYLLUM) One species, *P. peltatum*, i and along mountain streams, sw Oreg. to Tulare Co., Calif.; cymes o 1–5' scapes, appearing before the leaves; flowers white, aging to pin of 5 sepals, 5 petals, 10 stamens, 2–3 pistils fused at the base. Pelta leaves 4–16" wide, with toothed lobes.

MITERWORT or **BISHOP'S-CAP** (MITELLA) Leaves mostly basal o long petioles, heart-shaped, weakly lobed; stem naked or with 1– leaves, 1–2' tall, flowers in a 1-sided raceme, tiny but marvelous sculptured, of 5 sepals, 5 cleft petals, 5–10 stamens, 2 styles; 10 specie in N.A. *M. diphylla* grows in loamy or rocky woods, from sw Que. an N.H. to Minn.; s to uplands of S.C., Tenn., Miss., and Mo. *M. nu* inhabits cool woods or swamps, s Lab. to Mackenz., s to Mont., N.D. Minn., Wisc., n Ohio, and Pa.

FALSE MITERWORT (TIARELLA) Leaves palmately lobed or of leaflets, on long petioles with stipules; flowers in racemes on a fev leaved stem, 5-lobed calyx, 5 clawed petals, 10 stamens, 2 styles; species in N.A., all woodland plants. **Foam-flower,** *T. cordifolia,* grow from N.B. to Mich., s to Ga. and Ala.; **Sugar-scoop,** *T. unifoliata,* from Alaska to w Mont., s through Wash., Oreg., and the coastal mountain to cen. Calif.

ALUM-ROOT (HEUCHERA) Leaves long-petioled, palmately lobe and toothed, flowers small but showy, in narrow panicles, 5-lobe petal-like calyx, 5 petals, 5 stamens, 2 styles. About 40 N.A. species many in mountains. **Rock-geranium,** *H. americana,* grows in woods o shaded rocky places, e N.A., w to Okla. and ne Tex.; *H. micrantha,* i ravines and woods, s B.C. and n Ida. to cen. Calif.; **Coral-Bells,** *H sanguinea,* grows on moist shaded rocks in the mountains of s Ariz.

GOLDEN SAXIFRAGE or **WATER-CARPET** (CHRYSOSPLENIUM Low plants of cold wet places; leaves palmately lobed; flowers single o in leafy cymes, 4–5 lobes on calyx, no petals, 4–10 stamens, 2 styles; N.A. species. *C. americana* grows in NE, s to Ga., Md., and Ia.

LEATHER-LEAVED SAXIFRAGE (LEPTARRHENA) One species, *L pyrolifolia,* from Kamchatka Is. to Mt. Adams, Wash. Oval short-petioled toothed leaves; stems with 2–3 leaves, dense heads of flowers, 5-lobed calyx, 5 petals, 10 stamens, 2 pistils.

BENSONIA One species, *B. oregana,* grows in damp soil, Siskiyou Mts. of sw Oreg. Leaves round, with 5–7 toothed lobes; flowers on an 8" leafless scape, 5 irregular lobes on calyx, 5 threadlike petals, 5 stamens, and 2–3 pistils.

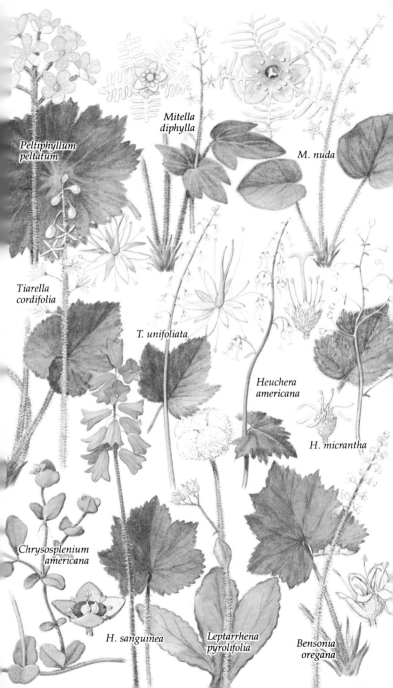

Peltiphyllum peltatum

Mitella diphylla

M. nuda

Tiarella cordifolia

T. unifoliata

Heuchera americana

H. micrantha

Chrysosplenium americana

H. sanguinea

Leptarrhena pyrolifolia

Bensonia oregana

STAR-FLOWER (LITHOPHRAGMA) Leaves long-petioled, often 3- to 5-lobed or divided; stems axillary, few-leaved; flowers in racemes, of 5 sepals, 5 entire to divided petals, 10 stamens, 3 styles; 12 species, of w N.A. **Prairie-star,** *L. parviflora,* grows in rocky places, B.C. to cen. Calif.; in Rocky Mts. to Colo.

GRASS-OF-PARNASSUS or **BOG-STARS** (PARNASSIA) Leaves simple, petioled; flowers single on scapes with 1 sessile leaf, of 5 sepals, 5 petals, 5 stamens, 5 clusters of staminodes, 4 stigmas; 11 N.A. species, of wet, often limy soil. *P. glauca* grows from Nfld. to Man., s to S.D., Ia., and Pa.

SUKSDORFIA Plants of wet rocks by mountain streams, basal leaves palmately notched or lobed, flowers in dense or open panicles, of 5 sepals, 5 petals, 10 stamens, 2 styles; 2 species, in w U.S. *S. violacea* ranges from e Cascades, Wash., to Mont. and nw Oreg.

JEPSONIA Leaves all basal, petioled, palmately toothed and lobed; flowers in terminal cymes on scapes, of 5 sepals, 5 clawed petals, 10 stamens, 2 styles. One variable species, *J. parryi,* of dry rocky sites and mesas, s Calif. mts.; Channel Is.

ELMERA Leaves round, weakly lobed, glandular-hairy; stems with 1–4 alternate leaves with stipules; flowers of 5 sepals, 5 entire or 5- to 7-lobed petals, 5 stamens, 1 style. One species, *E. racemosa,* an alpine plant, grows in rock crevices, s B.C. and Wash.

FRINGE-CUPS (TELLIMA) Leaves round, shallowly lobed and toothed, sparsely hairy; flowers of 5-lobed calyx, 5 fringed petals, 10 stamens, 2 styles. One species, *T. grandiflora,* grows on moist rocks, Alaska s to Sta. Lucia Mts. and n Sierra Nevada, Calif.

BOLANDRA Mountain plants of moist rocks; leaves palmately lobed, a leafy axillary stem, upper leaves sessile; flowers in a loose panicle, of 5 sepals, 5 petals, and 5 stamens; 2 stigmas; 2 species, in nw U.S. *B. californica* grows in the cen. Sierra Nevada.

YOUTH-ON-AGE or **THOUSAND MOTHERS** (TOLMIEA) Leaves glandular-hairy; clustered 1–3′ flower stems; calyx of 5 unequal lobes; 4 threadlike petals; 3 stamens; 2 stigmas. One species, *T. menziesii,* of mountain woods, stream banks, from s Alaska to n coastal Calif.

TELESONIX Low glandular-downy plants of moist rock crevices; flowering stems to 6″, bracted, flowers clustered in the axils, of 5 sepals, 5 petals, 10 stamens, 2 styles. One species, *T. jamesii,* ranges from e Ida. to S.D., s to s Nev. and Colo.

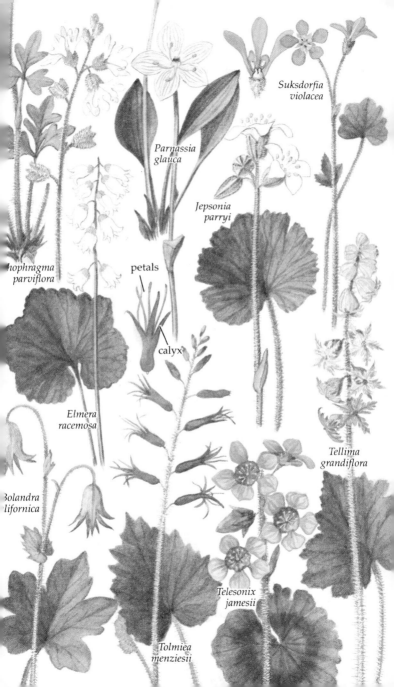

Suksdorfia
violacea

Parnassia
glauca

Jepsonia
parryi

hophragma
parviflora

petals

calyx

Elmera
racemosa

Tellima
grandiflora

Bolandra
lifornica

Telesonix
jamesii

Tolmiea
menziesii

ROSE FAMILY (ROSACEAE)

Leaves usually alternate, simple or compound, with stipules; flowers single or in racemes, cymes, or panicles; flower parts in 4's or 5's, the calyx saucer- or bell-like, few to many stamens and pistils; 25 genera with herbaceous species in N.A.

ROCK-SPIRAEA (PETROPHYTUM) Low mat-forming plants with horizontal woody stems and simple silky leaves; flowers in racemes, of 5 sepals, 5 petals, 20 stamens, 3–5 pistils; 3 species, on rocks in mountains, w N.A.; *P. caespitosum*, in most w mountains.

GOAT'S-BEARD (ARUNCUS) Plants to 7' tall, leaves pinnately compound, flowers on spikes in an open panicle (male and female on separate plants), of 5 sepals, 5 petals, 15–30 stamens, 3–5 pistils; 2 species, of e and w N.A. woodlands. *A. dioicus* ranges from Ia. to Pa., s to Okla. and Ga.

MEADOW-QUEEN (FILIPENDULA) Plants to 10' high, leaves pinnate; flowers in a panicle, 4–5 sepals and petals, 20–40 stamens, 5–15 pistils; 4 species in N.A., 3 e and 1 in nw Oreg. **Queen-of-the-prairie,** *F. rubra*, grows in NE, w to Ia., s to Ga.

INDIAN-PHYSIC (GILLENIA) Plants to 3' or more, leaves of 3 sessile doubly toothed leaflets; stipules small or leaflike; flowers in a loose panicle, of 5 sepals and petals, 10–20 stamens, 5 pistils; 2 species, of e N.A. **Bowman's-root,** *G. trifoliata*, grows in woods, s Ont. to Mich., s to Ga. and Ala.

LUETKEA One species, *L. pectinata*, a mat-forming plant; leaves finely dissected; flowering stem leafy, 2–6" high, flowers of 5 sepals, 5 petals, 20 stamens, 5 pistils; grows on moist rocky or sandy slopes, from Alaska to n Calif., e to the Canadian Rockies.

BURNET (SANGUISORBA) Stems branched, with pinnate leaves; flowers in a long-stalked head; calyx turban-shaped, of 4 petal-like lobes, no petals, 2–12 stamens, 1–3 pistils; 8 species in N.A. **American Burnet,** *S. canadensis*, 1–7' high, grows in bogs, ne N.A. s in mts. to Ga.; **Sitka Burnet,** *S. sitchensis*, 8"–4' tall, in swamps and salt marshes, from Alaska and Yuk. to Ida. and Oreg.

BRAMBLE (RUBUS) A large genus, mostly woody; 4 N.A. herbaceous species, spineless, flowers of 5 sepals and petals, many stamens and pistils. **Cloudberry,** *R. chamaemorus*, 4–12" high, has simple leaves and single flowers; grows in peat, Arctic, s to L.I. and s Canada. **Dwarf Raspberry,** *R. pubescens*, 8–16" tall, has 3–5 palmate leaflets, 5–7 flowers; grows in damp sites, s Canada, n U.S.

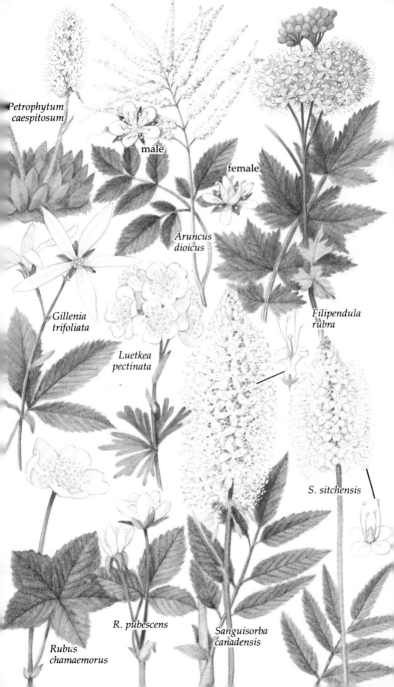

*Petrophytum
caespitosum*

male

female

*Aruncus
dioicus*

*Gillenia
trifoliata*

*Luetkea
pectinata*

*Filipendula
rubra*

S. sitchensis

R. pubescens

*Sanguisorba
canadensis*

*Rubus
chamaemorus*

DRYAS Low matted plants with a caudex; leaves simple, entire or toothed; solitary flowers, of 8–10 sepals and petals, many stamens and pistils; 3 N.A. species. *D. octopetala* is a mountain plant, Alaska to Oreg., e to Colo.; *D. integrifolia* grows in arctic N.A., alpine s to Mont., Alta., w Nfld., and se Que.

DEWDROP (DALIBARDA) One species, *D. repens*, a creeping woodland plant of e N.A., s in mountains to N.C.; leaves simple, heartshaped with wavy edges; 2 kinds of flowers—erect sterile ones with 5 petals; low, closed fertile ones without petals.

AGRIMONY or **COCKLEBUR** (AGRIMONIA) Hairy 1–7′ plants; pinnate leaves, small and large leaflets intermixed; leafy stipules; flowers in spikes, a 3-cleft bract at the base of the calyx, hooked bristles on the throat; 5 sepals, 5 petals, 5–15 stamens, many pistils; 8 species in N.A. *A. gryposepala* grows in s Canada, s to Calif., Ariz., N.D., Kans., N.C., and n N.J.

Note: *The next 7 genera have 5 scale-like to leaflike bracts on the calyx, just below and alternating with the sepals.*

STRAWBERRY (FRAGARIA) Stemless plants; long-petioled leaves in a rosette, of 3 coarsely toothed leaflets; flowers in cymes on hairy scapes, of 5 sepals, 5 petals, 20 stamens, many pistils. About 8 N.A. species. *F. virginiana* grows on open slopes and borders of woods, from Alaska to Nfld., s to Mexico, Tex., Ia., and Ga.

BARREN STRAWBERRY (WALDSTEINIA) Plants easily mistaken for Strawberry, but leaves 3- to 5-lobed or divided, flowers yellow; 3 species in N.A. *W. fragarioides* ranges w to Minn. and Mo.

AVENS (GEUM) Leaves mostly pinnately divided, with large terminal lobes; flowers single or in cymes on leafy stems, of 5 sepals and petals, many stamens and pistils; 18 species in cold and cooler regions of N.A.

White Avens or **Redroot,** *G. canadense*, 8″–4′ tall, has glandular hairs on the upper stem, simple or 3-cleft upper leaves; grows in woods, fields, at roadsides, N.D. to Que., s to Ga. and Tex.

Large-leaved Avens, *G. macrophyllum*, 1–3′ tall, is bristly hairy on the lower stem; grows in woods and fields, from Alaska to Lab., s to n U.S. states; in mts. to Calif. and Ariz.

Water Avens, Purple Avens, or **Chocolate-root,** *G. rivale*, has a few 3-lobed stem leaves, nodding flowers; in wet soil or peat, B.C. to Lab., s to Minn., Pa., and N.J.; in w mts. to N.M.

Long-plumed Purple Avens or **Prairie-smoke,** *G. triflorum*, has finely dissected basal leaves, 2″ hairy tails on the fruits; grows in fields or gravel, B.C. to Ont., s to Wash., Utah, N.M., Ill.

Dryas octopetala

Dryas integrifolia

Dalibarda repens

Fragaria virginiana

Waldsteinia fragarioides

Agrimonia gryposepala

Geum canadense

G. rivale

G. macrophyllum

G. triflorum

SIBBALDIA A low creeping tufted plant from a caudex; leaves of 3 leaflets, each with 3 teeth at the tip. Flowers in dense cymes, of 5 sepals, 5 tiny petals, 5 stamens, 5–20 pistils. One species in arctic N.A. *S. procumbens* ranges s as an alpine plant to s Calif., Utah, Colo., N.H., and Gaspé Pen., Que.

IVESIA Leaves mostly basal, pinnate, finely dissected; flowers in dense or open cymes, of 5 sepals and petals, 5 or 20 stamens (rarely 10 or 15), 1–15 pistils, surrounded by a ring of bristles; 20 species, mostly alpine, of w N.A. *I. gordonii* grows on high rocky ridges and at lower elevations along rivers, from s Wash. to n Calif., e to Mont. and Colo.; *I. lycopodioides*, alpine, grows in cen. Sierra Nevada, e to Nev.

HORKELIA Plants with silky and glandular hairs; multiple short leafy stems from a caudex; pinnate leaves with toothed leaflets; flowers in dense cymes, of 5 sepals, 5 white to cream or pink petals, 10 (rarely 20) stamens, 3–50 or more pistils. About 20 species, of w N.A., chiefly Calif. *H. cuneata*, 6–12″ high, grows in fields and sandy woodlands, s half of Calif.

CINQUEFOIL or **FIVE-FINGER** (POTENTILLA) Plants with palmately or pinnately compound leaves, 3 to many leaflets, mostly toothed; flowers solitary or in cymes, often yellow, of 5 sepals and petals (rarely 4), few to many stamens (often 20), many pistils. Over 120 species are described for temperate and arctic N.A.

Old-field Cinquefoil, *P. simplex*, has supple hairy stems that arc and root at the tip; in dry open soil and woods, N.S. to Minn., s to N.C. and Tex.

Three-toothed Cinquefoil, *P. tridentata*, has 3–5 teeth at the tip of its 3 leaflets; in dry soil, Lab. to Mackenz., s to Ga., Ia., N.D.; mts., s Oreg. to s Calif.

Silverweed, *P. anserina*, has one or both sides of the leaflets silvery-silky; grows in gravel, sand, Alaska to Nfld., s to Calif., Ariz., N.M., Ia., Ind., N.Y.

Tall Cinquefoil, *P. arguta*, is 1–3′ high, with brownish clammy glandular hairs; n B.C. to N.B., s to e Ariz., N.M., Okla., Mo., Ill., Ind., Ohio, W.Va., D.C.

Marsh Five-finger, *P. palustris*, 4–24″ tall, has 5–7 leaflets; 1 to many flowers; grows in wet soil, from Lab. to Alaska, s to N.J., Ohio, Wyo., and Calif.

Sulfur Cinquefoil, *P. recta*, is a European species; stems 6–28″, very leafy; grows in dry soil, Nfld. to Minn., s to Va., Tenn., Tex.; spreading rapidly.

P. thurberi, 12–16″ high, has 5–7 fine-toothed leaflets, silky beneath with fine hairs; grows in coniferous forests at 6000–9000′ in Ariz. and N.M.

Golden-hardhack or **Widdy,** *P. fruticosa*, 8″–3′, is shrubby, with shreddy bark; in wet or dry soil, Alaska to s Lab., s in all of the U.S. except SE and Tex.

I. lycopodioides

ibbaldia
ocumbens

Ivesia
gordonii

Horkelia
cuneata

otentilla
implex

P. anserina

P. arguta

P. tridentata

P. thurberi

P. palustris

P. recta

P. fruticosa

LEGUME FAMILY (LEGUMINOSAE)

Leaves alternate, simple or compound, with stipules; flowers regu
or zygomorphic, with 1 simple pistil that becomes a legume in frui
very large family, divided into 3 subfamilies.

I. MIMOSA SUBFAMILY (MIMOSOIDEAE)

Leaves pinnately twice-compound; tiny regular flowers in heads; cal
5-lobed; 5 petals, often fused; 5 to many stamens, much longer th
the petals; 6 N.A. genera with herbaceous species.

CALLIANDRA Flowers in dense heads; about 20 stamens, fused ir
tube at the base; 5 herbaceous species, in sw U.S. *C. humilis*, 8" hig
grows in dry soil, from w Tex. to Ariz.

ACACIA Tiny cream or white flowers in round half-inch heads on
loose leafy panicle; 2 herbaceous species, in s U.S. **Fern Acacia**, *A. hir*
2–4' tall, grows in open areas, Fla. to Mo. and Ariz.

CAT'S-CLAW or **SENSITIVE BRIER** (SCHRANKIA) Stems sprawlin
with curved spines; leaflets closing if touched; flowers in ½–1" globes
species, in s U.S. *S. uncinata*, n to Neb. and N.C.

MIMOSA One herbaceous species, **Powder-puff** or **Vergonzosa**, *M*
strigillosa, similar to *Schrankia* but with stiff bristles, no prickles; grow
in sandy soil, se U.S. to Okla. and Tex.

DESMANTHUS Stems erect or spreading, 8"–3' tall; stipules brist
tiny flowers, few per head, with 5–10 stamens; 10 species, mostly in
U.S. **Prairie-mimosa** or **Prickle-weed**, *D. illinoensis*, grows often in cla
from Ala. to Tex., n to Ohio, N.D., and Colo.

NEPTUNIA Stems unarmed, sprawling; yellow flowers, 10 stamen
Two species, of s U.S. *N. pubescens* has sterile petal-like stamens in th
lower flowers; grows in dry or sandy soil, Fla. to Tex.

II. SENNA SUBFAMILY (CAESALPINIOIDEAE)

Leaves pinnately once- or twice-compound; flowers zygomorphic, of
free or fused sepals, 5 free petals, 5–10 stamens.

SENNA (CASSIA) Leaves once-compound, 2–40 leaflets; flowers mostl
in axillary racemes; 10 stamens; 25 herbaceous species.

Two-leaved Senna, *C. bauhinioides,* has woolly 4–16" stems;
ranges from Tex. to Ariz.

Wild Senna, *C. hebecarpa*, 3–4
high, grows on heavy soil, ne U.S.
s to w N.C., e Ky. and Tenn.

Partridge-pea, *C. fasciculata,* 4' tall,
opens 1 flower a day; Mass. to
S.D., s to Fla. and Tex.

Coffee Senna or **Styptic-weed,** *C*
occidentalis, is an escape, Va. to
Kans., s to Fla. and Tex.

Acacia
hirta

Calliandra
humilis

Mimosa
strigillos

Neptunia
pubescens

Schrankia
uncinata

Desmanthus
illinoensis

Cassia
fasciculata

Cassia
hebecarpa

Cassia
occidentalis

Cassia
bauhinioides

RUSH-PEA (HOFFMANSEGGIA) Leaves oddly twice-compound, with 5–11 pinnae, 4–11 pairs of leaflets; flowers in terminal racemes, 5-lobed calyx, 5 petals (the uppermost different); 10 stamens; about 10 species, of cen. and sw U.S. *H. glauca,* 4–12″ high, is common from w Texas to Calif., n to Kans.; *H. jamesii,* 8–16″, is widespread from Kans. and Colo. to Tex. and Ariz.

III. PEA SUBFAMILY (PAPILIONOIDEAE)

Leaves simple or once-compound; flowers zygomorphic, sepals fused in a tube; usually 5 petals—the standard (upper petal) larger, the wings (2 lateral petals) clawed, and the keel (2 lower petals) partly fused; 10 or fewer stamens, inside the keel with the pistil. About 54 genera with herbaceous species in N.A.

FALSE LUPINE (THERMOPSIS) Leaves palmately compound of 3 leaflets, with leafy stipules; yellow flowers in long terminal racemes; 9 species, of e and w U.S. *T. montana,* 16–28″ high, grows in mountain meadows, e Wash. and e Oreg. to Mont., Nev., Utah, and Colo. **Aaron's Rod,** *T. villosa,* with hairy pods, grows in openings in upland woods, from w N.C. and Tenn. to Ala. and Ga.

LUPINE (LUPINUS) Leaves palmately compound, of 3–18 leaflets, stipules adhering to the petiole; flowers in terminal racemes; calyx 2-lipped, the lower lip longer; standard erect, often a vertical groove down the center; 10 stamens, with alternately long and short anthers. Over 150 species are described for N.A.

Late Lupine, *L. formosus,* has 1–3′ erect or reclining stems, 7–9 silky leaflets; flowers vary from white to blue or violet; in open fields and woods, Calif.

Annual Lupine, *L. concinnus,* has 2–6″ stems, 5–8 densely hairy leaflets on a long petiole; racemes 1½–3″ long; abundant in the spring, sw sandy deserts.

Gray's Lupine, *L. grayi,* is usually unbranched, 8–14″ tall, 5–9 leaflets, covered by dense silky hairs; racemes 4–6″ long; canyons and valleys, n Sierra Nevada.

Wild Lupine, *L. perennis,* 8–28″ tall, has 7–11 leaflets on the lower leaves; 3–12″ racemes; in dry open woods, clearings, Me. to Fla., w to Minn. and Ill.

Texas Bluebonnet, *L. subcarnosus,* is branched at the base, the branches reclined, 6–16″ long; 5 cr 6 (rarely 7) leaflets, silky beneath; mostly in deep sandy loam, s-cen. Tex.

BUR-CLOVER or **MEDICK** (MEDICAGO) Plants 1–3′ tall, pinnately compound leaves with 3 leaflets, the rounded tips toothed; flowers axillary, solitary, in small clusters, or in spikes; 10 stamens, 9 fused at the base, 1 free; Eurasian; 10 species are escapes in N.A. **Black Medick** or **Nonesuch,** *M. lupulina,* is now found throughout most of temperate N.A. **Lucerne** or **Alfalfa,** *M. sativa,* is widespread except in the SW.

Hoffmanseggia glauca

H. jamesii

Thermopsis montana

T. villosa

Lupinus formosus

L. concinnus

L. grayi

Medicago lupulina

M. sativa

L. perennis

L. subcarnosus

SWEET CLOVER (MELILOTUS) Similar to *Medicago* (p. 112) but often taller; flowers in spike-like racemes. Eurasian; 6 escapes, 3 throughout N.A. **White Sweet Clover,** *M. alba,* 1–10′, has 30–80 flowers per raceme; in **Sour Clover,** *M. indica,* 4–20″ tall, the stipules of the lower leaves partly encircle the stem; **Yellow Sweet Clover,** *M. officinalis,* 16″–7′ contains coumarin and has been used for flavoring cheese.

CLOVER (TRIFOLIUM) Leaves mostly palmately compound, often o 3 leaflets, toothed toward the tip; flowers axillary and/or terminal, in clusters, heads, or spike-like racemes, rarely solitary; calyx-tube with 5 bristle-like teeth; 10 stamens, 9 fused at the base, 1 free. About 95 species, mostly in w N.A.

Rabbit-foot Clover, *T. arvense,* crowds its flowers in cylindrical heads to 2″ long; feathery bristles on calyx hide the flowers; leaves silky. European, now established from Que. to Fla., w to the Pac.; rare in the SW.

Shamrock, *T. dubium,* is a low much-branched trailing plant; leaves pinnately trifoliate, the leaflets to ½″ long; 5–18 flowers in ⅜″ heads; European, now from N.S. to Fla., w to B.C. and Calif.

Large-headed Clover, *T. macrocephalum,* has stout stems to 1′; sparsely hairy, with 5–9 leathery palmately compound leaflets, 1–2″ flower heads. Grows in wet meadows, from B.C. and Ida. to ne Calif. and Nev.

Small-headed Clover, *T. microcephalum,* has a 7- to 10-lobed involucre below the tiny heads;

stems erect or reclining, 8–16″ long, 3-foliate leaves. Grows in open grassy sites, B.C. and Mont. to Baja Calif. and Nev.

Buffalo Clover, *T. reflexum,* is an erect 4–20″ plant, branched from the base, hairy toward the top; flowers in 1–2″ globes, the standard red, the other petals red or white; ranges from s Ont. to S.D., s to Fla. and Tex.

Crimson Clover, *T. incarnatum,* 4–32″ tall, with dense spike-like heads 1–4″ long; the standard is much longer than the wings or keel; European, now common in NE, local to Pac. coast.

Red Clover, *T. pratense,* has 30–90 flowers per head, the heads to 1½″ long, subtended by a pair of leaves; only the bumblebee's tongue is long enough to enter the keel. Throughout N.A.

DEER VETCH and **TREFOIL** (LOTUS) have several kinds of leaves—odd-pinnately compound of 5–15 or more leaflets, or of 3 palmate leaflets, or sessile simple leaves; stipules leaflike or glandlike; flowers solitary, in pairs, or in umbels; 10 stamens, 9 fused at the base, 1 free. About 60 species, mostly in w N.A. **Bird's-foot Trefoil,** *L. corniculatus,* has many 6–24″ stems, tiny 3-foliate leaves, leaflike stipules; Eurasian, now widespread in N.A. *L. crassifolius* has 16–40″ hollow stems and 9–15 1″ leaflets; nw Wash. to s Calif. *L. rigidus* has 1–3′ wiry stems, 3–5 leaflets; grows in desert, s Calif. to Utah and Ariz.

M. indica

T. dubium

Trifolium arvense

M. officinalis

Melilotus alba

T. microcephalum

T. reflexum

T. incarnatum

T. macrocephalum

Lotus corniculatus

L. rigidus

L. crassifolius

T. pratense

SCURF-PEA (PSORALEA) Leaves of 1–7 leaflets, even-pinnate, odd-pinnate, or palmately compounded; stipules leafy; herbage and caly dotted by glands with a heavy or tarlike odor. Flowers in short or spike-like racemes; lower lobe of calyx longer and broader than the 4 uppe lobes; standard tapered to a short claw; 10 stamens, 9 fused at the base 1 free or missing. About 40 herbaceous species in N.A.

Silver Scurf-pea, *P. argophylla*, 10″–2′ high, is silvery silky-white throughout; palmate leaves of 3–5 leaflets; flower spike of 1–3 separate whorls of flowers. Sask. to Wisc., s to Mo. and N.M.

Breadroot, *P. esculenta*, 4–16″, has palmate leaves with 5–7 leaflets; long spreading hairs; turniplike taproot. Grows in dry prairies, Alta. to Man. and Wisc., s to Mo., Tex., and N.M.

California Tea, *P. physodes*, is erect 12–32″ high, with sparse black hairs; leaves pinnately 3-foliate flowers in 1″ heads. Grows in open forests, V.I. and e Wash. to s Calif

Sampson's Snakeroot, *P. psora lioides*, has 1–3′ slender erec stems, pinnately 3-foliate leaves ½–1″ flower spikes, elongating to 4″ at flowering. Fla. to Tex., n to Va. and Ill.

FALSE INDIGO (AMORPHA) Erect bushy plants; leaves odd-pinnate, with bristly deciduous stipules, leaflets with stipels; herbage and calyx often gland-dotted. Flowers in dense spike-like racemes, of 1 petal, the standard; 10 exposed stamens. About 20 species, of temperate N.A.; 9 are herbaceous. **Lead-plant,** *A. canescens*, is gray from fine hairs; leaves of 11–51 leaflets; many racemes in a dense cluster 3–10″ long at the stem tips; ranges from Sask. to Mich., s to Ind., Ark., Tex., and N.M. **Fragrant False Indigo,** *A. nana*, 1–3′ tall, has leaves of 21–41 leaflets; usually solitary terminal racemes; grows in dry prairies, Man. and Sask. s to Ia., Okla., and N.M. *A. herbacea*, to 3′, has up to 41 leaflets; the stem, petioles, lower side of leaflets, and calyx silvery; grows in pine-lands, Coastal Plain, Fla. to N.C.

DALEA Leaves odd-pinnate (rarely palmately 3-foliate), gland-dotted, with stipules and stipels; flowers in terminal heads, spikes, or racemes, of 1 petal, the standard; 9–14 stamens, the filaments fused in a tube, 4 stamens petal-like, 5–10 fertile. About 30 herbaceous species in warmer N.A.; most are silky. **Golden Dalea,** *D. aurea*, has 12–20″ erect stems, pinnate leaves of 5–7 leaflets; flower spikes ½–1″ long; ranges from S.D. to Wyo. and Tex. **Silky Dalea,** *D. mollis*, has spreading basal branches 1–8″ long, pinnate leaves with 9–13 leaflets, ½–1″ flower spikes, feathery teeth on calyx; grows in Colorado Desert (s Calif., Baja Calif., sw Ariz.). *D. jamesii* has many upright 4″ stems from a caudex, palmately 3-foliate leaves, dense flower spikes to 1″ long; ranges from s Ariz. and w Tex. to Kans. and Colo.

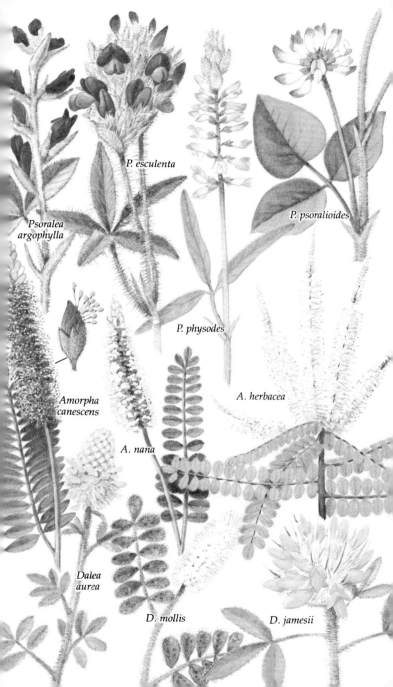

P. esculenta

Psoralea
argophylla

P. psoralioides

Amorpha
canescens

A. nana

P. physodes

A. herbacea

Dalea
aurea

D. mollis

D. jamesii

PRAIRIE-CLOVER (PETALOSTEMUM) Herbs similar to *Dalea* (p. 116) with odd-pinnate leaves of 3 to many leaflets, tiny stipules; flowers with 1 petal, the standard; 9 stamens—4 sterile and petal-like, 5 fertile; about 27 N.A. species. **White Prairie-clover,** *P. candidum*, 12–28″ tall lacks hair, has leaves of 5–7 leaflets, dense cylindrical 1–4″ spikes of flowers; each flower subtended by a pointed bract much longer than the calyx; grows in prairies, Alta. and Sask. to Minn. and Ind., s to Miss. and Ariz. *P. villosum*, 1–2′, is branched at the base and bushy, densely hairy; leaves of 9–17 leaflets; terminal 1–4″ spikes of flowers, each subtended by densely hairy bracts; grows in sandy soil, from Mont. and Sask. to Mich., s to Mo., Tex., and N.M.

MILK-VETCH and **LOCO WEED** (ASTRAGALUS) Herbs, some with a caudex, some stemless, with odd-pinnate leaves of 3 to many leaflets, with stipules and no stipels. Flowers in axillary racemes or spikes, rarely in umbels or solitary; calyx tubular, 5-toothed; 5 typical petals, the standard clawed and its edges rolled back, the keel blunt-tipped and wings adhering to its base; 10 stamens, 9 with fused filaments, 1 free. Over 375 species, often variable, have been described for N.A.; most are western, some local, others widespread. Some accumulate selenium and are poisonous, causing "loco disease" in livestock.

Rattle-vetch, *A. canadensis*, 1–5′ tall, has ½″ flowers in thick cylindrical 6″ racemes; in open woods, stream banks, Que. to B.C., s to Ga., Tex., and Utah.

A. ceramicus has underground stems, leaves often just the midrib; 2- to 15-flowered racemes; grows in dry, sandy soil, Ida. to S.D., s to Neb., N.M, Ariz.

Ground-plum, Buffalo-bean, or **Indian-pea,** *A. crassicarpus*, has a group of 4–24″ half-reclining stems, 15–33 leaflets; unripe fruits resemble green plums. Mont. to Man., s to Tex., N.M.

Texas or **Woolly Loco Weed,** *A. mollissimus*, the first recognized loco weed; low and leafy, covered by soft straight hair; Ariz. to Tex., n to Wyo.

Pink Lady-fingers, *A. utahensis*, is stemless, the leaves arranged in a symmetrical clump, covered by silvery down; e Oreg. and e Calif. to Mont., Wyo., and Utah.

LOCO WEED (OXYTROPIS) Like *Astragalus* but the tip of the keel is sharp-pointed. About 36 species in N.A. *O. lambertii*, to 10″, silky with forked hairs, has 9–23 stiff leaflets; grows in dry prairies, gravel, Mont. to Man. and Minn., s to Ariz. and Tex.; common and readily eaten by livestock; the most destructive of loco weeds, addictive, often fatal. *O. deflexa*, 1–12″, silky-hairy, has 25–41 leaflets; grows in moist soil, Alaska to e Wash. and S.D., s to N.M. *O. splendens*, 4–14″ high, leaflets in clusters or whorls on the rachis; racemes of 20–80 flowers; ranges from Alta. and Man. to w Minn., s to N.D. and N.M.

Astragalus canadensis

A. ceramicus

A. crassicarpus

A. utahensis

P. villosum

Petalostemum candidum

A. mollissimus

Oxytropis lambertii

O. deflexa

O. splendens

LICORICE (GLYCYRRHIZA) One native species, *G. lepidota*, 2–3′ tall leaves odd-pinnate, of 15–19 leaflets, sprinkled by tiny scales when young, gland-dotted and sticky when old; flowers as in *Astragalus* (p 119), but the 2 top calyx teeth are short or partly united, every other stamen smaller; var. *glutinosa* is glandular-hairy. Prairies, meadows low places, from B.C. to s Calif., e to w Ont., nw Mo., Tex.

CROWN VETCH (CORONILLA) Spreading, branched hairless plant to 2′ high, with odd-pinnate leaves of 15–25 leaflets, axillary umbels c 10–20 flowers. Eurasian and n African; 1 species, *C. varia*, has escaped Me. to S.D., s to Mo. and N.C., and in w Oreg.

SWEET VETCH (HEDYSARUM) Leaves odd-pinnate, with stipules flowers in axillary racemes; keel nearly straight, longer than the wings the tip obliquely blunt; 8 N.A. species. *H. alpinum* has many 4–24″ leaf stems from a caudex, leaves of 13–23 leaflets, 1–6″ 1-sided racemes Alaska and boreal Canada, s to s Canada, mts. of Me. and Vt. *H. boreale* 8–20″, with 11–13 leaflets; Alta. and Sask. to Ariz. and Tex.

VETCH (VICIA) Vines, leaves with stipules, even-pinnate, of 2–1 leaflets, end of rachis a tendril. Flowers axillary, single or in racemes lowest teeth of calyx longer; the wings adhere to the middle of the keel style slender; 30 species.

Common Vetch, *V. angustifolia*, has 4–24″ stems, branched at the base; 2–5 pairs of leaflets; flowers in pairs. European, now in s Canada and most of the U.S.

Tufted Vetch, *V. cracca*, is Euro pean, now from B.C. to Nfld., s over n U.S. to n Calif. and Va. stems 2–7′, 8–12 pairs of leaflets racemes of 10–40 flowers.

American Vetch, *V. americana*, is 3′ long, with 4–9 pairs of leaflets; 3- to 9-flowered racemes. On damp shores, meadows, se Alaska to w Que., s to all but the SE.

Large Yellow Vetch, *V. grandiflora*, is also European, now on road-sides and fields, Del. to Fla. and Miss.; flowers in pairs; 3–7 pairs of leaflets.

VETCHLING or **WILD PEA** (LATHYRUS) Much like *Vicia* but the style is dilated; a few are upright herbs; 45 species in N.A.

L. eucosmus has 3–4 pairs of thick leaflets 1–2″ long; 2- to 5-flowered racemes. In dry open woods, Colo., Utah, N.M., Ariz.

Pacific Pea, *L. vestitus*, climbs to 10′, has 4–7 pairs of leaflets; 4- to 20-flowered racemes; grows in mts., w Oreg. to s Calif.

Everlasting Pea, *L. latifolius*, a European escape, ranges from N.Eng. to Va., Kans., Tex.; w Oreg. to n Calif.; has winged stems, 2 leaflets; high-climbing.

L. venosus has 4-angled stems to 7′; leaflets 8–14, often scattered on the rachis; 5- to 19-flowered ra-cemes; Sask. to s Que., s to Ga., La., Ark., Okla, and e Tex.

lycyrrhiza lepidota

Coronilla varia

Hedysarum alpinum

H. boreale

Vicia angustifolia

V. americana

V. cracca

V. grandiflora

L. latifolius

L. vestitus

L. venosus

Lathyrus eucosmus

CANAVALIA Erect or strong-twining trailing herbs; leaves odd-pinnate, of 3 leaflets, with stipules and stipels; flowers in axillary racemes calyx 2-lipped, upper lip much longer; 10 stamens, 9 fused in a tube, 1 partly free; 2 species in se U.S. **Bay-bean,** *C. maritima*, has trailing or twining 2–10′ stems, rounded leaflets 2–4″ long; grows on beaches from Fla. to Tex.

DIOCLEA One N.A. species, *D. multiflora*, a downy high-climbing twiner; odd-pinnate leaves with 3 round 1–6″ leaflets, abrupt sharp tips, racemes axillary; calyx 4-lobed; ranges from Ga. and Fla. to e Tex., n to Ky. and Ark.

KUDZU (PUERARIA) Stems hairy, becoming woody, very high-climbing, 65–100′; odd-pinnate leaves with 3 entire or lobed leaflets; axillary 4–12″ racemes. Asian; 1 species, *P. lobata*, has escaped in se U.S. and now reaches e Tex., Pa., and Tenn.

WILD BEAN (STROPHOSTYLES) Stems 1–4′, erect when young, trailing or twining later; leaves pinnately 3-foliate, with stipules and stipels; flowers in few-flowered axillary heads; 3 N.A. species. **Amberique Bean,** *S. helvola*, grows in sandy soil, from S.D. to Que., s to Fla. and Tex.

LADY'S-FINGERS (ANTHYLLIS) European; 1 species, *A. vulneraria*, is wide-ranging but local, N.D. to Que., s to Mo. and Pa.; a downy 8–12″ plant; odd-pinnate leaves with 1–13 leaflets; flowers yellow to red, in paired heads subtended by an involucre.

ALICIA (CHAPMANNIA) One species, *C. floridana*, grows in dry pinelands of Fla.; stems 2–4′, sticky-hairy; odd-pinnate leaves with 3–7 tiny leaflets; terminal racemes with 2 kinds of flowers—showy males with 10 stamens, females lacking petals and stamens.

INDIGO (INDIGOFERA) Downy-gray plants; leaves odd-pinnate, with stipules, 5–15 leaflets; racemes axillary; calyx 5-toothed; keel with lateral pouches; 10 stamens, filaments fused, 1 half-free; 9 species in N.A. **Scarlet Pea,** *I. miniata*, salmon-pink to scarlet, grows in sandy soil, Fla.; e Tex. to s Kans.

RATTLEBOX (CROTALARIA) Stems erect or prostrate, leaves simple or 3-foliate; racemes bracted, terminal or axillary; calyx of 5 unequal lobes; standard large, heart-shaped; keel scythe-shaped; 10 stamens, filaments fused. 13 species, most in s U.S. **Rabbit-bells,** *C. angulata*, forms carpets 3′ wide in sandy pinelands, from La. to Fla. and se Va. *C. spectabilis*, to 7′ high, is a tropical escape, grows in se U.S., n to e Va. and se Mo.

Canavalia maritima

Dioclea multiflora

Pueraria lobata

Anthyllis vulneraria

Strophostyles helvola

Chapmannia floridana

Indigofera miniata

Crotalaria angulata

Crotalaria spectabilis

SOPHORA Leaves odd-pinnate, stipules deciduous; racemes terminal or axillary; calyx 5-lobed; stamens 10, free; 2 herbaceous species. **White Loco,** *S. nuttalliana,* forms colonies of 12–20″ silky-gray shoots from a rhizome; grows on prairies, dry hills, S.D. to Wyo., s to Kans., Tex., N.M., Ariz., and s Utah.

FALSE INDIGO (BAPTISIA) Stems stout, solitary at the base, bushy higher up; leaves palmately 3-foliate; racemes terminal or axillary; calyx 4- or 5-toothed; 10 stamens, all free. About 25 species (and many hybrids), in e N.A. **White False Indigo,** *B. leucantha,* 3–7′ tall; grows in most of e U.S. and s Ont. **Plains False Indigo,** *B. leucophaea,* 12–32″ high, has nearly sessile leaves, white or yellow flowers; grows in sandy soil, s Mich. to Minn. and Neb., s to La. and e Tex. **Rattle-weed,** *B. tinctoria,* 1–3′ tall, inhabits dry open woods and clearings, e U.S.

BUTTERFLY-PEA (CENTROSEMA) Twining vines, leaves pinnately 3-foliate, with stipules and stipels; flowers solitary or in 2's; back of standard spurred; keel broad; 10 stamens, 9 fused in a tube, 1 free; 3 N.A. species, 2 restricted to Fla. *C. virginianum,* with 8″–5′ stems, grows in sandy soil, se U.S., n to N.J.

BUTTERFLY-PEA (CLITORIA) Vines much like *Centrosema,* but no spur on the standard and keel narrow; 2 N.A. species, 1 only in Fla. *C. mariana* grows in dry soil, from Fla. to se Ariz. (but not in N.M.), n to Ia. and s N.Y.

COLOGANIA Stems 4″–5′ long, erect, reclining, or twining; leaves pinnately 3-foliate, with stipules and stipels; flowers axillary, solitary, in 2's, or in umbels; calyx 4-lobed; 10 stamens, 9 in a tube, 1 free; 3 species in sw U.S. *C. angustifolia* is downy; has long narrow leaflets; ranges from w Tex. to Ariz.

POTATO BEAN (APIOS) Twining vines; odd-pinnate leaves of 3–9 leaflets, with stipules and stipels; dense axillary racemes; 5 tiny calyx-teeth; standard broad; keel scythe-shaped, slender, at times coiled. Rootstock with tubers; 2 species (1 rare) in e N.A. *A. americana* grows in se Canada and e U.S., w to Colo.

HOG PEANUT (AMPHICARPA) One species, *A. bracteata;* stems 8″–7′ long, brown-haired, twining; leaves pinnately 3-foliate; 2 kinds of flowers: (1) perfect on the upper branches, calyx-tube 4-lobed; 10 stamens, 9 in a tube, 1 free; (2) those on basal creeping branches lack well-developed petals, have a few free stamens, are self-fertile, sometimes flower underground. Grows in damp woodlands, se Canada and e U.S., w to Man., Mont., and Tex.

Baptisia leucantha

B. leucophaea

Sophora nuttalliana

B. tinctoria

Centrosema
virginianum

Clitoria mariana

Cologania angustifolia

Apios
americana

Amphicarpa bracteata

BUSH-CLOVER (LESPEDEZA) Leaves pinnately 3-foliate, with stipules, no stipels; flowers in 2's or in racemes, calyx 5-lobed; 10 stamens, 9 fused in a tube, 1 free. Spring flowers showy; often lacking petals in summer and fall; 20 species in N.A.

Dusty Clover, *L. capitata,* an erect plant 2–7' tall, has 10–30 flowers per head; grows in dry open soil, e and cen. U.S.

Prairie Clover, *L. violacea,* has weak, nearly erect 8–28" stems, delicate 4- to 6-flowered racemes; in most of ne and cen. U.S.

Trailing Bush-clover, *L. procumbens,* 1–6' stems, softly hairy all over; grows in dry woods, clearings, e and cen. U.S.

Slender Bush-clover, *L. virginica,* 1–5', is very leafy, soft-hairy or downy; has 4- to 8-flowered racemes; grows in e N.A.

SNOUT-BEAN (RHYNCHOSIA) Erect, trailing, or twining herbs; leaves pinnately 1- or 3-foliate, resin-dotted, with stipules, some with stipels; flowers axillary, few or in racemes; calyx 2-lipped; 10 stamens, 9 in a tube, 1 free; 10 species, in s U.S. **Dollar-leaf,** *R. reniformis,* is erect, to 9" high; leaves 1-foliate, round; Coastal Plain, N.C. to Fla. and Tex.; *R. latifolia* twines, has 3-foliate leaves, racemes to 1' long; grows in sandy soil, s Mo. and Okla. to La. and Tex.

MILK-PEA (GALACTEA) Low trailing or twining herbs, odd-pinnate leaves of 1–7 leaflets, with stipules and stipels; flowers few to many in axillary racemes; calyx 4-lobed; 10 stamens, 9 in a tube, 1 free; 17 species, in s U.S. *G. regularis* grows in sandy soil, from Fla. to Tex., n to N.Y. and Kans.

HOARY PEA (TEPHROSIA) Erect or reclining herbs, odd-pinnate leaves of 5–31 leaflets, with stipules; racemes axillary or terminal; calyx 5-lobed; standard broad, silky on the back; 9 stamens in a tube to halfway up, 1 free at both ends, but fused to the others at the middle; 17 species, of e and s U.S. **Goat's-rue,** *T. virginiana,* is silky-hairy, with erect simple 12–28" stems, dense 1–4" terminal racemes; grows in sandy soil, N.H. to Fla., w to Wisc., Kans., and Tex.

ZORINA Wiry-stemmed herbs; palmate leaves of 2 or 4 leaflets; stipules broad, attached just above the petiole base; flowers in spikes, each flower subtended by 2 large bracts; 3 species, in s U.S. **Viperina,** *Z. bracteata,* has 4 leaflets; forms large mats on dry sandy soil, Coastal Plain, se Va. to Tex.

ERYTHRINA One species, **Cardinal-spear,** *E. herbacea,* with spiny 2–7' stems, pinnately 3-foliate leaves, with stipules and stipels; 2" seemingly tubular flowers; Coastal Plain, N.C. to Tex.

L.
virginica

L.
procumbens

L. violacea

Lespedeza
capitata

Galactea
regularis

R. latifolia

Rhynchosia
reniformis

Tephrosia
virginiana

Zorina
bracteata

Erythrina
herbacea

FLAX FAMILY (LINACEAE)

FLAX (LINUM) Herbs with simple sessile entire leaves, alternate, opposite, or whorled; flowers in S-shaped cymes, flower parts in 5's, 1 pistil, 5 styles; 35 species in N.A. **Prairie Flax,** *L. lewisii,* 4–32", has densely leafy stems from a caudex; ranges from Alaska to s Calif., e to n Ont. and Tex.; *L. rigidum,* 4–20", is bushy, has stiff angled branches; Alta. to Minn., s to Mo. and n Texas; **Common Flax,** *L. usitatissimum,* 1–3', has fringed inner sepals; European, now found in most of N.A.

WOOD-SORREL FAMILY (OXALIDACEAE)

WOOD-SORREL (OXALIS) Low plants with sour watery sap; leaves basal or alternate, simple to pinnate or palmately divided, often of 3 leaflets, notched at the tip. Flowers on scapes, solitary or in umbels, of 5 sepals, 5 petals, 10 stamens, 1 pistil, 5 styles; 31 species in N.A. **Yellow Wood-sorrel,** *O. dillenii,* to 2' high, is clump-forming; se U.S., w to Tex. **Wood-shamrock,** *O. montana,* creeps by a rhizome; leaves and scapes all basal; grows in damp woods, s Nfld. to Man., s to Pa. and Mich.; in mountains to N.C. and Tenn. In **Pink Wood-sorrel,** *O. violacea,* leaves and scapes are from a bulb; grows in woods and prairies, from Fla. to N.M., n to Mass., N.D., and Colo.

GERANIUM FAMILY (GERANIACEAE)

Leaves basal or alternate, lobed or divided, with stipules; flowers solitary or in cymes, of 5 sepals, 5 petals, 5 or 10 stamens; 1 pistil, 5-lobed; 5 long styles; 2 genera in N.A.

CRANE'S-BILL (GERANIUM) Stems much-branched; leaves palmately lobed, the lobes often pinnately divided; 10 stamens (rarely 5) alternately long and short. About 33 species in N.A. *G. carolinianum,* to 2' tall, is bushy-branched, has densely hairy stems and petioles; grows in dry woods, fields, Me. to B.C., s to Calif. and Fla. **Wild Geranium,** *G. maculatum,* has 2–6" 5-lobed basal leaves, a scape-like stem ending in 2–3 large leaves and a terminal corymb; inhabits woods and meadows, Man. to Me., s to Kans., Mo., Tenn., and Ga. **Dove's-foot,** *G. molle,* is downy, with slender weak stems, 2-lobed petals; European, now ranges over s Canada and the U.S.

STORK'S-BILL (ERODIUM) Leaves palmately lobed to pinnately divided; flowers in umbels; 10 stamens—5 fertile, 5 lacking anthers; 9 species in N.A. **Pin-clover** or **Alfileria,** *C. cicutarium,* to 2', has evergreen rosettes of pinnate leaves; much-branched at the base; ranges from Alaska to Que., s in most of the U.S. *E. texanum* has simple 3-lobed leaves, horizontal stems to 20"; grows in open areas, Tex. to s Utah and se Calif.

*Linum
lewisii*

*L.
usitatissimum*

L. rigidum

*Oxalis
dillenii*

O. violacea

O. montana

*Geranium
carolinianum*

G. maculatum

*Erodium
cicutarium*

E. texanum

G. molle

CALTROP FAMILY (ZYGOPHYLLACEAE)

Plants with zigzag stems, diverse leaves with stipules, mostly solitary flowers of 4–5 sepals and petals, 5, 10, or 12–15 stamens, 1 pistil, 1 style. 5 herbaceous genera in N.A.

PEGANUM Globose plants with forked branches, dense simple alternate pinnately lobed leaves; solitary flowers, of 4–5 sepals and petals, 12–15 stamens; 2 species in N.A. *P. harmala*, to 1' high, is an Afro-Asian escape, Tex. to Ariz. and Nev.

FAGONIA One species, *F. californica*, from Utah and Ariz. to s Calif.; to 16" high, base woody, leaves palmately 3-foliate; stipules sharp; flowers clustered, of 5 sepals, petals, and stamens.

CALTROP or **PUNCTURE-VINE** (TRIBULUS) Stems spreading to 10' from a central root; leaves paired, even-pinnate, of 6–14 leaflets; 1 leaf of each pair alternately smaller; flowers solitary, of 5 sepals, 5 petals, 10 stamens with glands between them; a 5-lobed pistil; fruit with 10–20 stout spines; 2 species, both Eurasian, in N.A. *T. terrestris* grows in dry or sandy soil, from Fla. to Calif., n to e Wash., S.D. and s N.Y.

KALLSTROEMIA Similar to *Tribulus* but lacking intra-staminal glands, pistil 10-lobed, fruit not spiny; 7 N.A. species. *K. parviflora* ranges from Miss. to se Calif., n to Colo. and Ill.

MILKWORT FAMILY (POLYGALACEAE)

Leaves simple and entire, sessile or short-petioled, alternate, opposite, or whorled. Flowers zygomorphic; 5 sepals, 3 petals, 6 or 8 stamens, 1 pistil, a 2-lobed stigma; 2 N.A. genera.

MILKWORT (POLYGALA) Three sepals usually green, 2 petal-like; base of petals united, lower petal keel-like, sometimes 3-lobed; stamens fused in a tube. About 60 N.A. species.

P. incarnata, 5–24", has a stiff erect slender grooved stem; grows in dry open soil, s Ont. to Wisc. and Neb., s to Fla., Tex.

Yellow Bachelor's-button, *P. lutea*, grows in damp or wet sand or peat, Coastal Plain, La. to Fla., n to L.I. and e Pa.

P. obscura, 5–16", is many-stemmed from a woody base; gray-downy; grows on dry slopes, from cen. and w Tex. to Ariz.

Seneca-Snakeroot, *P. senega*, 4–20", has several stems from a thick base; in limestone soil, Alta. to Que., s to Ark. and Ga.

P. ramosa, 4–18", has terminal panicles 1–6" wide; grows in damp pinelands and wet fields, Fla. to Tex.; Coastal Plain to N.J.

Fringed Polygala, *P. pauciflora*, 3–4" high, has 1–4 1" flowers; in woods, Que. to Man., s to Minn. and N.Eng., mts. to Ga.

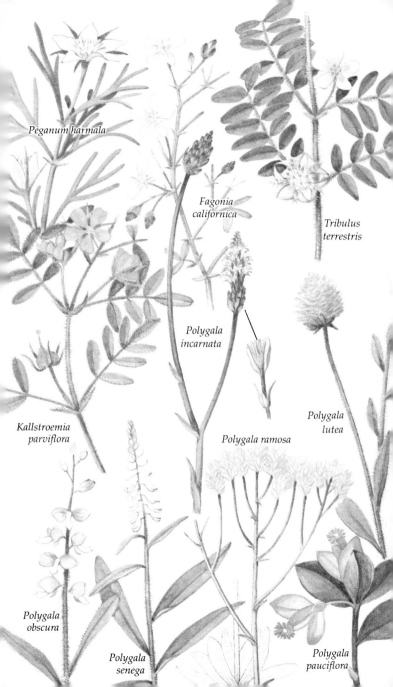

Peganum harmala

Fagonia californica

Tribulus terrestris

Polygala incarnata

Polygala lutea

Kallstroemia parviflora

Polygala ramosa

Polygala obscura

Polygala senega

Polygala pauciflora

SPURGE FAMILY (EUPHORBIACEAE)

Plants usually with milky juice; leaves simple in the herbaceous species, most with tiny stipules. Flowers male or female; ovary 3-lobed, with 3 styles, 3 or 6 stigmas; 19 genera with herbaceous species in N.A.; many are weeds; others have colored leaves resembling petals.

JATROPHA Leaves entire or palmately lobed, alternate or whorled; flowers in cymes, of 5 sepals, 5 petals, males with 8–10 stamens; 3 herbaceous species, in sw U.S. *J. macrorhiza*, 1–3' high, has palmately 3- or 5-lobed leaves; w Tex. to Ariz.

SPURGE-NETTLE (CNIDOSCOLUS) Herbs with stinging hairs; leaves palmately 3- to 5-lobed; flowers in terminal forking cymes; calyx of 5 petal-like lobes, no petals, males with 10–30 stamens; 3 N.A. species. **Tread-softly,** *C. stimulosus*, 5–24", has fragrant flowers; grows in dry sandy soil, se U.S.

STILLINGIA Erect plants with alternate entire leaves, glandular stipules. Flowers in terminal and axillary bracted spikes; calyx cuplike, no petals, males of 2 stamens; 8 species of s U.S. **Queen's-delight,** *S. sylvatica*, 1–3', grows in sandy soil, Fla. to N.M., n to Kans., se Va.

SPURGE (EUPHORBIA) Diverse plants with milky sap, flowers lacking sepals and petals, grouped in calyx-like involucres with horned or petal-like glands on the rim; males of 1 stamen. A huge genus, mostly weedy; a few are showy.

Flowering Spurge, *E. corollata*, has several 3' stems; flowers in broad forking umbels; grows in dry soil, e and cen. U.S.

Wild Poinsettia or **Fire-on-the-mountain,** *E. cyathophora*, 8–20" tall, is found from Fla. to Ariz., n to S.D. and Va.

Cypress Spurge, *E. cyparissias*, is densely tufted; stems 4–28", very leafy; a European escape, Mass. to Va. and Colo.

Caper-spurge or **Mole-plant,** *E. lathyris*, to 5', has opposite clasping leaves; a European escape, N.Eng. to N.C. and Ohio.

Wolf's-Milk, *E. escula*, 1–3', has many flowering branches, a large terminal umbel; Wash. and Alta. to Que., s to Neb. and Pa.

Snow-on-the-mountain, *E. marginata*, 1–3', is native, Mont. to Minn., s to the border; cultivated and escaped to the Atlantic.

BOX FAMILY (BUXACEAE)

PACHYSANDRA One species, **Allegheny Spurge,** *P. procumbens*, grow in woods, Ky. to w Fla. and La. Stems 5–10", reclined, a few simple leaves at the tip, a few many-flowered spikes near the base; flowers ill-scented, with 1–3 bracts; calyx 4- to 5-lobed; no petals; males of 4 stamens; female flowers at the base of the spike with 3 styles.

Stillingia sylvatica

Cnidoscolus stimulosus

Jatropha macrorhiza

E. cyathophora

E. escula

Euphorbia corollata

E. cyparissias

Pachysandra procumbens

E. marginata

E. lathyris

RATANY FAMILY (KRAMERIACEAE)

RATANY (KRAMERIA) Leaves alternate, simple, entire; flowers zygomorphic, of 4–5 petal-like sepals; 5 petals—3 long-clawed, 2 short and thick; 4 stamens; 1 pistil, in fruit a downy bur; 2 herbaceous species both with trailing stems, in s U.S. **Prairie-bur,** *K. lanceolata,* has silk 4"–6' stems, short narrow leaves; common from Kans. to Ariz. and Tex

RUE FAMILY (RUTACEAE)

DUTCHMAN'S-BREECHES (THAMNOSMA) One species, *T. texana* to 1', with simple alternate gland-dotted leaves, flowers in racemes yellow or purple, of 4 sepals, 4 petals, 8 stamens, a 2-lobed pistil; frui like inflated "dutchman's breeches"; grows from Tex. to Ariz.

MALPIGHIA FAMILY (MALPIGHIACEAE)

JANUSIA One species, *J. gracilis,* a wiry-stemmed twiner; leaves op posite, simple, entire; flowers solitary or in axillary clusters, of 5 sepals 5 petals, a 3-lobed ovary; some have 2-lobed ovary, are self-fertile and do not open; ranges from w Tex. to Ariz.

CROWBERRY FAMILY (EMPETRACEAE)

CROWBERRY (EMPETRUM) Low creeping plants with woody stems and narrow simple rigid evergreen leaves, resembling herbs; flowers axillary, of 3 petal-like sepals, no petals, 3 stamens, 1 pistil with a 6- to 9-rayed stigma; 4 species in n N.A. **Black Crowberry** or **Curlew-berry,** *E. nigrum,* is circumboreal, s in peat to n tier of states and to n Calif.; isolated on e L.I. **Purple Crowberry,** *E. atropurpureum,* has cobweb-like hairs; grows on acid soil, s Lab. and s Que. to mountains of n N.Eng.

TOUCH-ME-NOT FAMILY (BALSAMINACEAE)

JEWEL-WEED or **TOUCH-ME-NOT** (IMPATIENS) Herbs with watery juice, simple leaves; zygomorphic axillary pairs of flowers, of 4 petal-like sepals, 1 forming a spurred sac; 2 2-lobed petals, 5 stamens, 1 pistil; fruits explode if touched; 10 species in N.A., of moist or wet soil, often in shade. *I. pallida* ranges from sw Nfld. to Sask., s to Ga. and Okla.; *I. capensis* from Nfld. to Alaska, s to Fla., Tex., and nw Oreg.

CACAO FAMILY (STERCULIACEAE)

BROOM-WOOD (MELOCHIA) One herbaceous species, **Chocolate-weed,** *M. corchorifolia,* on the Coastal Plain, Fla. to se Tex. and S.C. Stem to 5' with wandlike branches, simple alternate leaves, irregularly toothed or lobed; dense axillary clusters of flowers, of a 5-lobed calyx, 5 petals, 5 stamens with filaments fused at the base, a 5-lobed pistil.

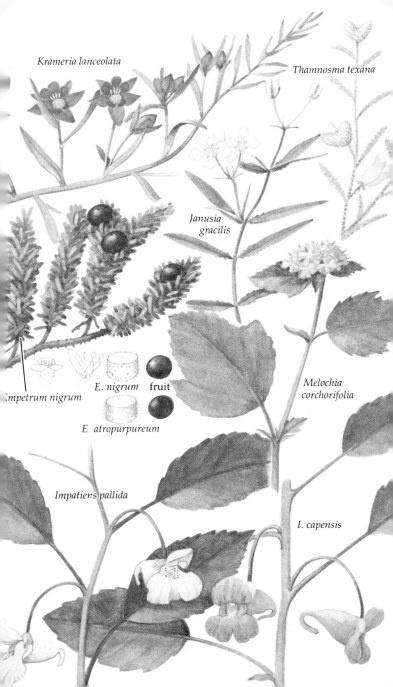

Krameria lanceolata

Thamnosma texana

Janusia gracilis

Empetrum nigrum

E. *nigrum*   fruit

E. *atropurpureum*

Melochia corchorifolia

Impatiens pallida

I. *capensis*

MALLOW FAMILY (MALVACEAE)

Plants with simple alternate leaves with stipules; flowers axillary or in terminal spikes; 5 sepals, united at base, often within an involucre; 5 petals; many stamens, fused in a column that unites with the petal bases; several pistils, united in a ring; 21 genera in N.A. with herbaceous species.

MALLOW (MALVA) Leaves palmately lobed; flowers axillary, single or clustered; involucre 3-leaved; petal tips notched; anthers at top of column; many styles, stigmatic on the inner side; Old World, 8 species now in N.A. **Musk-mallow,** *M. moschata*, 8–28″ high, is common, Nfld. to B.C., s to Oreg., Neb., Mo., Tenn., and Md. **High Mallow**, *M. sylvestris*, to 40″ tall, grows in e N.A., w to N.D. and Tex.

POPPY-MALLOW (CALLIRHOË) Leaves palmately lobed; long-stalked solitary flowers, with or without a 3-leaved involucre; petals square-tipped, ragged-toothed; stamens and styles as in *Malva*; 7 N.A. species. *C. alcaeoides* grows on barrens and plains, from Ill. to Neb., s to Ala., Tenn., Mo., Okla., and Tex. *C. digitata*, of dry plains, ranges from Tex. n to Kans., Mo., and Ind. *C. involucrata* grows in plains, open woods, scrublands, from N.D. to Wyo., s to Mo., Tex., N.M., and Utah.

GLADE-MALLOW (NAPAEA) One species, *N. dioica*, 5–10′ high; large leaves of 9–11 dissected lobes, hairy underneath; small flowers in large terminal clusters, male and female on separate plants; males with 15–20 anthers; females with a short column of antherless filaments, 8–10 styles, stigmatic along the inside; rare, in moist ground, from Pa. to Minn., s to Va. and Ia.

WILD HOLLYHOCK (ILIAMNA) Erect bushy herbs; leaves maplelike; flowers in terminal spikes; involucre 3 narrow bracts; basal edges of petals densely hairy; column stellate-hairy at base; stigmas terminal; 7 N.A. species. *I. grandiflora*, to 6′ high, grows in damp sites, s Utah and Colo. to n Ariz. and N.M.

GLOBE-MALLOW (SPHAERALCEA) Herbage stellate-hairy; leaves toothed or palmately dissected; flowers in racemes or panicles; involucre usually of 3 bractlets; column divided at top into many filaments; styles 5 or more, stigmas terminal; about 22 species, of w U.S. **Desert-mallow,** *S. ambigua*, to 40″ tall, has 3-lobed leaves; ranges from sw Utah to s Calif. *S. angustifolia*, to 6′, has narrow unlobed toothed leaves; grows from w Kans. and Colo. s to Tex. and Ariz. **Scarlet Globe-mallow,** *S. coccinea*, has 20″ reclining stems; Man., s to w Ia., Tex., N.M., and Ariz.

Malva
moschata

M. sylvestris

Callirhoë
alcaeoides

digitata

C. involucrata

Napaea
dioica

Sphaeralcea
ambigua

Iliamna
grandiflora

S. angustifolia

S. coccinea

MODIOLA One species, *M. caroliniana,* a low creeping hairy herb; leaves palmately 3- or 5-lobed; flowers solitary; involucre of 3 leafy bracts; stamens 10–20; stigmas terminal; ranges from Fla. to Va. and Calif.

ANODA Sparsely to densely hairy herbs; upper leaves halberd-like at base; flowers single or in panicles; calyx naked, stigmas terminal; 9 N.A. species. *A. cristata,* to 3' tall, has variable leaves; ranges from cen. Calif. to Tex., n to Ia. and se Pa.

SIDA Leaves entire or palmately divided; flowers solitary, in few-flowered cymes or in leafy terminal panicles; calyx usually naked; styles 5 or more, stigmas terminal; about 22 species in N.A., some weedy. **Dollar-weed** or **Alkali-mallow,** *S. hederacea,* has reclining stems; ranges from Wash. and Ida. s to Mex., e to Kans. and Tex.; **Virginia Mallow,** *S. hermaphrodita,* 4–10', has palmately 3- to 7-lobed leaves; rare, grows in moist soil, s Mich. to Pa., s to Md., w Va., and e Tenn.

MALVASTRUM Leaves scalloped or palmately divided; flowers axillary or in bracted terminal spikes; involucre of narrow or leafy bracts; styles 5 or more, stigmas terminal; 11 species, of s U.S. **Desert Five-spot,** *M. rotundifolium,* 4–16" high, grows in dry sandy soil, w Ariz., s Nev., and s Calif.

CHECKER-MALLOW (SIDALCEA) Leaves palmately divided; flowers in terminal spikes, mostly without bracts or involucres; stamens in a double tube, with anthers at 2 levels; styles 5–10, stigmatic along the inside; about 25 species, of w N.A. *S. neomexicana,* 8–30" tall, grows in wet meadows, from Oreg. to Wyo., s to Mex.

SALT MARSH-MALLOW (KOSTELETZKYA) Leaves palmately veined or lobed; involucre of few to many broad or narrow bracts; column anther-bearing below the top; 5 terminal stigmas; capsule 5-celled, 1 seed per cell; 2 N.A. species. *K. virginica,* to 3' high, is found in brackish to nearly fresh water, Fla. to Tex. and L.I.

ROSE-MALLOW (HIBISCUS) Capsule with several seeds per cell, otherwise as *Kosteletzkya;* 19 herbaceous species in N.A.

Scarlet Hibiscus, *H. coccineus,* 3–10' high, leaves 3- or 5-lobed, flowers 5–8" wide; in coastal swamps, Fla. to Ala. and Ga.

Wild Cotton, *H. moscheutos,* 3–8' tall, lower and middle leaves 3-toothed or entire; flowers white or cream; in swamps, se U.S.

Swamp-rose, *H. palustris,* 3–8', middle stem leaves 3-lobed, flowers pink to purple or white; fresh or salt marshes, ne U.S.

Flower-of-an-hour, *H. tronium,* sprawling plant to 2' high, 3- or 5-parted leaves; flowers 2–3"; African, now in s Canada and U.S.

*Sida
hederacea*

*Anoda
cristata*

*Modiola
caroliniana*

*Sida
hermaphrodita*

*Sidalcea
neomexicana*

*Malvastrum
otundifolium*

*Hibiscus
tronium*

*Kosteletzkya
virginica*

H. coccineus

H. moscheutos

H. palustris

ST. JOHN'S-WORT FAMILY (GUTTIFERAE)

Plants with opposite entire dotted leaves; flowers solitary or in cymes, of 4–5 sepals, 4–5 petals, few to many stamens, 1 pistil; 3 genera in N.A., some species woody.

ASCYRUM Flowers of 4 sepals, outer 2 leaflike, inner 2 small; 4 petals; many free stamens; 5 species, mainly of se U.S. **St. Peter's-wort,** *A. stans,* 12–32″, grows in sand, SE n to L.I., w to Okla. and Tex. **St. Andrew's Cross,** *A. hypericoides,* to 4′ tall, is shrubby; grows in dry sand or bogs, e U.S., w to Okla. and Tex.

ST. JOHN'S-WORT (HYPERICUM) Flowers of 5 sepals, 5 petals, stamens in 3–5 bundles; 25 herbaceous species in N.A. **Common St. John's-wort,** *H. perforatum,* 1–3′ high, is bushy-branched; European, now from Nfld. to B.C., s to Calif., Mont., Colo., Ark., Tenn., and N.C. **Marsh St. John's-wort,** *H. virginicum,* to 2′, has clasping leaves, 3 tufts of stamens; grows in wet soil, s Lab. to Man., s to Fla., and Tex. **Orange Grass** or **Pineweed,** *H. gentianoides,* to 2′, grows in dry gravel or sand, e U.S., w to Texas.

CROOKEA One species, *C. microsepala,* to 4′ high; wiry stems and branches; 1″ flowers of 4 equal sepals, 2 narrow and 2 broad petals; grows in s Ga. and n Fla. pinelands.

ROCK-ROSE FAMILY (CISTACEAE)

Leaves simple, entire; alternate, opposite, or whorled; flowers of 5 sepals; 3 or 5 petals or none; few to many stamens; 1 pistil.

ROCK-ROSE and **FROSTWEED** (HELIANTHEMUM) Leaves dilated, not overlapped; early flowers of 5 petals, 10–100 stamens; later ones with no petals, 3–8 stamens; 15 N.A. species. **Frostweed,** *H. bicknellii,* has clustered 2′ stems from a caudex; grows in dry open woods and plains, Me. to Minn., S.D., and Colo., s to Md., Mo., Kans., and in mts. to N.C. **Rock-rose,** *H. corymbosum,* 4–10″, has leaves silvery beneath; Coastal Plain, Fla. to Miss. and N.C.

HUDSONIA Low bushy plants with tiny overlapped leaves; flowers axillary, 5 sepals, 5 petals; 3 N.A. species. **Golden Heather,** *H. ericoides,* grows from sea level to mountain tops, Nfld., P.E.I., N.S. to Del.; **Poverty-grass,** *H. tomentosa,* on dunes, ranges from s Lab. to n Alta., s to N.C., Ind., Ill., Minn., and Sask.

MEADOW-FOAM FAMILY (LIMNANTHACEAE)

MEADOW-FOAM (LIMNANTHES) Low basally branched herbs of moist places; leaves pinnately divided; flowers single, the parts in 5's; 7 species, of w N.A. *L. douglasii* grows in Calif. and Oreg.

Ascyrum stans

A. hypericoides

Hypericum perforatum

Hypericum virginicum

Hypericum gentianoides

Crookea microsepala

Helianthemum bicknellii

Helianthemum corymbosum

Hudsonia ericoides

Hudsonia tomentosa

Limnanthes douglasii

VIOLET FAMILY (VIOLACEAE)

Leaves simple, alternate, with stipules; nodding solitary flowers in the leaf axils; flower parts in 5's; 1 pistil. In summer most species produce self-fertile flowers of 5 sepals, 2 tiny petals, 2 stamens; 2 N.A. genera.

GREEN VIOLET (HYBANTHUS) Tall leafy-stemmed herbs to 3' with downy entire or toothed leaves; petals nearly equal, lowermost slightly cup-shaped, stamens fused in a tube enclosing the ovary; 3 N.A. species. *H. concolor* inhabits woodlands, from Wisc. and s Ont. to N.Y. and Conn., s to Kans., Miss., and Ga. *H. verticillatus* grows in dry fields, forest edges, on rocky slopes, Kans. and Colo. to Tex. and Ariz.

VIOLET (VIOLA) Stemmed or stemless herbs; leaves with large stipules; sepals with earlike lobes; lower petal spurred; stamens distinct, lower 2 with spurs inside the petal spur. About 80 species in N.A.

Bird's-foot Violet, *V. pedata,* grows in dry sunny sites, on sandy or clay soil, from Fla. to Tex., n to N.H. and Minn.

Marsh Blue Violet, *V. cucullata,* grows in wet meadows, swamps, and bogs, Nfld. to Minn., s to Neb., Ark., upland Ga., and Tenn.

Common Blue Violet, *V. papilionacea,* grows in e N.A., w to Wyo. and Tex.; pale-gray **Confederate Violet** is form *albiflora.*

Missouri Violet, *V. missouriensis,* grows in river forests and bottomlands, from N.M. to s Tex. and Ark., n to Minn. and Ind.

Northern Bog-violet, *V. nephrophylla,* grows in moist soil, B.C. to Nfld., s to Calif., Ariz., N.M., N.D., Ia., Wisc., Conn.

Woolly Blue Violet, *V. sororia,* grows in woodlands, e half of Tex. to n Fla., n to Que. and N.D.

Triangle-leaved Violet, *V. emarginata,* grows in dry to moist open woods and clearings, from Mass. to Kans., s to Ga. and Okla.

Arrow-leaved Violet, *V. sagittata,* grows in damp to dry open woods, Tex. to Ga., n to N.H., Minn.

Prairie Violet, *V. pedatifida,* grows in prairies and dry openings, from Alta. to n Ohio, s to Mo., Okla., N.M., and cen. Ariz.

Alpine Marsh-violet, *V. palustris,* is circumboreal, s to alpine and subalpine moist sites, N.Eng., Colo., Utah, and Oreg.

American Dog-violet, *V. conspersa,* grows in meadows, damp woods, Que. to Minn., s to N.Eng., mts. to Md., Ga., Ala.

Hooked-spur Violet, *V. adunca,* grows in dry open woods, fields, Alaska to Lab., s to Calif., Ariz., N.M., S.D., e to N.Y.

Long-spurred Violet, *V. rostrata,* grows in rich woods, sw Que. and Vt. to Wisc., s to n N.J., Pa., W.Va., mts. to Ga. and Ala.

Wood Violet, *V. palmata,* grows in rich deciduous woods and on shaded limestone, from s N.H. to Minn., s to Fla. and Miss.

Hybanthus concolor

H. verticillatus

Viola pedata

V. cucullata

V. missouriensis

V. papilionacea

V. nephrophylla

V. sororia

V. emarginata

V. sagittata

V. pedatifida

V. palustris

V. adunca

V. rostrata

V. palmata

V. conspersa

Wild Pansy, *Viola arvensis*, 6–18″, is a European escape, partial to disturbed soil; Nfld. to Mich. and Alta., s to Ga. and Mo.

Pansy or **Heart's-ease,** *V. tricolor*, has branched stems to 2-½′ high; European, now in fields in much of N.A.

Beckwith's Violet, *V. beckwithii*, grows in brush, pine forests, dry soil, e Oreg. and Ida., s, e of the Sierra Nevada, to Inyo Co., Calif., e to Nev., Utah.

Sweet White Violet, *V. blanda*, creeps by runners, forming carpets; in rich deciduous woods, sw Que. and N.H. to Minn., s to Del., Md., Ill.; mts. to Tenn., Ga.

Halberd-leaved Yellow Violet, *V. hastata*, has an erect slender 4–12″ stem from a fleshy rhizome, 2–4 leaves at stem tip; grows in deciduous woods, Fla. and Ala. n to Pa., W.Va., and n Ohio.

Smooth Yellow Violet, *V. pensylvanica*, has stems 4–12″ high bearing 1–5 basal leaves; damp woods, cool shaded slopes, Que. to Man., s to Del., Md., mts. of N.C. and Tenn., Mo. and Okla.

Canada Violet or **Tall White Violet,** *V. canadensis*, has several 8–16″ stems from a rhizome; in deciduous woods, sw Que. and w N.H. to Mont., s to Md., mts. to S.C., Ala., N.M., Ariz.

Lance-leaved Violet, *V. lanceolata*, is a low mat-forming herb; grows in damp or flooded clay, sand, or peat; in the open or light shade, from Fla. to e Tex., n to C.B. and N.B., s Que., s Ont., Minn., Neb.

Primrose-leaved Violet, *V. primulifolia*, has thready rhizomes tipped by crowns of leaves; grows in wet to dry open sites, Fla. to Tex., n to N.S., n Ind., Okla.

Viola purpurea has 2–8″ stems; back of 2 upper petals is purple; on dry open or forested slopes, Wash. to s Calif., e to Mont., Colo., Utah, and Ariz.

Johnny-jump-up, *V. rafinesquii*, is 1–6″ tall, with basal and stem leaves; a Eurasian escape to dry fields, roadsides, Ga. to Tex., n to N.Y., Ia., Neb.; in s Rocky Mts.

Round-leaved or **Early Yellow Violet,** *V. rotundifolia*, has barely unrolled its leaves at flowering; in rich woods, ne U.S. and s Ont., w to Ohio, s in mts. to n Ga.

Viola sheltonii has finely dissected leaves, which are purple underneath; grows in loam in open woods or brush at 2500–8000′ in mts., s Calif. to Wash.

Cream Violet, *V. striata*, has stems 4–12″ tall at flowering, later to 28″ with many branches; in low woods, meadows, Ga. to Ark., n to Wisc., s Ont., and N.Y.

Kidney-leaved Violet, *V. renifolia*, its young leaves downy-white on both sides, is in cool woods, up to subalpine barrens, Alaska to Nfld., s to nw Conn., Mich., Wisc., Minn., S.D., Colo., and B.C.

Downy Yellow Violet, *V. pubescens*, 4–18″ tall, sometimes has a basal leaf (var. *eriocarpa* has 4–8 basal leaves). In rich woods, ne Tex. to N.C., n to Que., Ont.

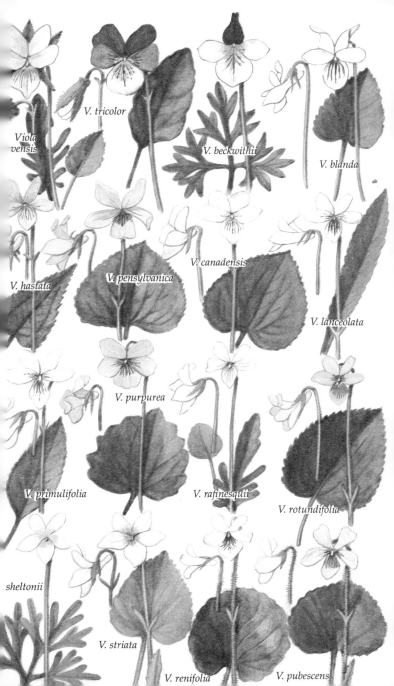

V. tricolor

Viola vensis

V. beckwithii

V. blanda

V. hastata

V. pensylvanica

V. canadensis

V. lanceolata

V. purpurea

V. primulifolia

V. rafinesquii

V. rotundifolia

sheltonii

V. striata

V. renifolia

V. pubescens

TURNERA FAMILY (TURNERACEAE)

PIRIQUETA Slender erect herbs with single alternate leaves, single axillary flowers, the parts in 5's, 1 pistil, 3 styles, fringed at the tip; 4 species, 3 only in Fla. *P. caroliniana*, to 16" high, grows in pinelands from Fla. to S.C.

PASSION-FLOWER FAMILY (PASSIFLORACEAE)

PASSION-FLOWER (PASSIFLORA) Vines, climbing by tendrils; leaves alternate, simple, entire or palmately lobed, with stipules; petioles often gland-bearing. Flowers axillary, of 5 petal-like sepals, 5 petals, a fringed corona, 5 stamens fused in a tube, 1 pistil, 3 styles; 14 N.A. species, of e and s U.S. **Apricot-vine**, *P. incarnata*, grows in open woods, old fields, from Va. to Mo., s to Fla. and Tex.; edible fruits are called maypops. **Yellow Passion-flower**, *P. lutea*, grows in shade in low moist woods, Pa. to Ill. and Kans., s to Fla. and Tex.

STICK-LEAF FAMILY (LOASACEAE)

Plants with stinging and/or barbed hairs; leaves alternate, simple, entire to lobed; flowers single and axillary, or in terminal heads or cymes; 5 sepals, rarely 4 or 6–7; petals equal in number to sepals; stamens 5 to many, sometimes petal-like; 1 pistil, 1 style; 4 herbaceous N.A. genera.

CEVALLIA One species, *C. sinuata*, to 2' tall, herbage woolly, with long stinging hairs; flowers in long-stalked heads opposite the leaves; grows in the open, often by roads, w and s Tex. to Ariz.

ROCK-NETTLE (EUCNIDE) Herbage woolly; flowers of 5 sepals, 5 petals united at base, many stamens; 2 species in sw U.S., in dry rocky areas. *E. bartonioides* has low spreading stems; grows in cen. and w Tex.; *E. urens*, 1–2' erect stems, 2–5' prostrate stems; stinging hairs, s Utah, s Nev., w Ariz., and se Calif.

STICK-LEAF or **BLAZING-STAR** (MENTZELIA) Leaves sessile or petioled, lobed or entire, with barbed hairs; flowers axillary or in bracted terminal cymes; 5 sepals, 5–10 petals, few to many stamens (petal-like in some). About 53 species in s and w U.S.

Stick-leaf, *M. oligosperma*, 1–3', matted or bushy, leaves oval to 3-lobed; ranges from Ill. to S.D. and Colo., s to La., Tex.

M. micrantha has tiny flowers in terminal corymbs with many broad bracts; Calif. Coast Ranges and Islands to Baja Calif.

Blazing-star, *M. decapetala*, to 40" tall, opens its 6" flowers an hour after sunset; Alta. and Sask., e of Rocky Mts., to Tex.

M. laevicaulis, 1–4' tall, has petal-like outer stamens; in desert and mts., Wash. to Mont. and Wyo., s to s Calif., Utah.

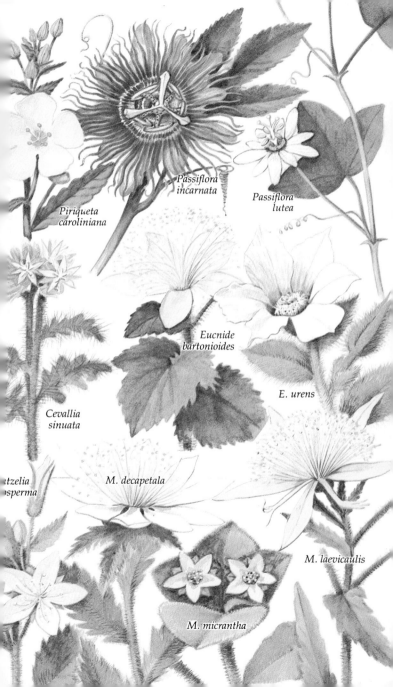

Piriqueta
caroliniana

Passiflora
incarnata

Passiflora
lutea

Eucnide
bartonioides

E. urens

Cevallia
sinuata

tzelia
osperma

M. decapetala

M. laevicaulis

M. micrantha

LOOSESTRIFE FAMILY (LYTHRACEAE)

Leaves simple and entire, mostly opposite; flowers axillary or clustered; tubular calyx, 4- to 6-toothed, with extra teeth between; petals 4–7; stamens 4–18; 1 style, stigma round, rarely 2-lobed; 7 N.A. genera with herbaceous species; 4 are weedy.

SWAMP-LOOSESTRIFE (DECODON) One species, *D. verticillatus*, with 4- to 6-sided arching 2–8' stems that root at the tip; leaves opposite or whorled; flowers in axillary clusters; calyx of 5–7 erect teeth and 5–7 horns; 5 petals; 10 stamens of 2 lengths. Grows in wet soil, se Que. and s Ont. to Minn., s to Fla. and Tex.

LOOSESTRIFE (LYTHRUM) Stems 4-sided; leaves opposite, alternate, or whorled; calyx 4- to 7-toothed with 4–7 tiny teeth between; 4–6 petals, 8–12 stamens; 11 species in N.A., in low moist or wet habitats. **Winged Loosestrife,** *L. alatum*, to 4' tall, has wings along the corners of the stem; N.Eng. and s Ont. to N.D., s to Ga., La., and Okla. **Hierba del Cáncer,** *L. californicum*, 2–5', has a creeping woody rootstock; Tex., n to Kans., w to Calif. **Spiked Loosestrife,** *L. salicaria*, 3–10', has dense whorls of flowers in a leafy spike; an aggressive European escape, Nfld. and Que. to Minn., s to Va. and Mo.; also in Pac. NW.

CUPHEA Sticky-hairy herbs; leaves entire; flowers solitary or in terminal spikes or racemes; calyx swollen or spurred on the top, 6-lobed, with 6 tiny teeth between; 6 unequal petals; 6–14 stamens; stigma 2-lobed; 6 species, of e and s U.S. **Clammy Cuphea** or **Blue Waxweed,** *C. viscosissima*, 4–28" tall, traps small insects on the stem; grows in fields, roadsides, stream banks, from N.Eng. to Ia. and Kans., s to Ga. and Tex.

MELASTOMA FAMILY (MELASTOMATACEAE)

MEADOW-BEAUTY or **DEER-GRASS** (RHEXIA) Low erect plants with 4-sided stems, sometimes winged; leaves simple, opposite, often with bristly edges; flowers single or in cymes, calyx 4-lobed; 4 petals; 8 stamens; 1 pistil, 1 style, 1 stigma; 12 species, in e and se N.A.; grows in moist or wet peat, sand, or gravel.

Common Meadow-beauty, *R. virginica*, to 40", grows throughout e U.S. (except Fla.), n to N.S. and Ont., w to Kans. and Tex.

R. mariana, to 28" high, varies from white to pale rose or crimson; Coastal Plain, e Tex. to Fla. and se Mass.; inland to Okla., Mo., s Ill., and s Ind.

R. lutea, to 20" tall, usually much-branched, has glandular hairs edging lobes of calyx; e N.C. to n Fla., w to Tex.

R. alifanus, wandlike stems to 40", large 2" flowers in an open panicle-like cyme; in bogs, savannas, and wet pinelands, e N.C. to Fla., w to Tex.

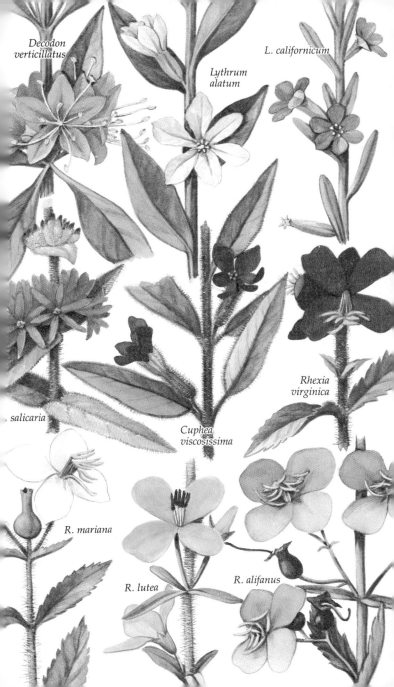

*Decodon
verticillatus*

*Lythrum
alatum*

L. californicum

salicaria

*Cuphea
viscosissima*

*Rhexia
virginica*

R. mariana

R. lutea

R. alifanus

EVENING-PRIMROSE FAMILY (ONAGRACEAE)

Herbs, sometimes woody at the base, with simple alternate or opposite leaves, the blades entire, toothed, or pinnately lobed; flowers axillary, regular or slightly zygomorphic, the parts often in 4's or 5's, in 2's, 3's, or 6's in some; calyx tubular; stamens as many or twice as many as petals; 1 pistil, 1 style, stigma round or 2- to 4-lobed; 13 genera in N.A.

PRIMROSE-WILLOW and **WATER-PRIMROSE** (JUSSIAEA) Leaves alternate and entire; flowers yellow, calyx 4- to 6-lobed, 4–6 petals, twice as many stamens as petals: 9 species in N.A. **Primrose-willow,** *J. decurrens*, to 10' tall, has wings running down the stem from the leaf bases; grows in wet places, Okla. and Mo. to Va., s to Fla. and Tex. **Creeping Water-primrose,** *J. repens*, has creeping or floating stems, rooting at the nodes; found in water or mud, Fla. to Tex., n to Kans. and Del.; s Oreg. to s Calif.

FALSE LOOSESTRIFE (LUDWIGIA) Herbs with alternate or opposite leaves, entire or fine-toothed; flowers axillary or in heads, 4-lobed calyx, 4 or no petals, 4 stamens; 23 N.A. species.

Seedbox, *L. alternifolia*, to 4' tall, has alternate leaves, cubical capsules with a hole in the top; in swamps, Mass. and Ont. to n Fla., w to Ia. and n Tex.

Spindle-root, *L. hirtella*, is an erect hairy herb to 40", leaves alternate, sessile; roots fascicled, spindle-shaped; Coastal Plain, e Tex. to Fla. and N.J.

L. alata, 2–5', has wing-angled stems, alternate leaves, sessile axillary flowers lacking petals; inhabits brackish or tidal marshes, La. to Fla., n to se Va.

Marsh-purslane, *L. palustris*, has creeping stems to 20", opposite leaves, sessile flowers without petals; in shallow water or wet soil, much of temperate N.A.

ZAUSCHNERIA Bushy shaggy-haired plants, woody at base, with narrow leaves and racemes of scarlet flowers; calyx 4-lobed, base of tube bulbous; 4 petals, notched or 2-lobed; 8 stamens; 4 species, of w U.S. **California-fuchsia,** *Z. californica*, 1–3' high, with 1–2" flowers; grows on dry slopes, s Calif. to sw Oreg.

STENOSIPHON One species, *S. linifolius*, 2–10' tall, slender; leaves entire, 1–2" long, shorter on upper stem; flowers in a long spike, 4-lobed calyx-tube thready; 4 petals; 8 stamens; stigma 4-lobed; grows on limestone, Colo. and Neb., s to Ark. and Tex.

BOISDUVALIA Soft-hairy herbs with simple alternate entire leaves, sessile axillary flowers of 4 notched petals, 8 stamens; 6 species, in w N.A. *B. densiflora*, 6–40" tall, grows in moist soil, Pacific N.A., e to Mont. and Nev.

J. repens

*Jussiaea
decurrens*

*Ludwigia
alternifolia*

L. hirtella

L. alata

L. palustris

*Boisduvalia
densiflora*

*Zauschneria
californica*

*Stenosiphon
linifolius*

WILLOW-HERB (EPILOBIUM) Erect, sprawling, or creeping herbs with simple nearly sessile leaves, alternate or opposite, entire or toothed. Flowers solitary and axillary or in terminal spikes or racemes; calyx 4-lobed; 4 rounded petals; 8 stamens; stigma club-shaped or 4-lobed about 40 species in N.A.

River-beauty, *E. latifolium,* is a matted plant with upward-arching stems 4–20″ long, crowded thick fleshy leaves; grows in damp places, arctic N.A., s to Nfld., se Que., S.D., Colo., and Wash.

Fireweed or **Wickup,** *E. angustifolium,* 4″–10′ high; main leaves alternate, lower ones scale-like; it invades burned woodlands, cleared land; subarctic N.A., s to n half of U.S.; in mts. to N.C., N.M., Ariz., and s Calif.

E. alpinum is a tufted or matted plant to 22″ high from short creeping branches arising from a much-forked crown; flowers milk-white, sometimes pink-tipped; found at brook edges, arctic N.A., s to alpine areas of Me., N.H., Colo., Utah, Nev., and Calif.

E. palustre, a boreal species, has erect stems and branches 4–22′ tall, incurved hairs on upper stem, nodding stem-tips, becoming erect at flowering; grows in wet sites, Lab. to Alaska, s to N.Y., Minn., S.D., Colo., Oreg.

E. coloratum has erect or ascending stems to 40″, bushy at the top, stem leaves have a short petiole, thin blades with short irregular teeth; in low wet places, S.D. to Que., s to Ga., Ark., n Tex.

CLARKIA Herbs with wandlike basal branches, alternate entire or toothed leaves; flowers solitary and axillary or in terminal spikes; calyx 4-lobed; 4 petals, entire or 3-lobed; 4 or 8 stamens, alternately shorter or rudimentary; stigma 4-lobed. About 35 species in w N.A.

C. purpurea is variable; flowers ½–2″ wide, the petals white, pink, lavender, or wine-red, with or without a red or purple blotch; leaves 1–3″ long; in open soil, Wash. to s Calif., Ariz.

C. pulchella, 6–18″ high, has a downy stem and smooth leaves; flowers 2″ or more wide; 3-lobed petals on toothed claws; 4 of the 8 stamens are rudimentary; grows in open ground, from Wash. to se Oreg., e to w Mont.

C. rhomboidea, 1–4′, has simple or sparingly branched stems, 1–3″ leaves; 1″ flowers, all petals held to one side, slightly 3-lobed; in dry or disturbed soil, from S.D. to Wash., s to Ariz. and Baja Calif.

C. dudleyana, to 28″ high; a downy narrow-leaved plant with fine-toothed leaves; flowers 1–2″ wide with 8 stamens. Grows on dry slopes, foothills of the s Sierra Nevada and other mts. of s Calif.

Farewell-to-spring, *C. amoena,* 1–3′, a slender branched herb with satiny 1–3″ flowers, lilac-crimson or red-pink; lobes of calyx are united and turn to one side when the flower opens; B.C. to San Francisco Bay region.

E. angustifolium

Epilobium latifolium

E. alpinum

E. coloratum

E. palustre

Clarkia purpurea

C. pulchella

C. rhomboidea

C. dudleyana

C. amoena

EVENING-PRIMROSE (OENOTHERA) Herbs with alternate entire to toothed or pinnately divided leaves; flowers mostly solitary in the upper leaf axils, rarely in 2's or clusters, opening near sunset or near sunrise. Calyx of 4 lobes; 4 petals; 8 stamens, alike or alternately longer; stigma entire or 4-lobed. Possibly 100 or more species in N.A.

Common Evening-primrose, *O. biennis,* has a rosette to 2' wide of long-petioled hairy leaves; much-branched stems 3–4' high (rarely to 10') with sessile leaves; flowers 2–4" wide, stigma 4-lobed; e N.A., w to w B.C. and Ariz.

Prairie Evening-primrose, *O. albicaulis,* has erect stiff-hairy stems to 20", often with reclining basal branches, 1–3" flowers, opening white, fading to pink; stigma 4-lobed; grows in sandy soil, S.D. and Mont. to Tex., Ariz.

Seaside Evening-primrose, *O. humifusa,* 4–30", is a hoary bushy plant; basal leaves pinnately lobed, stem leaves entire or with wavy toothed edges; flowers solitary, ½–1" wide, opening yellow, changing to reddish; sandy seabeaches, La. to Fla., n to N.J.

Missouri Primrose or **Glade-lily,** *O. missouriensis,* 12–20", has lance-like smooth or downy leaves 1–4" long, entire or with teeth near the tip; flowers 2–4" wide, calyx-tube 2–5" long with 1–2" lobes; in rocky or sandy soil, Kans. and Neb., s to w Mo., Ark., and Tex.

Yellow Desert-primrose, *O. primiveris,* is usually stemless with a rosette of 1–5" downy leaves, entire to irregularly toothed or lobed; flowers 1–3" wide, fading to reddish; stigma 4-lobed; on desert flats, Trans-Pecos, Tex., w to sw Utah, s Nev., Ariz., and s Calif.

Rose Sundrops, *O. rosea,* 16–40", a slender shrubby plant with 1–2" leaves with short distinct petioles, the edges wavy or lobed; 1" solitary rosy flowers in the axils of the upper leaves; grows along streams and in weedy places, Tex. to Ariz.

White Evening-primrose, *O. speciosa,* to 20" tall, a stiff-hairy plant with 1–4" wavy-lobed leaves, 2–3" white or rose-purple flowers; native Mo. and Kans. to Tex., but widely cultivated and escaped, Ill. to La., e to Va. and Fla.

O. clavaeformis has a rosette of 8" entire to pinnately divided leaves; stems to 20" high with smaller leaves, a cluster of 1" flowers; the stamens curve inward, forming a cage around the stigma. In desert washes, s Oreg. to Ariz. and Baja Calif.

O. lavandulaefolia, 3–8" high, a low tufted plant, its stems and 1" leaves gray from stiff hairs; flowers 1–2" wide, the diamond-shaped petals aging to reddish; stigma club-shaped. On dry slopes and flats, S.D. and Wyo. to Tex., and Wyo. to e Nev. and n Ariz.

Yellow Evening-primrose, *O. serrulata,* 4–20" tall, a hoary plant, simple to branched and clump-forming; leaves 1–3" long, shallowly toothed; flowers ½–2" wide; stigma disk-like; from N.Eng. to Alta., s to Wisc., Mo., Tex., N.M., and Ariz.

O. albicaulis

O. humifusa

Oenothera biennis

O. rosea

O. missouriensis

O. primiveris

O. speciosa

O. lavandulaefolia

O. clavaeformis

O. serrulata

GAURA Somewhat weedy herbs, sometimes woody at base, with alternate entire to deeply lobed sessile leaves; flowers in a terminal raceme with tiny leaves; flower parts in 4's, rarely 3's; petals clawed, unequal or all to one side; 8 stamens; stigma 4-lobed, rarely 3-lobed, surrounded by a ring or cup on the style; 21 species, in e and s N.A.

Morning Honeysuckle, *G. biennis,* to 12', is downy and hairy, with a 2' basal rosette; spikes of white flowers, fading to pink. In damp soil, w Que. to Minn., s to Va., w N.C., Tenn., and Mo.

Lizard-tail or **Velvet-leaved Gaura,** *G. parviflora,* to 10', a coarse erect plant densely glandular-hairy; grows on dry prairies, Wash. and Mont. to Ind., s to Ariz., La.; local to N.Eng.

Scarlet Gaura, *G. coccinea,* 4–20" tall, a low well-branched plant growing from a caudex, with stiff hairs; in dry prairies, at roadsides, s-cen. Canada to s Nev., Ariz., and Tex.; e to N.Y.

Woolly Gaura, *G. villosa,* 2–6' tall, a bushy plant, densely hairy toward the base; 2 layers of hair, those underneath stiff or glandular; ranges from Kans. to Tex. and e N.M.

ENCHANTER'S NIGHTSHADE (CIRCAEA) Leaves opposite, with slender petioles; small flowers in racemes; calyx 2-lobed; 2 petals, in some deeply forked; 2 stamens; fruits burrlike; 3 N.A. species. *G. alpina,* to 1' high, grows in cool moist woods and openings, Lab. to Alaska, s to s N.Y., mountains to Ga. and Tenn., Mich., Ill., Ia., S.D., Colo., Utah, and Wash. *C. quadrisulcata,* to 40", grows in rich woods, N.S. and w N.B. to N.D., s to Ga., Tenn., Mo., and Okla.

PARSLEY FAMILY (UMBELLIFERAE)

Herbs, often with hollow stems (a few stemless), alternate mostly compound leaves, the petioles expanded or sheathing the stem at the base; flowers usually in simple or compound umbels; if compound, secondary ones termed umbellets; the whole inflorescence often subtended by an involucre, the umbellets subtended by bractlets termed an involucel. The small flowers have a tubular entire or 5-toothed calyx, 5 petals and 5 stamens, attached to a disk on top of the ovary; 2 styles, base often thickened, surrounded by the disk; 79 genera in N.A., some weedy. Many species cannot be identified by flowers and leaves alone; identification depends on anatomical details of fruits and seeds. **NOTE: Some species are poisonous; do not taste or eat wild plants of this family.**

WATER-PENNYWORT (HYDROCOTYLE) Low aquatic or marsh plants with creeping stems; simple round, peltate, or kidney-shaped leaves with petioles; flowers in simple umbels; 7 species in N.A. *H. ranunculoides* grows in s U.S., n to Pa., Ark., Okla., and Wash.

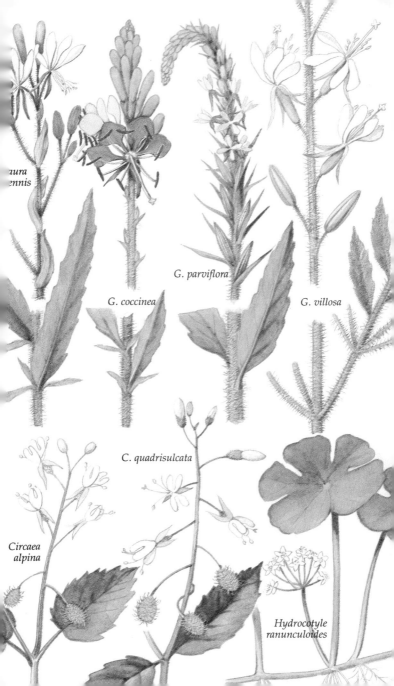

*aura
ennis*

G. parviflora

G. coccinea

G. villosa

C. quadrisulcata

Circaea
alpina

Hydrocotyle
ranunculoides

BOWLESIA One species in N.A., *B. incana*, a low or prostrate her with forked stems 4–20″ long or high, simple opposite palmately 5- t 7-lobed leaves, simple 2- to 6-flowered umbels; flowers white or purple grows in swamps, wet woods, lawns, from s Calif. to Fla.

WILD CELERY (APIASTRUM) One species, *A. angustifolium*, to 2(tall, has finely dissected leaves to 2″ long, flowers in compound umbe lacking involucres and involucels, the rays unequal, to 2″ long; grow in sandy soil, through Calif. and s Ariz.

SWEET CICELY (OSMORHIZA) Mostly hairy herbs with branche stems; leaves ternate, the leaflets toothed or pinnately lobed; flower white, purple, or yellow-green, in few-rayed compound umbels, invo lucre and involucels of a few recurved leafy bracts or absent; herbag and root licorice-scented if bruised; 9 species, in e and w N.A. **Swee Jarvil,** *O. claytonia*, 1–3′ tall, grows in woods, on wooded slopes, s Que. to s Sask., s to w L.I., upland to N.C. and Ala., e Kans., and nw Ark. **Anise-root,** *O. longistylis*, to 4′ high, is found in rich woods, Canada s to Ala. and Tex., w to Alta., Colo., and N.M.

VENUS′-COMB (SCANDIX) is European; 1 species, *S. pecten-veneris* is now found throughout the U.S. and in B.C.; a bristly herb 6–13″ high often branched at base; leaves twice or thrice pinnate; umbels simple o 2- to 3-rayed, involucre usually lacking, involucels of 2 bractlets fusec at base, lobed above; "combs" to 3″ long.

GLEHNIA One species in N.A., *G. leiocarpa*, grows on sandy sea beaches, Alaska to n Calif., its short stem and petioles usually buried, the 3-parted leaflets lying on the sand; flowers in headlike umbellets on woolly rays, with conspicuous involucels.

HEDGE-PARSLEY (TORILIS) Hairy herbs, stems branched, mostly erect; leaves once or twice pinnate; umbels compound, involucre a few small bracts or none; involucels of thready bractlets; rays 6–12; fruits flat-oval, tiny, bristled. Eurasian, now 3 species in N.A. *T. japonica*, 1– 3′, grows in open woods, waste ground, from Fla. to Calif., n to N.Y., Ia., and Kans.

WILD CARROT (DAUCUS) Erect branching bristly or hairy herbs; leaves thrice pinnate; umbels compound, becoming concave; involucre and involucels of many 3-forked or pinnate bracts; 2 species in N.A. **Queen Anne's Lace,** *D. carota*, 1–5′, has white or rosy flowers, central one red or dark purple; European, in s Canada and all of U.S. **Rattle-snake-weed,** *D. pusillus*, 1–3′, has twice pinnate-lobed involucre bracts; s U.S., w coast to B.C.

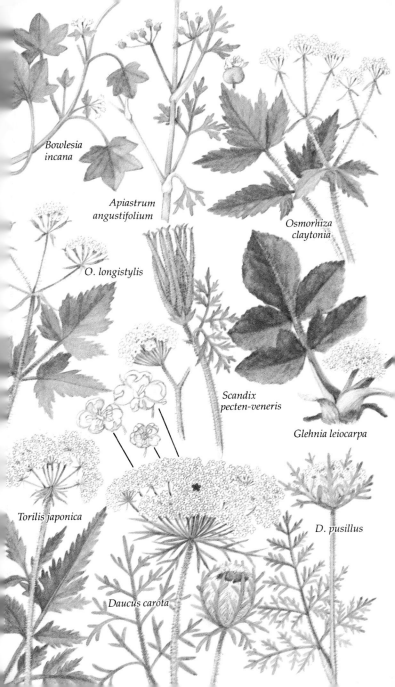

*Bowlesia
incana*

*Apiastrum
angustifolium*

*Osmorhiza
claytonia*

O. longistylis

*Scandix
pecten-veneris*

Glehnia leiocarpa

Torilis japonica

D. pusillus

Daucus carota

FENNEL (FOENICULUM) One species, *F. vulgare*, 3–10′ tall, a European escape in much of the U.S.; a smooth herb with leaves thrice or pinnate, lobes threadlike, petioles broad, clasping; umbels compound rays 15–40, involucre and involucels lacking.

ALETES Low tufted herbs, leaves once or twice pinnate, or ternate leaflets round to thready, often lobed and spine-toothed; umbels terminal, compound; involucre often lacking, involucels 2-parted, unequal; 5 species in sw U.S. *A. acaulis,* 2–14″, grows in the Rocky Mts. Colo., s to Ariz., N.M., and Tex.

THOROUGH-WAX (BUPLEURUM) Slender herbs with forking or a ternate branches, simple entire leaves, clasped or joined round the stem; umbels compound, involucre leafy or none, involucels of broad leafy bracts. Eurasian, 3 species in N.A. *B. rotundifolium* grows in fields e U.S., w to S.D. and Tex.

WATER-HEMLOCK (CICUTA) Leaves once or thrice pinnate, or ternate; leaflets toothed; umbels compound, many-rayed, often no involucre, involucels a few slender bractlets; calyx-teeth prominent; 7 N.A. species, in moist soil, all poisonous. **Spotted Cowbane,** *C. maculata,* 2 6′ tall, grows in e N.A., w to Man. and Tex.

POISON HEMLOCK (CONIUM) One species, *C. maculatum,* in N.A. a smooth erect Eurasian herb 20″–10′ high, the grooved branching hollow stems often spotted; leaves twice to 4-pinnate, fernlike, fetid umbels compound, involucre and involucels of narrow bracts; Que. to Fla., w to Pac. Fatal to taste.

HEMLOCK-PARSLEY (CONIOSELINUM) Similar to *Conium;* involucre of narrow bracts or none; involucels of narrow bractlets; 5 N.A. species. *C. chinensis,* 4″–5′ high, grows from Alaska to B.C.; w Ont. to Lab., s to Pa. and Mo., upland to N.C.

PERIDERIDIA Erect herbs with tuberous roots; leaves once or twice pinnate, or ternate; umbels compound, involucre (if present) and involucels of narrow papery or papery-edged bristly bracts; calyx-teeth prominent; flowers white or pink; 13 N.A. species. **Yampa** or **Wild Caraway,** *P. gairdneri,* grows in moist soil, from S.D. to N.M., w to B.C. and s Calif.

LOVAGE (LIGUSTICUM) Smooth herbs with large aromatic roots, large ternately compound leaves; compound umbels, involucre and involucels a few narrow bractlets or none; flowers white or pink; 11 species in cool areas of N.A. **Chuchupate** or **Osha,** *L. porteri,* 20–40″ tall, grows in mts., Ariz. and N.M., n to Nev. and Wyo.

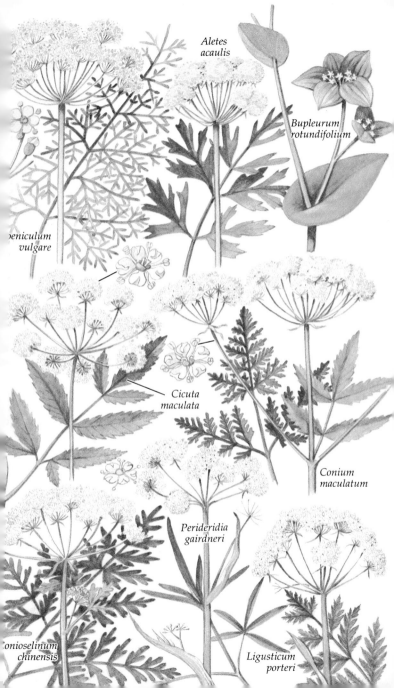

*Aletes
acaulis*

*Bupleurum
rotundifolium*

*Feniculum
vulgare*

*Cicuta
maculata*

*Conium
maculatum*

*Perideridia
gairdneri*

*Conioselinum
chinensis*

*Ligusticum
porteri*

WATER-PARSNIP (BERULA) One species in N.A., *B. erecta*, 8"–3' tal
a slender erect or reclined branched hairless herb; aerial leaves od
pinnate, leaflets toothed; submerged leaves 3- or 4-pinnate with thread
lobes; umbels compound, involucre leafy, often toothed, involucels
entire bractlets. Grows in swamps and streams, all of s Canada and th
U.S.

LILAEOPSIS Dwarf creeping or floating herbs of muddy shores, wit
hollow grasslike jointed petioles in place of leaves; simple few-flowere
umbels; 4 species, 2 in e, 2 in w N.A. *L. chinensis* grows along the coas
w N.S. to Fla. and Miss.

WATER DROPWORT (OENANTHE) One species in N.A., *O. sarmen
tosa*, in slow water or marshes, Alaska to Ida. and s Calif.; a branchin
weak-stemmed herb to 4', rooting at the nodes; leaves twice pinnate
leaflets toothed to divided; umbels compound, 10- to 20-rayed; involu
cre often lacking, involucels conspicuous.

OREOXIS Low tufted herbs, leaves once or twice pinnate, segment
narrow; umbels compound, few-rayed; umbellets headlike; involucre
of 1 bract or none, involucels of narrow bractlets; 3 species, in s Rock
Mts. *O. alpina*, to 7" high, ranges from Wyo. and Utah to n N.M. and n
Ariz.

CYMOPTERUS Short-stemmed or stemless herbs, smooth or hairy
leaves at or near the ground, diverse (from palmate, ternate, or pinnate
to multi-compound); umbels compound, some rays often sterile, ray
with umbellets few and spreading; involucre lacking or present, dry o
leafy; involucels 2 unequal dry or leafy bractlets; flowers white, yellow,
or reddish-purple; 31 species, in w N.A. **Chimaya**, *C. fendleri*, ranges
from Tex. to Ariz., n to Colo. and n Utah.

PTERYXIA Much like *Cymopterus* but tufted; umbels compound, the
rays unequal; involucel bractlets usually all to one side; about 5 species,
in w U.S. *P. petraea*, 6–18" tall, ranges from se Oreg. and s Ida. to s Calif.,
Nev., and n Ariz.

PSEUDOCYMOPTERUS Similar to *Cymopterus*; 2 species, of w U.S.;
flowers yellow or red-purple. **Mountain-parsley,** *P. montanus*, to 33",
grows in rocky places, Wyo. and Utah to Ariz. and w Tex.

HARBINGER-OF-SPRING or **PEPPER-AND-SALT** (ERIGENIA) One
species, *E. bulbosa*, a woodland herb ranging from s Ont. and w N.Y. to
Wisc., s to Ala., Miss., and Mo.; stem simple, 4–10" high, leaves twice
or thrice ternate, umbel simple.

Berula erecta

Oenanthe sarmentosa

Lilaeopsis chinensis

Oreoxis alpina

Cymopterus fendleri

Pteryxia petraea

Pseudocymopterus montanus

Erigenia bulbosa

ANGELICA Stout herbs, leaves ternately or pinnately compound, upper leaves of petioles only or often with petioles much longer than the blades; umbels compound, terminal; involucre a few bracts or none, involucels of many small bracts or none; flowers greenish or white. About 21 species in e and w N.A. **Alexanders,** *A. atropurpurea*, 3–10' tall, grows in damp or wet soil, s Lab. to Wisc., s to Md. and ne Ia.

HOG-FENNEL (OXYPOLIS) Slender erect hairless herbs of wet places; leaves pinnate to ternate, or only petioles; umbels compound, involucre and involucels a few slender bracts or lacking; flowers white or purple; 6 N.A. species. **Cowbane,** *O. rigidior*, 2–5' high, has variable leaflets; ranges from N.Y. to Minn., s to Fla. and Tex. Poisonous.

LOMATIUM Herbs of dry ground, most short-stemmed or stemless, leaves variously much-divided; umbels compound, without involucres, involucels present or lacking; flowers white, pink, yellow, or reddish; about 78 species, mostly w N.A. *L. orientale* has 4–12" flower scapes; grows from Minn. to Mont., s to Ia., Kans., N.M., and Ariz. *L. dissectum* has a leafy stem to 5' high; ranges from B.C. to Colo., s to Ariz. and Calif.

PARSNIP (PASTINACA) is European; *P. sativa* is naturalized in almost all but arctic N.A. An erect herb 1–3' tall, leaves pinnately compound, umbels compound, no involucre or involucels.

COW-PARSNIP (HERACLEUM) Stout boreal herbs with large compound leaves, compound umbels, involucre deciduous, involucels many-leaved; flowers white or purplish, outer petals of outer flowers larger and 2-lobed; 2 species in N.A. **Masterwort,** *H. lanatum*, 3–9', is woolly, has a grooved stem, ternate leaves; grows in rich or low ground, Lab. to Alaska, s to N.Eng., mts. to Ga., Ohio, Kans., N.M., Ariz., and Calif.; up to subalpine areas.

ERYNGO (ERYNGIUM) Creeping or erect herbs, stemmed or stemless. Usually with leathery toothed, cut, or prickly leaves, bracted sessile flowers in dense heads; 31 N.A. species.

E. aquaticum, 16"–5' high, grows in fresh to brackish swamps, ponds, or streams, Coastal Plain, Fla. to La., n to N.J.

Mexican Thistle, *E. heterophyllum*, 8–24" high, a stout erect branching herb; grows in sandy soil in mts., w Tex. to Ariz.

Rattlesnake-master or **Button-snakeroot,** *E. yuccifolium*, 2–6', grows in dry or moist soil, Conn. s to Fla., w to Minn. and Tex.

E. leavenworthii, 20–40", is a slender erect herb with forked branches; plains and prairies, from e Kans. and Ark. to Tex.

Lomatium dissectum

Angelica tripurpurea

Oxypolis rigidior

Pastinaca sativa

Heracleum lanatum

L. orientale

Eryngium aquaticum

E. yuccifolium

E. heterophyllum

E. leavenworthii

MEADOW-PARSNIP (THASPIUM) Leaves simple or ternate, blade broad, toothed; flowers stalked, in compound umbels, greenish, yellow, or purple; 3 species, in e N.A. *T. barbinode*, 16"–4', has bearded nodes; ranges from s Ont. to Minn., s to Ga. and Okla.

ZIZIA resembles *Thaspium* but the central flower in each umbellet is sessile; 3 species, primarily of e N.A., extending to the Pac. NW. **Golden Alexanders**, *Z. aurea*, inhabits meadows and moist woods, Que. to Fla w to Sask. and Tex.

RANGER'S-BUTTONS or **WHITE-HEADS** (SPHENOSCIADIUM) One species, *S. capitellatum*, to 5', has large pinnately dissected leaves, heads of sessile flowers at the tips of 4" woolly rays; grows in swampy places in mountains, Baja Calif. to Oreg. and Ida.

BLACK SNAKEROOT or **SANICLE** (SANICULA) Leaves palmate, umbels irregular, involucre and involucels leafy; umbellets headlike; male flowers stalked, perfect ones sessile; 17 species in s Canada and the U.S. *S. gregaria*, 1–3' tall, grows in woods, w N.B. to Minn. and S.D., s to n Fla. and Tex.

OROGENIA Low herbs; leaves ternate; umbels of 1–10 1" rays, no involucre, involucels 1 or more bractlets, short-stalked flowers in heads; 2 species, in nw U.S. *O. linearifolia*, 2–6", grows on open slopes, s Wash to w Mont., s to Oreg. and w Colo.

PRAIRIE-PARSLEY (POLYTAENIA) Stout erect branched herbs; leaves bipinnate or ternate-pinnate with large lobed leaflets; umbels compound, no involucre, narrow involucels; 2 species, in s-cen. N.A. *P nuttallii*, 20–40" tall, grows in dry prairies and open woods, from N.D. to Ind., s to Tex., La., and Ala.

TREPOCARPUS One species, *T. aethusae*, 1–3' high, a slender erect herb with finely divided leaves, ternate or ternate-pinnate; lateral compound umbels opposite the leaves; flowers few per umbellet, tiny; grows in dry soil, S.C. to Ark., s to Ala. and Tex.

HONEWORT or **WILD CHERVIL** (CRYPTOTAENIA) One species, *C. canadensis*, in N.A.; 1–3' tall, leaves thin, 3-foliate; umbels compound, no involucre, unequally few-rayed, involucels of tiny bracts or none; grows in woods, w N.B. to Man., s to Ga. and Tex.

YELLOW PIMPERNEL (TAENIDIA) One species, *T. integerrima*, of e N.A.; 2–4' tall, leaves 2- to 3-ternate, leaflets entire; umbels compound, no involucre or involucels; 15–20 rays, central ones sterile and half the length of the fertile rays.

Sphenosciadium capitellatum

Thaspium barbinode

Zizia aurea

Sanicula gregaria

Orogenia linearifolia

Polytaenia nuttallii

Trepocarpus aethusae

Cryptotaenia canadensis

Taenidia integerrima

GINSENG FAMILY (ARALIACEAE)

Plants similar to the *Umbelliferae* but flowers usually have more than 2 styles; 5 petals; 5 stamens, alternate with the petals. Two genera in N.A. with herbaceous species.

ARALIA Leaves alternate, pinnately decompound; flowers in umbels in a panicle or corymb; 4 herbaceous species in N.A. **Spikenard** or **Pretty Morrel,** *A. racemosa,* to 10' or more, has large spicy-aromatic roots; grows in rich woods, Que. to Man., s to Ga., Tex., and Ariz. **Bristly Sarsaparilla,** *A. hispida,* 8"–3' tall, has 2 to many umbels in a terminal corymb; grows in open woods and clearings, Nfld. and s Lab. to Man., s to w N.C., Ill., and Minn. **Wild Sarsaparilla,** *A nudicaulis,* has a single long-stalked leaf 8–16" high, a short stem tipped by 2–7 umbels; in woods, Nfld. to B.C., s to Ga., Mo., Colo., and Ida.

GINSENG (PANAX) Stems simple, erect, with a single whorl of 3 palmate leaves and a solitary simple terminal umbel; roots tuberous, used in Chinese medicine; 2 species in N.A. **American Ginseng,** *P. quinquefolius,* usually has 5 leaflets, most flowers with 2 styles; grows in rich woods, Que. to Man., s to n Fla., La., and Okla. **Dwarf Ginseng** or **Ground-nut,** *P. trifolius,* has 3–5 sessile leaflets, most flowers with 3 styles; in woods and damp clearings, P.E.I. to Minn., s to n Ga., Ohio, and Neb.

DOGWOOD FAMILY (CORNACEAE)

DOGWOOD or **CORNEL** (CORNUS) Two herbaceous N.A. species, both low creeping herbs with simple opposite or whorled leaves on 1' flowering stems; flowers terminal, perfect, calyx 4-toothed, 4 petals, 4 stamens, 1 style. **Bunchberry, Crackerberry,** or **Pudding-berry,** *C. canadensis,* has upper leaves much larger than the lower ones; grows in woods, damp openings, s Greenl. to Alaska, s to n N.J., S.D., N.M., and Calif. **Swedish Dwarf Cornel,** *C. suecica,* has more uniform sessile leaves; grows in woods, marshes, and bogs; circumboreal, s to Nfld., Que., B.C.

LENNOA FAMILY (LENNOACEAE)

Root parasites, lacking chlorophyll; 6- to 9-lobed flowers in heads or spikes. Two genera, in sw U.S. deserts.

PHOLISMA One species, *P. arenarium,* in s Calif.; stems 4–8" bearing a 3" thick spike, sometimes branched, of tiny flowers.

SAND-ROOT or **SAND-SPONGE** (AMMOBROMA) One species, *A. sonorae,* a buried scaly stem topped by a "sponge" bearing masses of small flowers; grows in Ariz. and s Calif.

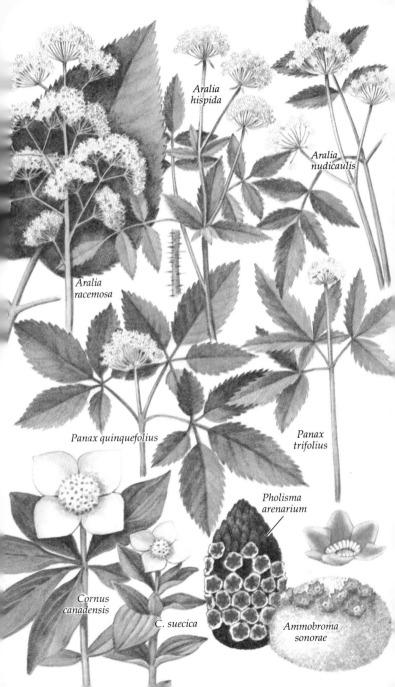

Aralia hispida

Aralia nudicaulis

Aralia racemosa

Panax quinquefolius

Panax trifolius

Pholisma arenarium

Cornus canadensis

C. suecica

Ammobroma sonorae

WINTERGREEN FAMILY (PYROLACEAE)

Plants with simple evergreen leaves, or root parasites or saprophyt without chlorophyll; sepals and petals mostly 5, stamens usually 10 pistil; 10 genera in N.A.

WAXFLOWER or **PIPSISSEWA** (CHIMAPHILA) Stem to 1' high, leaf flowers in a corymb; 5 pink or white petals; 10 stamens, filamen dilated, hairy; 3 N.A. species. **Prince's-pine,** *C. umbellata,* grows in d woods, Que. to Alaska, s to Calif., Ariz., N.M., Minn., n Ill., and Ohi mts. to Ga.

WINTERGREEN (PYROLA) Stem leafy only near base; flowers sing or in racemes, of 5 petals, 10 stamens, filaments naked; 12 N.A. specie **One-flowered Wintergreen,** *P. uniflora,* grows in cool woods, from La to Alaska, s to Pa., W.Va., Minn., N.M., Ariz., and Calif. **Pink Winte green,** *P. asarifolia,* grows in moist soil throughout w N.A., e acros Canada and n U.S. to N.Y. **Wild Lily-of-the-valley,** *P. rotundifolia,* found in damp places, ne N.A., s to N.C. and Ky., w to Minn.

NOTE: The next 6 genera are saprophytes or root parasites, lackin chlorophyll, with fleshy stems and scale-like leaves.

MONOTROPA Calyx of 2–5 bracts, 2–5 scaly petals swollen at the base 8 to 10 stamens; 3 N.A. species. **Indian-pipe** or **Corpse-plant,** *M uniflora,* 6–12", has a single pink or white flower; ranges from Nfld. t Alaska, s to n Calif., e to Fla. **Pinesap,** *M. hypopithys,* has 4–16" raceme of aromatic flowers; Nfld. to B.C., s to cen. Calif., ne Tex., and Fla.

PINE-DROPS (PTEROSPORA) One species, *P. andromedea,* 1–3', is a root parasite of conifers; P.E.I. to B.C., s over n half of U.S.

PIGMY-PIPES or **SWEET PINESAP** (MONOTROPSIS) One species *M. odorata;* 2–4" spikes of fragrant flowers; grows in sandy pinelands se U.S.

FRINGED PINESAP (PLEURICOSPORA) One species, *P. fimbriolata,* flower parts mostly in 4's; inhabits deep woods, Pac. NW and Sierra Nevada.

CANDYSTICK (ALLOTROPA) One species, *A. virgata,* 4–20", 5 sepals, no petals, 10 stamens; grows in coniferous forest humus, Sierra Nevada and Coast Ranges of Calif., at lower elevations to B.C.

SNOW-PLANT (SARCODES), One species, *S. sanguinea,* with 6–12" translucent spikes of rose, carmine, or blood-red flowers; grows in mountain forests of s Calif., n to Oreg., e to Nev.

Chimaphila umbellata

Pyrola uniflora

Pyrola asarifolia

Pyrola rotundifolia

Pterospora andromedea

Allotropa virgata

Sarcodes sanguinea

Monotropa hypopithys

Monotropsis odorata

Monotropa uniflora

Pleuricospora fimbriolata

HEATH FAMILY (ERICACEAE)

Woody plants of acid soils; leaves simple, entire or toothed; flowers 4- to 7-parted or lobed, stamens as many or twice as many as petals; 1 style. A few are dimunitive or herblike.

BEARBERRY (ARCTOSTAPHYLOS) Mat-forming plants with papery shredding bark, alternate entire leaves, scaly-bracted flowers in terminal clusters. *A. uva-ursi* is circumboreal on exposed rock and sand, s to Calif., N.M., Minn., Ill., and Va.

MOUNTAIN HEATHER (CASSIOPE) Dwarf alpine shrublets with tiny overlapping leaves, solitary nodding flowers; 5 N.A. species. **White Heather,** *C. mertensiana*, forms mats 2–12″ tall; ranges from Alaska to Calif. and Nev., e to Canadian Rockies and Mont.; **Lapland Heather,** *C. tetragona*, is circumboreal, s in Rocky Mts. to Glacier Nat. Park, on Pac. Coast to Okanogan Co., Wash.

GAULTHERIA Creeping plants; leaves alternate, evergreen; flowers axillary, nearly white; 6 N.A. species. **Creeping Snowberry** or **Maidenhair-berry,** *G. hispidula*, is a delicate matted plant, its leaves bristly beneath; grows in mossy woods or bogs, Lab. to B.C., s to Ida., Minn., Wisc., Mich., mts. to N.C. **Teaberry** or **Checkerberry,** *G. procumbens*, grows in sterile woods and clearings, Nfld. to Man., s to Minn., Wisc., Ga., and Ala.

TRAILING ARBUTUS or **GROUND LAUREL** (EPIGAEA) One species in N.A., **Mayflower,** *E. repens*, a low trailing evergreen with alternate leaves and spicy-fragrant flowers in small terminal or axillary clusters that emerge from scaly bracts; grows in sandy or peat woods or clearings, Lab. to Sask., s to Fla., Miss., and Ia.

AMERICAN LAUREL (KALMIA) Evergreen shrubs with entire leaves; 2 are small. **Wicky,** *K. hirsuta*, to 2′ tall, grows on sandhills or pinelands, Fla. to Miss. and s Va. **Bog Laurel,** *K. polifolia*, is a somewhat matted plant with 2-edged stems; Lab. to Alaska, s to Calif., Ida., Colo., Minn., Mich., n N.J., and Pa.

ALPINE AZALEA (LOISELEURIA) One species, *L. procumbens*, a mat-forming dwarf evergreen shrub with opposite leaves; ranges from Greenl. to Alaska, s on peat or exposed rock to Nfld. and N.S., alpine regions of Que., Me., N.H., and Alta.

MOUNTAIN HEATH (PHYLLODOCE) Dwarf alpine evergreen shrubs with linear rough-edged leaves; 4 N.A. species. *P. empetriformis*, 6–10″ tall, ranges from Alaska to Calif., Ida., and Mont.; *P. glanduliflora*, from Alaska to Oreg. and Wyo.

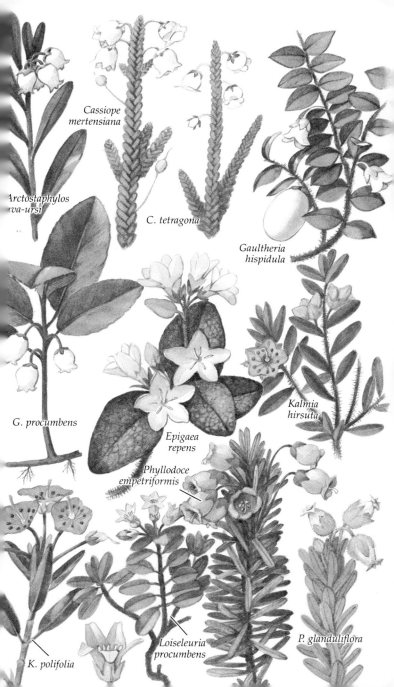

Cassiope mertensiana

C. tetragona

Arctostaphylos uva-ursi

Gaultheria hispidula

G. procumbens

Epigaea repens

Kalmia hirsuta

Phyllodoce empetriformis

K. polifolia

Loiseleuria procumbens

P. glanduliflora

DIAPENSIA FAMILY (DIAPENSIACEAE)

Low or tufted plants; leaves simple; flowers solitary or in racemes; flower parts in 5's, stamens attached to the petals, 1 style, a 3-lobed stigma; 4 N.A. genera.

DIAPENSIA One species, *D. lapponica*, forming low dense tussocks, circumboreal, s on bare ledges and gravel to Nfld. and alpine regions of Que., N.Eng., n N.Y.; a rose-flowered var. in Alaska.

FLOWERING MOSS or **PYXIE** (PYXIDANTHERA) Two species, in se U.S. *P. barbulata* creeps on sandy soil, N.J. to S.C.; leaves alternate, hairy near the base; flowers white or rose.

WANDFLOWER or **BEETLEWEED** (GALAX) One species, *G. rotundifolia*, with wavy-toothed heart-shaped evergreen leaves 2–6" wide from scaly rhizomes; flowers in spikes on naked scapes 1–3' tall; in open woods, Va. and W.Va. to Ga. and Ala.; cultivated n to Mass.

OCONEE-BELLS (SHORTIA) One species, *S. galacifolia*, a low herb with glossy evergreen oval leaves, bell-shaped 1" flowers; grows in moist woods, on stream banks, mts. of N.C., S.C., and Ga.

PRIMROSE FAMILY (PRIMULACEAE)

Leaves mostly simple, rarely pinnately dissected; flower parts usually in 5's, 1 style, 1 stigma; 12 N.A. genera.

SCARLET PIMPERNEL (ANAGALLIS) is European; *A. arvensis* is now widespread in old sandy fields of s Canada and the U.S.; a low spreading much-branched herb, leaves opposite or whorled, entire, sessile; solitary axillary flowers, scarlet, white, or sky-blue, closing as bad weather nears, hence called "Poor Man's Weather-glass" in England.

ANDROSACE Small herbs; leaves in basal rosettes, tiny flowers in umbels subtended by an involucre; about 7 species in cooler N.A. *A. occidentalis*, to 3" tall, grows on dry sand or gravel or in rocky woods, Ont. to B.C., s to Ind., Ill., Ark., Tex., N.M., Ariz., Sierra Nevada. *A. septentrionalis*, to 1' high, is an arctic plant; s to Que., mts. of w U.S.

SHOOTING-STAR (DODECATHEON) Hairless herbs with a cluster of basal leaves, simple naked scape with an umbel of nodding flowers, the petals reflexed; 15 widespread N.A. species. *D. amethystinum*, 4–12" high, grows in damp soil, e Pa. to Minn., s to Ky. and ne Mo. *D. media* grows in open woods or meadows, D.C. to Wisc., s to Ga. and Tex.

*Galax
rotundifolia*

*Diapensia
lapponica*

*Pyxidanthera
barbulata*

*Androsace
occidentalis*

*Shortia
galacifolia*

*Anagallis
arvensis*

*Androsace
septentrionalis*

*Dodecatheon
amethystinum*

*Dodecatheon
media*

DOUGLASIA Low cushion-forming plants with tiny lance-shaped leaves, 5-lobed tubular red or pink flowers, solitary or in umbels, on leafless scapes; 6 N.A. species, 3 confined to the Arctic. *D. montana*, 1" high, grows in the foothills and on open ridges in the mountains, B.C. to n Wyo.

SEA-MILKWORT (GLAUX) One species, *G. maritima*, a low succulent with opposite sessile entire leaves, tiny axillary flowers of 5 pink or red sepals, no petals; saline or brackish shores, marshes, or sands, Que. to Va.; Sask. to B.C., s to N.M.

LOOSESTRIFE (LYSIMACHIA) Tall leafy-stemmed herbs; leaves opposite or whorled, entire; flowers axillary, single or in racemes, calyx and corolla 5- to 6-parted; 16 species in N.A.

Fringed Loosestrife, *L. ciliata*, erect, simple or branched, 4"–4' tall; has long fringed petioles; Que. to B.C., s to Oreg., Colo., Tex., and Fla.

Swamp Candles, *L. terrestris*, 8"–4' tall, has conspicuously bracted terminal racemes; Nfld. to Minn., s to Ga., Ky., and Ia.; introduced s B.C., nw Wash.

Whorled Loosestrife, *L. quadrifolia*, has erect 4-angled 8"–3' stems, sessile stem leaves; Me. to s Ont. and Wisc., s to L.I., Ga., Ala., Ill., and Tex.

Tufted Loosestrife, *L. thyrsiflora*, has unbranched 8–31" stems, flowers in spike-like racemes; in swamps, Que. to Alaska, s to Calif., Colo., Mo., and Pa.

PRIMROSE (PRIMULA) Low boreal or alpine herbs, simple leaves in basal tufts; flowers in umbels on simple scapes; 20 N.A. species. **Bird's-eye Primrose,** *P. mistassinica*, grows in meadows, along streams, s Lab. to Alaska, s. to N.Y., Mich., Wisc., Ia., s Alta., and B.C. *P. parryi* has carrion-scented flowers; grows in Rocky Mts., Mont. and Ida. to N.M. and Ariz.

WATER-PIMPERNEL (SAMOLUS) Leaves simple, in a rosette, alternate on the stem; small flowers in axillary racemes; 4 N.A. species. *S. parviflorus*, to 2', grows in shallow water and wet soil throughout s Canada and the U.S.

WATER-VIOLET or **FEATHERFOIL** (HOTTONIA) One species, *H. inflata*, an aquatic herb; leaves dissected into threadlike lobes, clustered at base of the 1' inflated flowering stems; ranges from Fla. to Tex., n to N.Eng. and Mo.

STAR-FLOWER (TRIENTALIS) Low simple erect herbs, a whorl of leaves at the stem tip, thin stalked flowers of 5–9 sharp-pointed petals; 3 N.A. species. *T. borealis* ranges from Lab. to Sask., s to Va. and Minn.; *T. latifolia*, from B.C. to Calif.

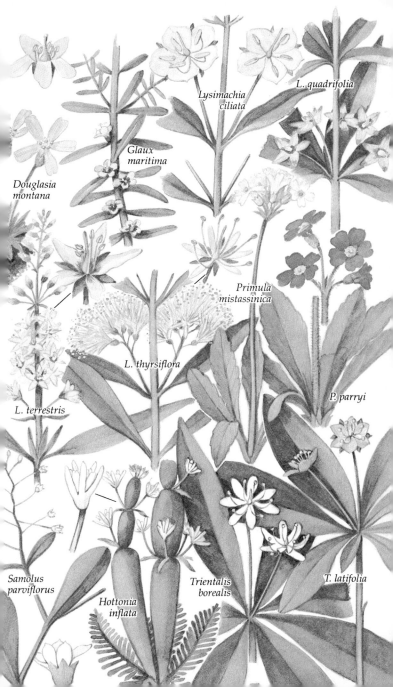

Lysimachia ciliata

L. quadrifolia

Glaux maritima

Douglasia montana

Primula mistassinica

L. thyrsiflora

P. parryi

L. terrestris

Samolus parviflorus

Hottonia inflata

Trientalis borealis

T. latifolia

LEADWORT FAMILY (PLUMBAGINACEAE)

Herbs with basal or alternate entire leaves; calyx and corolla 4- to 5-lobed or toothed; usually 5 styles; 3 N.A. genera.

THRIFT (ARMERIA) Leaves linear, in dense tussocks; flowers mixed with papery bracts in heads on 2–18″ naked stalks; 2 N.A. species; *A. maritima* grows on beaches and coastal bluffs, Arctic, s to Nfld.; on Pac. Coast to s Calif.

SEA-LAVENDER or **MARSH-ROSEMARY** (LIMONIUM) Salt-marsh herbs; leaves long-petioled, basal; stems naked, branching into panicles, flowers on l-sided branches, petals clawed; 6 N.A. species. *L. carolinianum* ranges from Fla. to Miss., n to N.H. *L. californicum* grows in Calif. coastal salt marshes.

LEADWORT (PLUMBAGO) One species, *P. scandens*, a vine-like herb with brittle branches to 4′, flowers in axillary clusters; grows in woods and thickets, s Fla., s Tex., and s Ariz.

OLIVE FAMILY (OLEACEAE)

MENODORA Herbs, some woody at base; leaves simple, entire or lobed, mostly alternate; flowers axillary, single or clustered, of 5–6 petals, 2 stamens; 6 N.A. species, of sw U.S. *M. scabra*, to 13″ high, has rough stems and leaves; ranges from s Colo. to Tex., Utah, and Baja Calif. *M. longiflora*, to 3′ tall, has 1″ flowers; grows in Tex. and s N.M.

LOGANIA FAMILY (LOGANIACEAE)

Leaves opposite, simple, entire, with stipules or a stipular membrane between; flowers 4- to 5-parted, 1 pistil, 1 style, stigma entire or 2-lobed; 3 herbaceous N.A. genera.

PINKROOT (SPIGELIA) Leaves united by stipules; flowers in 1-sided spike-like cymes; 5 species in s U.S. **Indian-Pink**, *S. marilandica*, 1-2′, grows in woods, Fla. to Tex., n to Mo. and Md.

MITERWORT (CYNOCTONUM) Herbs of moist soil; small stipules between the leaves, tiny flowers on one side of a coiled cyme; 2 N.A. species. *C. mitreola*, to 30″ high, grows from Fla. to Tex., n to se Va., Tenn., and Ark. *C. sessilifolium*, with sessile leaves, ranges from Fla. to Tex., n to se Va.

POLYPREMUM One species, *P. procumbens*, a small much-branched herb to 1′ high, the stems ribbed, leaves connected by a membrane, flowers 4-parted, solitary, sessile, in branch forks and at the stem tips; grows in sandy soil, Fla. to Tex., n to L.I. and se Mo.

*Armeria
maritima*

*Limonium
carolinianum*

L. californicum

*Plumbago
scandens*

M. longiflora

*Menodora
scabra*

*Spigelia
marilandica*

*Cynoctonum
mitreola*

*Polypremum
procumbens*

C. sessilifolium

GENTIAN FAMILY (GENTIANACEAE)

Hairless herbs with simple entire leaves, sessile and opposite or whorled (long-petioled and alternate in 2 genera); flowers solitary, clustered, or in cymes, the parts in 4's to 12's, 1 style, stigma entire or 2-cleft; 12 N.A. genera.

CENTAURY (CENTAURIUM) Flower parts in 4's or 5's, corolla tubular, stamens projected beyond the throat, spirally twisted, stigma headlike or bifid; 15 species in N.A. **Mountain Pink**, *C. beyrichii*, to 1' high, grows on rocky open slopes, n-cen. and w Tex. to Ark. **Rosita**, *C. calycosum*, 6"-2' high, grows in moist soil, Mo. to Tex., w to Utah, Nev., and Ariz. *C. umbellatum* is European, now escaped to moist sites, N.S. to Mich., s to Ga. and Ind.; nw Wash. to n Calif., e to Ida.

MARSH FELWORT (LOMATOGONIUM) One species, *L. rotatum*, of wet and saline soils; stem simple to bushy-branched, 1–10" high; leaves fleshy; 2–5 calyx lobes, corolla 5-lobed, a pair of fringed scales at the base of each lobe; 2 sessile stigmas; ranges from Lab. to se Me.; Hudson Bay to Alaska, s in Rocky Mts. to N.M.

SPURRED GENTIAN (HALENIA) Small upright herbs; corolla lacking folds or fringe, lobes erect, spurred at the base; 2 N.A. species. *H. deflexa* grows in damp cool woods, se Lab. to B.C., s to N.Y., Mich., n Ill., Minn., S.D., and n Mont. *H. recurva* grows in conifer forests and mountain meadows of Ariz.

COLUMBO (SWERTIA) Tall showy erect herbs with whorled leaves; corolla 4- to 5-lobed, a fringed glandular spot on each lobe; stigma 2-lobed; 15 N.A. species, mostly of w U.S. **American Columbo**, *S. caroliniensis*, 3–8' high, with leaves mostly in whorls of 4's, grows in dryish meadows, rich woods, and on limestone bluffs, Ga. to La., n to w N.Y., s Ont., Mich., and Wisc. **Deer's-ears**, *S. radiata*, to 6' tall, has leaves in whorls of 4 to 6, a 4-lobed corolla; grows in limestone soil, open pine forests, S.D. and Wash., s to w Tex., N.M., and Calif.

ROSE-GENTIAN (SABATIA) Erect slender herbs with leafy stems, some with basal leaves as well; flowers white, yellow, or rose-purple, the parts in 5's to 12's, corolla lobes much longer than the tube, stigma bifid; 18 species, of e N.A. **Rose-pink** or **Bitter-bloom**, *S. angularis*, to 3', has a basal rosette of leaves, a 4-angled stem; grows in open woods, prairies, and fields, Fla. to La. and Okla., n to s Ont., Mich., Wisc., and Mo. **Large Marsh-pink** or **Sea-pink**, *S. dodecandra*, to 2', is found in saline marshes and meadows, Fla. to Tex., n to s Conn.

*Centaurium
beyrichii*

C. calycosum

C. umbellatum

*Lomatogonium
rotatum*

*Halenia
deflexa*

H. recurva

*Swertia
caroliniensis*

*Sabatia
angularis*

*Swertia
radiata*

*Sabatia
dodecandra*

GENTIAN (GENTIANA) Herbs with short-petioled or sessile entir leaves, showy flowers, solitary or in cymes; corolla 4- to 5-lobed, ofte with plaited folds bearing teeth or appendages at the notches; 2 stig mas, on a short style or sessile. About 56 N.A. species.

G. algida, 2–8" high, a dwarf tufted herb with narrow basal leaves to 5" long, stem leaves to 2"; flowers in clusters of 1–3, mostly in pairs; in bogs and meadows, Colo. to Alaska.

Pleated Gentian, *G. affinis,* 6–16", has broad inch-long leaves, flowers in the upper leaf axils, each with a pair of bracts at the base; in damp soil, B.C. to Sask., s to Calif., Ariz., N.M., S.D., Minn.

Closed Gentian, *G. andrewsii,* has tufts of 12–31" stems, the lower leaves bracts, the uppermost 1–4" long, forming a 4- to 6-leaved involucre below the flowers; sw Que. to Sask., s to Ga. and Ark.

Closed-, Blind-, or **Bottle-gentian,** *G. clausa,* similar to *G. andrewsii* but often smaller, the calyx lobes herbaceous, with ciliated edges; in borders of woods, meadows, N.Eng. to Minn., s to Md., N.C., Tenn., and Mo.

Pine-barren Gentian, *G. autumnalis,* with slender 8"–2' stems. has 7–15 pairs of leaves; calyx lobes similar to the upper leaves; grows in pineland borders and pine barrens, N.J.; se Va. to S.C.

Fringed Gentian, *G. crinita,* 4–40" tall, sometimes with upright branches, and from 1 to 176 flowers; corolla of 4 rounded lobes, fringed with slender teeth; meadows, brooksides, low woods, cen. Me. to s Man., s to Ga., Ohio, Ind., and n Ia.

Yellowish Gentian, *G. flavida,* is stout plant with leaf bases clasp ing the stem; flowers in termina and sometimes axillary clusters in damp woods and meadows, Ont. to Man., s to N.C., Ark.

Stiff Gentian, Ague-weed, o **Gall-of-the-earth,** *G. quinquefolia* 12–31" tall; has a wing-angled sten and branches, clasping leaf bases in rich woods, damp fields, and gravelly banks, s Ont. to Mo., s t Fla., La.

Closed Gentian, *G. linearis,* 6–27 high, has 7–15 pairs of narrow leaves below the flowers; corolla lobes erect or incurved; in bogs, wet meadows, swampy woods, Lab. to s Ont., s to Md., Minn.

Narrow-leaved Fringed Gentian, *G. procera,* 6"–2' high, has keeled calyx lobes, the corolla lobes fringed at the sides with slender teeth, short-toothed on top; in wet soil, w N.Y. to Alaska, s to Ohio, Ia., and N.D.

Sampson's Snakeroot, *G. villosa,* has 1 to several 4–24" stems, blunt-tipped leaves, triangular corolla lobes; in open woods and pinelands, Fla. to La., n to N.J., Pa., s Ohio, and s Ind.

G. newberryi, 1–5", a dwarf alpine and subalpine plant, its stems horizontal with upturned tips and each with a single greenish flower, corolla lobes blue or violet; grows in moist meadows, Sierra Nevada and mts. of n Calif. and s Oreg.

Gentiana algida

G. affinis

G. andrewsii

G. clausa

G. crinita

G. autumnalis

G. flavida

G. quinquefolia

G. linearis

G. villosa

G. newberryi

G. procera

BARTONIA Herbs with thready stems 12–18″ tall, often somewh spiraled or twining, scales instead of leaves, tiny 4-parted flowers terminal panicles or racemes; 4 species, in e N.A. *B. virginica,* to 1′ ta grows in dry or wet acid soil, from Fla. to La., n to s Nfld., sw Qu n Ill., and Minn.

PENNYWORT (OBOLARIA) One species, *O. virginica,* a succule purplish-green saprophyte; stem simple or with few branches, 4–6″ t or less; leaves sessile, opposite, ½″ long; flowers solitary or in 3′s, tern nal and axillary, the parts in 4′s; grows in humus, hardwood forest Fla. to Tex., n to N.J. and s Ill.

CATCHFLY-GENTIAN (EUSTOMA) Erect herbs, often with a roset of basal leaves, stem leaves sessile, opposite, clasping the stem; shov long-stalked flowers, solitary or in panicles; calyx lobes keeled, corol 5- to 6-lobed, stigma 2-lipped; 2 species, of s U.S. *E. exaltatum,* to 2′ ta with blue, lavender, or white flowers, grows in pinelands, hammock and coastal sand, Fla. to s Calif. **Lira de San Pedro,** *E. grandiflorum,* 2′ high, is variously colored, from blue or violet to pinkish or yellov inhabits moist places in prairies and fields, from Okla. and Tex. to Ne and Colo.

MENYANTHES Boreal herbs of bogs and shallow water with thi creeping rhizomes, flowers in racemes on naked scapes, corolla deep 5- to 6-lobed, the whole upper surface bearded; stigma 2-lobed; 2 N. species. **Buckbean** or **Bogbean,** *M. trifoliata,* has long-petioled 3-folia leaves, 4–12″ scapes, 1″ white or rosy flowers; Lab. to Alaska, s to M and Neb., in the Rocky Mts. to Colo., Pac. N.W. to the Sierras of Cali **Deer Cabbage,** *M. crista-galli,* has simple kidney- or heart-shaped leave flowers in open cymes; ranges from nw Wash. to Alaska.

FLOATING-HEART (NYMPHOIDES) Aquatic herbs with rounde floating leaves notched at the base, on long petiole-like stems, sendin up near the leaf an umbel of flowers and often a cluster of spurlik roots; corolla 5-lobed, each lobe with a basal glandular appendag stigma 2-lobed; 3 species in N.A. *N. aquatica* has 1–6″ broadly oval c kidney-shaped leaves on stout petioles bearing purple glands; ofte lacks spur roots; grows from Fla. to Tex., n to s N.J. and Del. *N. cordat* has 1–2″ leaves on threadlike stems, a crested yellow gland at the bas of each corolla lobe; Nfld. to Ont., s to Fla. and La. **Yellow Floating heart,** *N. peltata,* is a European escape, locally spreading in s U.S., n t N.Y. and Mo., w to Tex.; its stems lack spur roots, corolla lobes ar fringed.

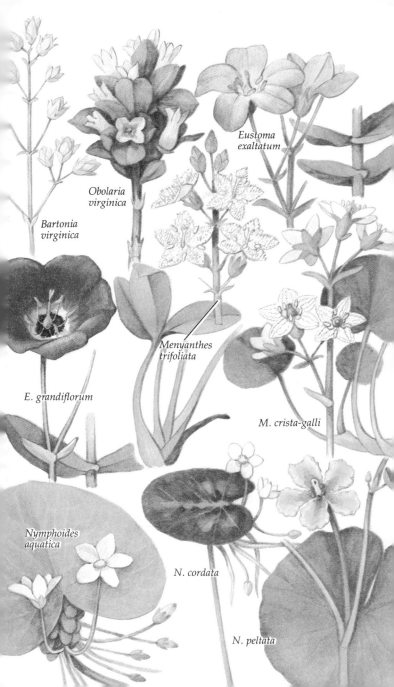

Bartonia
virginica

Obolaria
virginica

Eustoma
exaltatum

E. grandiflorum

Menyanthes
trifoliata

M. crista-galli

Nymphoides
aquatica

N. cordata

N. peltata

DOGBANE FAMILY (APOCYNACEAE)

Poisonous plants, most with acrid milky sap; leaves simple, entire, opposite (except in *Amsonia*); flower parts in 5's, corolla tubular, lobes overlapped at base; 2 ovaries with a united style and stigma; 9 genera with herbaceous species in N.A.

DOGBANE (APOCYNUM) Herbs with branched stems, sharp-pointed leaves, fibrous bark, small flowers in cymes; corolla bell-like, 5 triangular appendages inside; 6 N.A. species. **Spreading Dogbane,** *A. androsaemifolium*, to 20″ high, has terminal and axillary cymes, flowers all opening at once; grows in dry thickets, woodland edges, Nfld. to B.C., s to Ga. and Ariz. **Indian Hemp,** *A. cannabinum*, to 2′, has terminal cymes, the central one opening first; grows in open soil, thickets, s Canada and throughout U.S.

CLIMBING DOGBANE (TRACHELOSPERMUM) One species, *T. difforme*, a nearly herbaceous high-twining vine; leaves varying in shape, small flowers in axillary cymes; grows in swamps and on low ground, from Fla. to Tex., n to D.C., s Ind., Mo., and Okla.

ROCK-TRUMPET (MACROSIPHONIA) Low erect or diffusely branched plants, woody at base; leaves short-petioled or sessile; flowers trumpet-shaped, single or in 2's or 3's, axillary or terminal; 3 species in Tex. and the SW. *M. brachysiphon*, 4–12″ high, grows in dry soil, s N.M. and Ariz.

BLUE-STAR (AMSONIA) Herbs with alternate leaves, pale blue flowers in terminal panicled cymes; 20 species, in s U.S. *A. ciliata*, to 5′, has narrow leaves, often with long-haired edges; grows on sandhills, limestone, grasslands, Fla. to Tex., n to s Mo. and N.C. *A. illustris*, to 4′, is found in wet soil, s Mo. and e Kans. to Tex. *A. tabernaemontana*, to 40″, prefers woods or river banks, Va. to Kans., s to Ga. and Tex.; cultivated to Mass.

PERIWINKLE (VINCA) Erect or trailing herbs with solitary flowers in alternate leaf-axils; Eurasian, 4 species escaped in N.A. **Large Periwinkle,** *V. major*, a trailing evergreen, has upright flowering stems to 3′ high or more; grows on roadsides, woodland borders, s U.S., n to Va., and along the Pac. coast; **"Myrtle,"** *V. minor*, with creeping stems and glossy leaves, is found on roadsides, etc., throughout temperate N.A.

CYCLADENIA One species, *C. humilis*, 4–8″ high, with thick 1–3″ roundish opposite leaves with petioles, smooth and with a waxy "bloom," or densely woolly; flowers in axillary clusters; grows in rocky places, mountains of Calif.

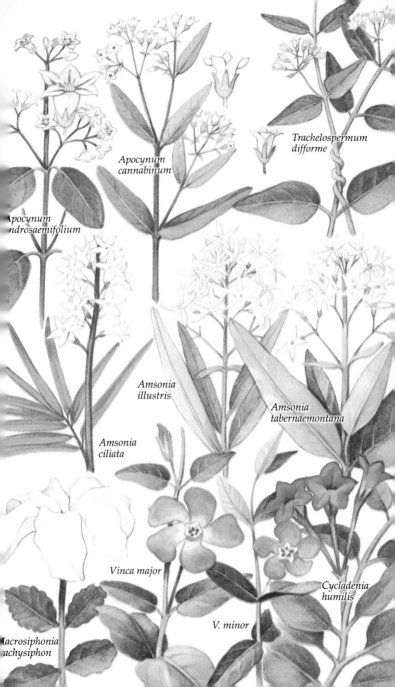

Apocynum cannabinum

Trachelospermum difforme

Apocynum androsaemifolium

Amsonia illustris

Amsonia tabernaemontana

Amsonia ciliata

Vinca major

Cycladenia humilis

V. minor

Macrosiphonia macrosiphon

MILKWEED FAMILY (ASCLEPIADACEAE)

Plants with milky sap, simple entire opposite leaves, flowers in umbels, flower parts in 5's; corolla lobes reflexed, a 5-lobed corona arising from the corolla or stamens; filaments fused in a tube, anthers adhering to the stigma; 2 ovaries, 2 styles united into 1 stigma; 5 genera in N.A.

ANGLE-POD (GONOLOBUS) Twining or trailing plants with slender simple or branched stems, heart-shaped leaves; flowers few to many in pairs or umbellate clusters, arising between the petioles; 25 N.A. species.

G. suberosus, hairy stems, leaves 2–6" long, 1–4" wide; 3- to 9-flowered umbels, much shorter than the petioles; in thickets, river banks, Fla. to e Va.

G. reticulatus has wiry downy stems decorated by long spreading hairs, 4" leaves, glandular petioles, ½" flowers; in open woods, cen., s, and w Tex.

G. carolinensis has downy stems, 2–4" leaves; its flowers, to 1" wide, are pollinated by flies; in rich thickets, Fla. to Miss., n to Md., W.Va., and Tenn.

G. biflorus is hairy and glandular throughout; ½" flowers in pairs, corolla lobes downy-white inside; in open woods or grassland, Tex. and Okla.

SILK-VINE (PERIPLOCA) One species in N.A., *P. gracea,* a European escape to thickets, Fla. to Tex., n to s N.Eng. and Kans.; stems to 16', flowers in long-stalked cymes, corona of 5 short rounded lobes and 5 long ascending linear appendages.

CYNANCHUM Twining vines with axillary inflorescences; corolla bell-shaped; corona of thin flat segments; 14 species in N.A. **Sand-vine** or **Honey-vine,** *C. laeve,* to 10' or more, has sweet-scented flowers in raceme-like clusters, corona segments divided into pairs; grows in thickets or fields, Pa. to Neb., s to Ga. and Tex. **Talayote,** *C. unifarium,* to 10' or more, has 3-lobed corona segments; in scrub and thickets, s and w Tex. **Black Swallowwort,** *C. nigrum,* is a European escape to thickets, roadsides, and fields, Me. to Pa., Ohio, and Kans.; its small dark purple flowers have a heavy fragrance.

SARCOSTEMMA Twining or trailing vines, becoming woody at base; stem simple to much-branched, leaves with tiny stipules, umbels extra-axillary, corona of 5 spherical sacs; 5 species in sw U.S. *S. hirtellum* has narrow downy leaves to 1½" long, 9–12 flowers per cluster; grows in desert washes, s Nev., w Ariz., and se Calif. *S. cynanchoides* has forms with narrow and heart-shaped leaves; found in sandy or rocky soil, Okla. and Tex., w to Utah and Calif.

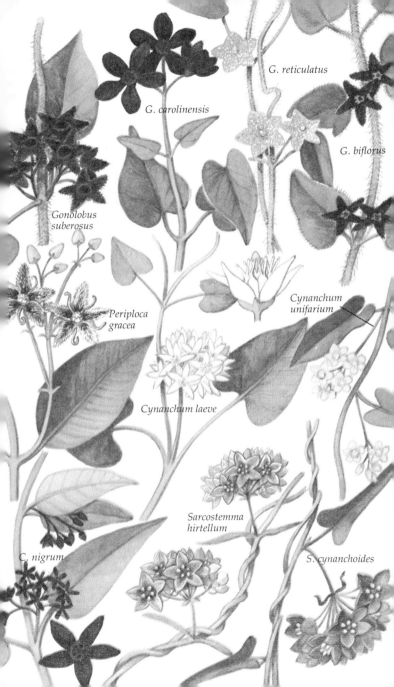

G. reticulatus

G. carolinensis

G. biflorus

Gonolobus suberosus

Periploca gracea

Cynanchum unifarium

Cynanchum laeve

Sarcostemma hirtellum

C. nigrum

S. cynanchoides

MILKWEED (ASCLEPIAS) Herbs with opposite or whorled leaves, rarely alternate; flowers in umbels; corona of 5 erect or spreading hoods, often horned within; stigma 5-angled or 5-lobed; 77 species in N.A.

Antelope-horn, *A. viridis,* 12–28″, umbels in clusters, flowers 1″ wide; in dry woods, fields, and prairies, Fla. to N.M., n to Neb., s Ill., s Ohio, and S.C.

Blood-flower or **Veintiunilla,** *A. curassavica,* to 3′, leaves short-petioled, 2–6″ long; flowers about ¼″ wide, in terminal or axillary umbels; grows in moist or wet soil, Fla. to Tex.; s Calif.

Poke Milkweed, *A. exaltata,* 2–5′ high, has 7–11 pairs of ovate leaves, 1–4″ wide, 4–12″ long; umbels terminal and in upper axils, loose, with nodding flowers; in rich woods and clearings, s Me. to Minn., s to Ga. and Ia.

Swamp Milkweed, *A. incarnata,* to 4′, stems solitary or clustered, very leafy, the leaves petioled, 3–6″ long, ½ to 1½″ wide, sometimes woolly underneath; in swamps or wet soil, e Canada s to Fla., w to Utah and N.M.

Purple Milkweed, *A. purpurascens,* has simple stems 16–40″ tall; leaves petioled, broadly oval, to 7″ long, 4″ wide; umbels terminal, solitary or in pairs; in open woods, fields, and roadsides, s Ont. to S.D., s to N.C. and Tex.

Four-leaved Milkweed, *A. quadrifolia,* has a slender 1–3′ stem with 1–2 whorls of 4 leaves at the middle and 1–2 pairs of leaves above; in dry woods, N.H. to s Ont. and Minn., s to N.C., Ala., and Ark.

Common Milkweed, *A. syriaca,* to 6′, with broad leaves, gray-woolly beneath, 4–10″ long, 2–7″ wide, in pairs; flowers ¼″ wide, in dense umbels; in dry fields, N.B. to Sask., s to Ga. and Kans.

Butterfly-weed or **Pleurisy-root,** *A. tuberosa,* is rough-hairy, 2–3′ tall, leaves alternate; corolla and corona orange to deep red or pale yellow; in dry open soil, s N.H. and Vt. to Minn. and Colo., s to Fla. and Tex.

White-flowered Milkweed, *A. variegata,* has slender simple 1–5′ stems, broadly oval opposite petioled leaves 3–6″ long, 1–3″ wide; umbels usually solitary and terminal; in dry soil, Conn. to s Mo., s to Fla. and Tex.

Green Milkweed, *A. viridiflora,* 3′ stems, often zigzag above; leaves 8–24, opposite or some alternate, variable in form; umbels solitary, mostly lateral; e Canada to Ga., w to Mont. and Ariz.

A. uncialis, a dwarf with stems 1–2″ long; leaves in whorls of 3 or more, lower ones oval, upper ones narrow, not over 1″ long; ½″ wide flowers in few-flowered umbels; in sandy soil, Wyo. to N.M. and Ariz.

Desert Milkweed, *A. erosa,* 3–7′, leaves opposite, sessile, clasping the stem, young leaves woolly; flowers 1″ wide in dense umbels; in desert washes, s Utah and w Ariz. to se Calif.

Asclepias viridis

A. exaltata

A. curassavica

A. incarnata

A. quadrifolia

A. purpurascens

A. syriaca

A. tuberosa

A. variegata

A. viridiflora

A. uncialis

A. erosa

MORNING-GLORY FAMILY (CONVOLVULACEAE)

Mostly twining herbs, some with milky sap; leaves alternate, simple (rarely compound); flowers terminal or axillary, single or in cymes; corolla funnel-form, 5-angled or 5-lobed; ovary 1- to 5-celled, 1–5 styles. 13 genera in N.A.

BINDWEED (CONVOLVULUS) Twining, trailing, or erect silky herbs; leaves simple, mostly entire, heart- or arrow-shaped, petioled; flowers single or in cymes; 1 style, 2 narrow stigmas; 28 species in N.A. **Field Bindweed** or **Possession Vine,** *C. arvensis,* has solitary long-stalked flowers; grows throughout s Canada and the U.S. **Hedge Bindweed** or **Wild Morning-glory,** *C. sepium,* has single or paired axillary flowers, Nfld. to B.C., s to Fla., Ariz., and Oreg. **Beach Morning-glory,** *C. soldanella,* grows on coastal beaches and dunes, s Calif. to B.C.

JACQUEMONTIA resembles *Convolvulus* but the 2 stigmas are thick and flattened; 5 N.A. species, all but one confined to s Fla. *J. tamnifolia* has flowers in headlike leaf-bracted cymes; its hairy stems reach 10' and twine; it often blooms when small; Coastal Plain, Fla. to e Tex.; n to Ark. and Va.

STYLISMA Small prostrate or ascending herbs, straight or twining; leaves entire, narrow, sessile or short-petioled; flowers solitary or few; 1 or 2 styles, 2 round stigmas; 6 species, in se U.S. *S. humistrata* grows in dry sandy open woods, Coastal Plain, Fla. to e Tex., n to Ark. and to se Va.

CRESSA Low densely downy herbs, forming colonies of erect or reclining freely branched stems; small entire sessile leaves; flowers solitary, axillary; 2 styles, 2 round stigmas; 2 N.A. species. *C. truxillensis,* 3–10' high, is found in salty or alkaline soil, w Tex. to Calif., n to se Oreg. and w Nev.

EVOLVULUS Low erect or reclining herbs, never twining; leaves sessile or nearly so, entire; flowers axillary, solitary or in few-flowered cymes; 2 styles, each with 2 threadlike stigmas; 6 N.A. species. *E. arizonicus* has ½" wide flowers in a branched inflorescence; sw N.M. and Ariz. *E. nuttallianus* is found on sterile plains and prairies, Ariz. to Mont. and Tenn. *E. sericeus* grows in wet sand or silt, from s Calif. to Fla.

MERREMIA Vines with palmately lobed or compound leaves; flowers axillary, single or in pairs; 2 styles, 2 round stigmas; 3 species in N.A. **Alamo-vine,** *M. dissecta,* grows mostly in pinelands, Coastal Plain, Fla. to Tex.

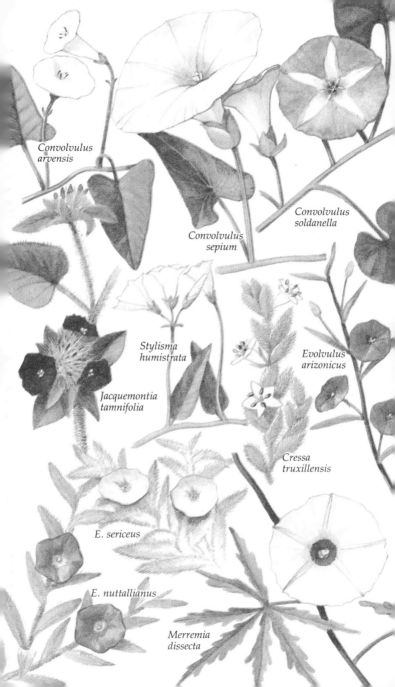

Convolvulus arvensis

Convolvulus sepium

Convolvulus soldanella

Stylisma humistrata

Jacquemontia tamnifolia

Evolvulus arizonicus

Cressa truxillensis

E. sericeus

E. nuttallianus

Merremia dissecta

MORNING-GLORY (IPOMOEA) Stems erect to trailing or twining; leaves long-petioled to sessile, simple and entire to deeply lobed or dissected; individual flowers are usually open less than 24 hours; 1 style; 1 stigma, round or of 2 or 3 round lobes. About 51 species in N.A.

Scarlet Creeper, *I. coccinea*, is a low-climbing vine, flowers 1" long, sepals long-awned at tip, corolla red with a yellow tube or all orange-red; a Trop. Am. escape, Fla. to Ariz., n to Kans., Mich., Mass.

I. hederacea is a slender twiner with down-pointed hairs; sepals broad, hairy, with long thin tips; fresh corolla sky-blue, quickly becoming rose-purple; tube white, 1" long; Fla. to Ariz., n to N.D. and N.Eng.

Bush Morning-glory, *I. leptophylla*, is a smooth decumbent to erect bushy herb to 4'; leaves 2–4" long on short petioles; flowers 3–4" long, lavender-pink with dark center or all red-purple; sandy prairies, Tex. to Neb., Colo., N.M.

Man-of-the-earth or **Wild Potato-vine,** *I. pandurata*, has trailing stems from large starchy roots; leaves heart-shaped, some with indented sides; flowers 2–3" long; in dry open or partly shaded soil, se U.S., n to Kans., Conn., s Ont., N.Y.

Railroad-vine or **Goat's-hoof Vine,** *I. pes-caprae*, has creeping stems rooting at the nodes, not twining; nearly round leaves, the tip notched, the 2 sides folded up; cymes several-flowered, tube 2–3" long; a sand-binding herb of beaches, Fla. to Tex. and Ga.

Common Morning-glory, *I. purpurea*, is a high-climbing vine with entire heart-shaped leaves (3-lobed in var. *diversifolia*); corolla purple, red, blue, white, or variegated; a Trop. Am. escape throughout the U.S.

Cypress Vine, *I. quamoclit*, is a twining vine with short-petioled leaves pinnately dissected into many narrow segments; cymes few-flowered, corolla deep scarlet, rarely white, tube narrow, to 1½" long; se U.S., n to Kans. and Va., sparingly escaped from cultivation farther north.

I. sagittata is a tightly twining low vine with narrow arrow-shaped leaves 2–4" long, to 2" wide across the base; flowers solitary; tube to 4" long; in wet prairies, swamps, and hammocks, Coastal Plain, Fla. to Tex. and N.C.

I. leptoloma is a slender twining or trailing herb; the leaves are palmately divided into 3 or 5 narrow lobes, and the 2 basal lobes are sometimes divided into 3 additional lobes; corolla may be blue, purple, or white on a 1–1½" white tube; grows in dry soil, N.M. and s Ariz.

I. shumardiana is a smooth erect to trailing or twining herb with narrow entire petioled leaves 1–3" long, ⅓–1½" wide; sepals oblong, tips rounded; corolla pink to white with a purple-red center, tube 2–3" long; in sandy or sandy-clay prairies, Okla. and n Tex.

Ipomoea coccinea

I. hederacea

I. leptophylla

I. pes-caprae

I. pandurata

I. purpurea

I. sagittata

I. quamoclit

I. shumardiana

I. leptoloma

PHLOX FAMILY (POLEMONIACEAE)

Leaves alternate or opposite, or opposite below and alternate on uppe
stem, simple and entire to toothed, lobed, or pinnately compoun
flower parts in 5's, corolla tubular with a 5-lobed border, 1 style, 3 line
stigmas; 14 genera in N.A.

COLLOMIA Stems simple or branched, leaves sessile, alternate, enti
or lobed; flowers in leafy-bracted heads; 11 species, mostly in w N./
C. debilis is a mat-forming herb; leaves entire or lobed, crowded at th
stem tips; ranges from w Wash. to w Mont., s to n Calif., ne Nev., cer
Utah, and w Wyo. *C. linearis*, 4–20", has narrow entire pointed leave
Man. to Mo., w to B.C. and Calif.; local e to N.B. and Que. *C. tinctor*
is sticky-glandular, 2–6" high, with narrow leaves; from cen. Wash. t
cen. Calif., e to Ida. and w Nev.

ERIASTRUM Leaves alternate, spine-tipped, narrow and entire or c
threadlike lobes; flowers in woolly heads; calyx of 5 awns joined by
membrane; 12 species, of w N.A. *E. diffusum* is branched to 4" tall an
6" wide, lower leaves 3-lobed, upper ones entire; w Tex. to s Utah an
Calif. *E. sparsiflorum*, 4–16" tall, is tufted by wool; leaves narrow, entir
or 2-lobed at base; grows in dry open places, Wash. to Ida., s to Cali
and Utah.

LANGLOISIA Low herbs with spine- or bristle-tipped pinnately lobe
leaves; flowers in small terminal clusters amid bristly bracts; som
species with zygomorphic flowers; 4 species, of w U.S. *L setosissim*
forms tufts 3–4" wide; its triangular leaflets have 3 long spines at th
tip; grows in dry open desert, Oreg. and Ida. to s Calif. and Ariz.

LINANTHUS Small plants with opposite entire or palmately lobe
leaves; flowers in dense cymes or heads; calyx teeth narrow, joined b
a membrane; about 35 species, in w N.A.

L. aureus, 2–4" high with a widely branched stem, has palmately lobed bristle-tipped leaves; it is common on dry plains and mesas from e N.M. to s Nev. and se Calif.

L. ciliatus, to 1' high, has palmately-lobed leaves, bristles on leaves, bracts, and calyx lobes; corolla lobes white to deep rose; grows in dry open places in the mountains, s Oreg. to s Calif. and Nev.

Mustang-clover, *L. montanus,* t
2', has palmately lobed leave
edged by hair; corolla lobes rose-
pink or white, with a red spot a
the base; grows in dry gravel,
Sierra Nevada, Calif.

L. nuttallii, 4–8" high, is a much-
branched bushy plant, ofter
bristly, woody at base; leaves palmately lobed, with clusters o
small leaves in the axils of the
larger ones; from Wash. to Wyo.,
s to s Calif. and N.M.

Collomia
debilis

C. linearis

C. tinctoria

Eriastrum
diffusum

E. sparsiflorum

Langloisia
setosissima

Linanthus
aureus

Linanthus
ciliatus

Linanthus
montanus

Linanthus
nuttallii

GILIA Stem erect, simple or branched; leaves alternate, entire or pinnately toothed, lobed, or dissected; flowers solitary or in sparse heads arranged in panicles; individual flowers or flower groups subtended by bracts; calyx teeth of equal length, bordered or united by membranes; corolla bell-like, funnel-form, or the lobes abruptly at right angles to a narrow tube; over 70 species, mostly in w N.A.

G. capitata, to 32", is a tall slender plant, often branched above; its basal and lower stem leaves are bipinnately divided; flowers white to blue-violet, ¼–½" long, in dense terminal heads; in dry sunny sites, s B.C. to Ida., s to s Calif.

Blue Desert-gilia, *G. rigidula,* is a branched plant to 10" high, its lower leaves divided into asymmetric stiff sharp-toothed lobes, upper ones with stiff sharp linear segments; in dry soil, w Neb. and Colo. to Tex., N.M., Ariz.

G. subnuda is a glandular-downy plant with a basal rosette of entire to pinnately lobed leaves and a few pinnately lobed stem leaves; corolla to 1" long; on sandy or rocky hills, Utah and Nev. to N.M. and n Ariz.

G. sinuata, 4–12" high, has a basal rosette of succulent woolly leaves; stem leaves entire or toothed, with clasping bases; flowers in tight 3-flowered heads or in loose panicles, pink or white to violet; grows in desert plains, e Wash. to Ida., s to se Calif. and N.M.

G. latiflora, 2–16" high, has 1 or more stems from a basal rosette of hairy, toothed or pinnately lobed leaves; stem leaves toothed or entire, with clasping bases; flowers to 1" long, in close or open clusters; in sandy places and fields, s Calif., sw Utah, w Ariz.

Scarlet Gilia or **Sky-rocket,** *G. aggregata,* to 7', has a simple downy-glandular stem from a rosette; leaves divided into narrow pinnate segments; 1" long flowers in a long slender panicle; on dry rocky open or lightly wooded slopes and drier meadows, s B.C. to Mont., s to s Calif. and the Trans-Pecos, Tex.

G. longiflora is a much-branched herb to 2' high; leaves spaced far apart, lower ones 2" long, with 7 narrow segments, upper ones entire; flowers solitary or in pairs, on a stout leafy panicle; calyx dotted by stalked glands; tube to 1½" long, corolla lobes white or lavender; in dry soil, Utah to Neb., s to Ariz., Tex.

G. spicata usually has an unbranched stem 4–14" high; leaves crowded, threadlike and entire or irregularly divided into threadlike segments; the ½" flowers in heads in a false spike; dry hills and plains, cen. Ida. to S.D., s to Kans., N.M., and Utah.

Standing Cypress, Spanish Larkspur, or **Texas Plume,** *G. rubra,* has a rosette and simple stem to 7'; leaves of threadlike segments; the 1" corolla is streaked or mottled inside with yellow; in dry sandy or rocky ground, Fla. to Tex. and N.C.; cultivated and escaped elsewhere.

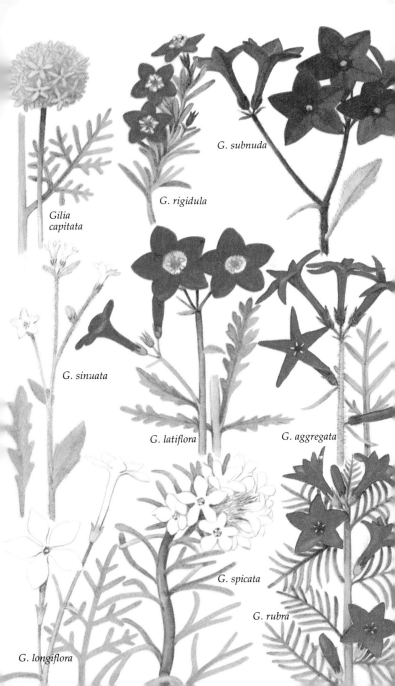

Gilia capitata

G. rigidula

G. subnuda

G. sinuata

G. latiflora

G. aggregata

G. spicata

G. longiflora

G. rubra

MICROSTERIS One species, *M. gracilis*, a branching herb 4–8″ high with glandular hairs; leaves entire, opposite below, alternate above, to 1″ long; flowers in axillary pairs, corolla tube yellow, lobes white, rose, or lavender; grows in dry to moderately moist open places, Alaska to Mont., s to Baja Calif. and N.M.

NAVARRETIA Mostly low branching herbs; leaves alternate, entire or pinnately lobed or divided, spine-tipped; tiny flowers in dense heads amid very spiny diversely lobed or dissected bracts; 30 species, in w N.A. *N. breweri*, 1–5″ high, is downy as well as spiny; leaves odd-pinnate, as are the floral bracts; grows in dry open places, Wash. to Ida. and Wyo., s to Calif. and n Ariz. *N. minima*, 1–4″, has prostrate or erect stems, flowers in tiny round heads; found in moist places, Wash. and Ida., s to n Calif., Nev., and n Ariz. *N. squarrosa*, 2–20″ high, is downy-glandular; leaves once- or twice-pinnate; floral bracts pinnate or palmate; plant has odor of skunk; s B.C. to cen. Calif.

GREEK VALERIAN or **JACOB'S-LADDER** (POLEMONIUM) Herbs of cool regions; leaves alternate and odd-pinnate; leaflets sessile; flowers in loose or compact terminal corymbs; corolla lobes rounded; stamens bearded at base; 20 N.A. species.

P. carneum 12–40″, larger leaves with 11–21 leaflets; long-stalked flowers in sticky-haired corymbs; corolla white, yellow, salmon, or purple; woodlands and forest openings, from sea level to moderate elevations in w Wash. to San Francisco Bay.

P. reptans 6–22″ high, has diffuse low-branching stems from a tufted base; basal and larger stem leaves with 11–17 pointed leaflets; few-flowered corymbs on long slender branches; in rich woods and bottoms, N.Y. to Minn., s to Ga. and Okla., escaped elsewhere.

Skunk-leaf, *P. delicatum*, is a delicate little glandular-hairy plant 2–8″ tall that emits a mephitic odor; larger leaves have up to 23 leaflets ⅛–¼″ long, corolla blue or white; in high mountains at alpine levels (10,000–12,000′ in Ariz.); Ida. to N.M. and Ariz.

P. pulcherrimum, 2–12″ high, has a basal rosette of leaves with 11–23 leaflets, relatively few stem leaves; flowers blue with yellow or white centers; at moderate to high elevations, in moist or shady places, or exposed sites above timberline, Alaska to Calif. and Colo.

P. viscosum, 2–20″, has leaflets palmately divided into 3 or 5 lobes; flowers blue, white, or yellow, in headlike corymbs; in open rocky places, commonly above timberline, Rocky Mts. region, Alta. and Wash. to n N.M.

P. pauciflorum, 6–24″ tall, is sparsely to freely branched; upper stems are glandular-hairy, somewhat sticky, with a musky scent; leaves with 11–21 leaflets; flowers solitary or in pairs, the tube to 1½″ long, with short lobes; in wooded canyons in mts., w Tex.; s Ariz.

N. squarrosa

Navarretia breweri

Microsteris gracilis

N. minima

lemonium
·neum

P. reptans

P. delicatum

P. pauciflorum

P. pulcherrimum

P. viscosum

PHLOX Stems erect to reclining or trailing, simple to much-branched; leaves simple and entire, mostly sessile, opposite or becoming alternate above; herbage often downy or downy-glandular; flowers solitary or in cymes, terminal or crowded in the upper axils, often bracted; calyx lobes toothed or awned, joined by a dry membrane; corolla lobes at right angles to the long narrow tube, ends round, pointed, or notched; stamens unequally attached. About 60 N.A. species.

P. andicola has erect crowded 5″ shoots, forming cushions; leaves awl-like; cymes kinky-hairy; corolla lobes white, yellow, or purple; se Mont. and sw N.D. to nw Kans., se Wyo., and ne Colo.

P. austromontana forms cushions 3–6″ high and as wide or wider; leaves awl-like; flowers terminal, 1–5 per cyme; corolla lobes white to pink or lavender; foothills to rather high in mts., Oreg. and Ida. to N.M., Calif.

P. carolina, 7–30″, has stems in a crown or from the axils of old decumbent branches; leaves narrow to lance-like, to 4″ long; corolla magenta to pink, rarely white; N.C. to Ala., n to Md., s Ind.

Blue Phlox, *P. divaricata,* has stems spreading or rising from a decumbent base; flowering stems erect, 6–20″ high; corolla lobes blue to purple, or white; Que. to S.D., s to se Tex. and Fla.

P. hoodii, 2″, is silvery green, its branches woolly; leaves tiny, stiff; flowers single, terminal; on dry mt. slopes, e Alaska to w Neb., s to Calif., nw Ariz.

Meadow Phlox or **Wild Sweet William,** *P. maculata,* 1–3′ tall, has leaves to 5″ long, 1″ wide; flowers purple or rarely white; meadows, bottomlands, Que. to Minn., s to Va., Mo.

Trailing Phlox, *P. nivalis,* forms mats to 2′ wide; leaves awl-like, crowded, to 1″ long; in pine and oak lands, Fla. to Tex., n to Va., n Ga., cen. Ala.

Drummond Phlox, *P. drummondii,* 6–18″ tall, is a much-branched erect hairy-glandular herb; lower leaves opposite, upper alternate, 1–3″ long; e Tex.; escaped, se Coastal Plain and elsewhere.

Gold-eyed Phlox, *P. romeriana,* to 14″, has lance-like mostly alternate leaves to 2″ long; flowers in asymmetric cymes, herbage densely soft-hairy; on dry rocky slopes, cen. Tex.

Creeping Phlox, *P. stolonifera,* is a weak glandular-hairy herb 5–12″ high; its long sterile stems root at the nodes; flowering stems erect, with 3–4 pairs of 1″ leaves; in woods, Pa. to s Ohio, s to w S.C. and n Ga.

Moss-pink or **Mountain Phlox,** *P. subulata,* forms mats 3′ wide; leaves awl-like, most ½″ long or less; flowers held just above the leaves; from L.I. and w N.Y. to s Mich., s upland to N.C., Tenn.

Sand Phlox, *P. bifida,* resembles Moss-pink but has fewer nodes; the lower leaves 1–2″ long; grows on dry cliffs, bluffs, and sandhills, from s Mich. to Ia., s to Ky., Mo., and e Okla.

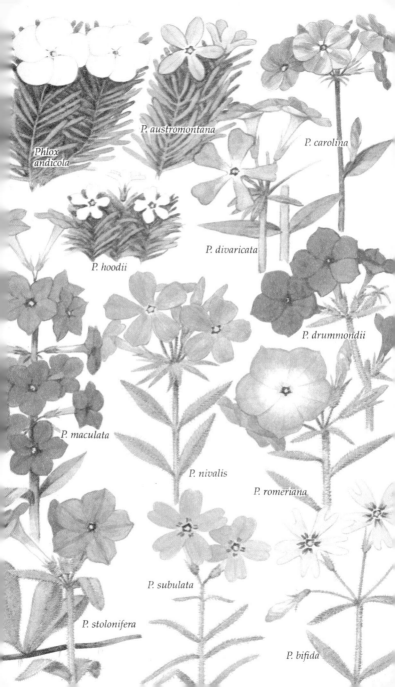

Phlox andicola

P. austromontana

P. carolina

P. hoodii

P. divaricata

P. drummondii

P. maculata

P. nivalis

P. romeriana

P. subulata

P. stolonifera

P. bifida

WATER-LEAF FAMILY (HYDROPHYLLACEAE)

Mostly hairy herbs; leaves opposite or alternate, simple or compound; flowers in S-shaped cymes, rarely solitary; flower parts in 5's; calyx deeply lobed; corolla bell-like, lobed; stamens attached to the corolla; pistil with 2 styles or 1 cleft style; 2 stigmas; 15 N.A. genera.

AUNT LUCY (ELLISIA) One species, *E. nyctelea*, a branched rough-hairy herb 4–16″ high; leaves mostly alternate, with 7–13 pinnate segments; flowers solitary, opposite the leaves, blue, purple, or white; grows in woods, damp soil, e N.A., w to Sask., and N.M.

HESPEROCHIRON Leaves in a rosette, simple, entire, petioled; flowers solitary, axillary; 2 species. *H. californicus* has oval leaves fringed by fine hair, 1″-long funnel-shaped flowers; grows in alkaline meadows and flats, Wash. to Baja Calif., e to w Mont., w Wyo., and ne Utah. *H. pumilus* has a bell-like corolla ¼–½″ long, densely hairy inside; grows in moist non-alkaline soil, Wash. to Calif., e to w Mont., Colo., and Ariz.

TURRICULA One species, *T. parryi*, 3–8′ tall, an erect sticky-hairy herb; leaves lance-shaped, sessile, alternate, the edges usually toothed; flowers in close axillary clusters along the nearly leafless upper stem; grows in dry soil, often appearing after fire, s Sierra Nevada and other mts. of s Calif.

LEMMONIA One species, *L. californica*, a low downy herb with simple entire alternate leaves to ½″ long; flowers tiny, sessile, solitary in the axils and in terminal clusters; filaments fused at base; 1 cleft style. Grows in sandy soil, inner coast ranges, s two-thirds of Calif.

WATER-LEAF (HYDROPHYLLUM) Plants mostly 1–3′, leaves large, petioled, cut-toothed or palmately or pinnately lobed or divided; flowers in open or headlike cymes; corolla tube with 5 linear nectaries opposite the lobes; 1 cleft style; 8 N.A. species.

H. appendiculatum is hairy; stem leaves palmately lobed, lobes toothed, lowest lobe pinnately divided; in rich woods, Ont. and Minn., s to sw Pa. and e Kans.

H. capitatum has long-petioled downy pinnately lobed leaves, lobes notched at the tip; blue or white flowers; s B.C. and Alta. to cen. Calif. and Colo.

H. macrophyllum is rough-hairy; leaves of 9–13 cut-toothed pinnate segments; calyx lobes very hairy; in rich woods, w Va. and W. Va. to Ill., s to Ga. and Ala.

Squaw-lettuce, *H. occidentale*, has pinnate leaves of 7–15 segments; cymes headlike, flowers white or blue-violet; Oreg. to Calif., e to Ida. and Ariz.

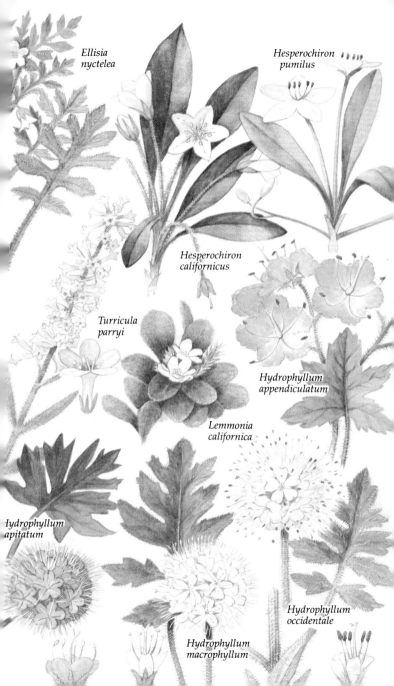

*Ellisia
nyctelea*

*Hesperochiron
pumilus*

*Hesperochiron
californicus*

*Turricula
parryi*

*Hydrophyllum
appendiculatum*

*Lemmonia
californica*

*Iydrophyllum
apitatum*

*Hydrophyllum
occidentale*

*Hydrophyllum
macrophyllum*

DRAPERIA One species, *D. systyla,* to 16″ high; stems rough-hairy; leaves simple and entire, petioled or sessile, alternate; flowers to ⅜″ long, in compact terminal cymes; 1 cleft style; grows on dry slopes in woods, Sierra Nevada and mts. of nw Calif.

NAMA Low downy herbs; leaves mostly alternate and entire; flowers in compact terminal cymes, or solitary in the axils; 2 styles, or 1 cleft style; 21 N.A. species, mostly in sw U.S. *N. aretioides* has horizontal hairy stems, narrow leaves, and solitary flowers; grows on dry sandy plains and hills, often with sagebrush, Wash. and Ida. to Inyo Co. Calif. *N. demissum* has hairy prostrate stems, the leaves crowded at the tips; flowers solitary, in false cymes; in sandy deserts, Utah, Ariz., and se Calif. *N. rothrockii,* to 12″ high, has bristly stems, bristly glandular 2″ leaves with scalloped or toothed edges, flowers in compact cymes; in dry sandy sites, Sierra Nevada, Calif., to w Nev.

HYDROLEA Erect aquatic or marsh herbs mostly 1–2′ tall; leaves alternate, simple, and entire, often with spines in the axils; blue flowers in axillary and terminal clusters; 2 styles; 5 species, in se U.S., *H. corymbosa* has sessile elliptic or lance-like leaves 1–2″ long; grows in swamps, along streams, Coastal Plain, Fla. to S.C. *H. ovata* is a stout erect hairy and spiny herb; leaves 1–2″ long, often with short petioles; grows in swamps and bayous, Ga. to Tex. n to se Mo. and Okla.

NEMOPHILA Weak-stemmed herbs; leaves alternate or opposite, toothed or pinnately lobed or divided; flowers solitary or in cymes, large if blue or purple, small if white; 1 cleft style; 11 species, 2 in e, 9 in w N.A. **Baby Blue-eyes,** *N. phacelioides,* is hairy or smooth-stemmed; leaves to 3″ long, pinnately divided into 9–11 oval segments; flowers single and axillary or in terminal cymes; grows in sandy soil of open woods, e and se Tex. to Ark. and Okla. *N. microcalyx* is sparsely hairy, its leaves pinnately divided into 3 or 5 lobes; inhabits moist woods, from w Fla. to Tex. n to e Va., se Mo. and Okla. **Five-spot,** *N. maculata,* has leaves pinnately divided into 3–9 lobes; flowers 1–2″ wide, a purple blotch on each corolla lobe; grows on w slopes of the Sierra Nevada, Calif.

WHISPERING BELLS (EMMENANTHE) One species, *E. penduliflora,* to 2′ tall, an erect branching hairy-stemmed herb with alternate and pinnately lobed leaves; flowers in loose terminal cymes, yellow or pink, the buds erect, nodding when open; the corolla becomes dry and papery but is held on the plant, and "whispers" in a breeze. Grows in dry soil, s Utah and Ariz. to Calif.

*Draperia
systyla*

*Nama
aretioides*

*Nama
demissum*

*Nama
rothrockii*

*Hydrolea
corymbosa*

H. ovata

*Nemophila
microcalyx*

*Nemophila
phacelioides*

*Nemophila
maculata*

*Emmenanthe
penduliflora*

EUCRYPTA Fragrant glandular-hairy herbs; leaves pinnately lobed or divided, upper ones alternate; white or blue flowers in loose clusters; 1 cleft style; 2 species, in sw U.S. *E. micrantha* has weak branching stems to 10″ high, leaves to ½″ long, lower ones toothed, upper ones of 7 or 9 lobes and clasping bases; grows in damp shady sites, w Tex. to s Utah and s Calif.

PHOLISTOMA Sprawling herbs with succulent 4-angled stems; upper leaves alternate, pinnately divided; flowers solitary in the axils or in loose terminal clusters; 1 cleft style; 2 species in sw U.S. **Fiesta-flower,** *P. auritum*, to 4′ tall, has broad-winged petioles that clasp the stem; climbs by hooked bristles on the stem, leaves, and calyx; grows in light shade, s Calif. and Ariz.

ROMANZOFFIA Low herbs; leaves mostly basal, with long petioles and roundish blades notched at base, the edges scalloped or toothed; white flowers in open cymes; 1 undivided style; 4 species, in w N.A. *R. sitchensis*, to 10″ high, has several stems from a short caudex; petioles dilated at base and overlapped at base of plant; grows in moist places, sea level to alpine, Alaska to nw Mont. and n Calif.

TRICARDIA One species, *T. watsonii*, to 1′ high; leaves simple and entire, in a basal rosette, petioled; tiny ¼″ flowers in a false raceme; corolla lobes white, striped with purple; 1 cleft style; after blooming, the calyx enlarges to 1″, enclosing the fruit; grows on dry slopes, s Utah, nw Ariz., and se Calif.

SCORPION-WEED (PHACELIA) Leaves mostly alternate, simple to variously lobed or divided; handsome blue, purple, or white flowers in S-shaped raceme-like cymes; 1 cleft style. About 140 species, largely of w N.A.

P. bipinnatifida, 10″–2′, has long-petioled bipinnately lobed leaves; in rich woods, Va. to se Ia., s to Ark., Ga., and Ala.

P. fimbriata, 8–16″ high, has pinnate lower leaves, upper ones pinnately lobed; corolla lobes deeply fringed; grows in upland woods, sw Va. to N.C. and Ala.

P. fremontii, 4–8″, has thickish pinnately lobed leaves, the lobes rounded, entire or lobed or toothed; grows in desert, s Utah, Nev., nw Ariz., and s Calif.

P. corrugata, 6″–3′, is a sticky glandular-hairy malodorous herb; leaves narrow, scalloped; Colo. and Utah to Ariz. and w Tex.

P. brachyloba, 4–20″, leaves 1–3″ long, mostly basal, pinnately lobed, lobes entire or toothed; herbage bristly, glandular; s half of Calif., e in deserts.

P. grandiflora, 20–40″, broad oval leaves to 4″ long, edges toothed; all herbage bristly hairy; flowers ½–1″ long; dry soil, Calif. coast; inland in s Calif.

Eucrypta micrantha

Romanzoffia sitchensis

Pholistoma auritum

Tricardia watsonii

Phacelia bipinnatifida

Phacelia fimbriata

Phacelia fremontii

Phacelia corrugata

Phacelia brachyloba

Phacelia grandiflora

BORAGE FAMILY (BORAGINACEAE)

Rough-hairy herbs with alternate simple entire or shallowly toothed leaves; flowers mostly on 1 side of S-shaped branches of a reduced cyme, the parts in 5's; corolla 5-lobed, the stamens attached to its tube; ovary 4-lobed, 1 style, 1 or 2 stigmas; 27 genera with herbaceous species in N.A.

HELIOTROPE (HELIOTROPIUM) Low bushy herbs; leaves entire, sessile or petioled; corolla funnel-form, or the lobes at right angles to the tube; anthers nearly sessile; 23 species in N.A.

H. convolvulaceum, 4–16″ high, has ash-gray young herbage from sharp stiff hairs; flowers fragrant; grows on dunes, sandy soil, Neb. and Wyo. to s Nev., Ariz., and Tex.

H. greggii has 6″ prostrate stems, sessile leaves; corolla of 5 round lobes and 5 smaller in-pointed triangular lobes; grows on sites where water collects temporarily, Tex. and N.M.

Seaside-heliotrope, *H. curassavicum,* has limp rubbery decumbent stems to 16″ long, succulent leaves; grows on sandy seabeaches, edges of fresh or salt marshes, throughout the U.S.

Turnsole, *H. indicum,* to 3′ tall, has long-petioled ovate leaves; cymes to 1′ long, with 2 ranks of blue, violet, or white flowers; Asian, now in se U.S., n to Okla., Mo., and Va.

BORAGE (BORAGO) is European; *B. officinalis* is an escape to waste ground, Nfld. to N.D., s to Va. and Ill., and w of the Cascades, Pac. NW; a coarse herb 12–20″ high, lower leaves petioled, corolla clear blue, throat closed by scales.

COMFREY (SYMPHYTUM) Rough-leaved Eurasian herbs; small nodding white, yellow, blue, or reddish flowers in single or paired false racemes; 4 species in N.A. **Common Comfrey,** *S. officinale,* to 40″ high, has winged leaf bases running down the stem; grows in damp waste places, e N.A.; also in Wash. and Mont.

VIPER'S BUGLOSS (ECHIUM) Erect herbs, 1–3′ tall, with sessile leaves, zygomorphic flowers in short cymes crowded along the upper stem; 2 species in N.A. **Blue-weed,** *E. vulgare,* with blue, pink, or white flowers, is local in w, common in e N.A.

GROMWELL and **PUCCOON** (LITHOSPERMUM) Leaves sessile; flowers solitary, or in leafy-bracted spikes; 18 species in N.A. **Corn-gromwell,** *L. arvense,* 8–28″ high, is European; its leaves lack lateral veins; in sandy soil, N.S. to B.C., s to Fla., La., and Calif. **Indian-paint,** *L. canescens,* 4–18″, is densely hoary; in dry soil or sand, s Que. to Sask., s to Ga. and Tex. *L. incisum,* 4–20″ tall, has showy early flowers, later ones small or cleistogamous; s Ont. to B.C., s to Ind., Tex., Ariz.

H. greggii

H. indicum

Heliotropium convolvulaceum

H. curassavicum

Echium vulgare

Borago officinalis

Symphytum officinale

Lithospermum arvense

L. incisum

L. canescens

FALSE GROMWELL (ONOSMODIUM) Erect branching herbs; leaves sessile, rib-veined; flowers white, greenish, or yellow, in terminal leafy S-shaped cymes; 3 N.A. species. *O. molle*, 2–4' high, a variable species, grows in open moderately dry sites, e N.A., w to the e base of the Rocky Mts., Mont. and N.M.

COLDENIA Low plants with forked stems, woody at base; numerous small entire leaves; sessile solitary or clustered flowers, opening in late afternoon; 7 herbaceous N.A. species. **Oreja del Perro,** *C. canescens,* to 4" tall and 1' wide, is woolly; solitary pink, blue, or white flowers; w Tex. and s N.M. *C. hispidissima* forms bristly mats 8–16" wide; flowers solitary, usually pink; ranges from cen. Tex. to Ariz. and s Utah.

ALKANET (ANCHUSA) Coarse hairy Eurasian herbs with blue flowers in leafy-bracted l-sided spikes; 3 species in N.A. **Common Alkanet,** *C. officinalis*, 1–3' tall, grows in waste places, Me. to Ohio, Mich., and N.J.; e of the Cascades, Pac. NW.

FORGET-ME-NOT (MYOSOTIS) Low mostly soft-hairy herbs with entire leaves, basal leaves petioled; small flowers in naked racemes; 10 species in N.A. **True Forget-me-not,** *M. scorpioides*, 12–28" tall, has angled succulent stems rising from a creeping base, rough-hairy leaves; European, found in quiet water or wet soil, e and Pac. N.A. **Garden Forget-me-not,** *M. sylvatica*, is a tufted herb, becoming 8–20" high; flowers blue, pink, or white, with a yellow eye; European, now escaped, Que. to Ont., s to N.Y. and Mich.; *M. verna*, 4–16" high, is a white-flowered native of rocky woods, prairies, e U.S.; Ida. to s B.C., s to Wyo. and Calif.; absent from most plains and Rocky Mt. states.

CRYPTANTHA Stems herbaceous or woody at base; basal leaves opposite, veinless; flowers white, rarely yellow, in bractless or bracted spikes or racemes; corolla with 5 inpointed appendages at the throat, and 5 rounded lobes; 1 headlike stigma; 113 species, in w N.A.; difficult to identify.

C. jamesii has loosely clustered 4–12" stems from a caudex, bristly or hairy leaves, terminal S-shaped cymes; in sandy soil, w S.D. and se Wyo. to Tex. and Ariz.

C. nubigena has several stems to 6" high amid a tuft of hairy-bristly leaves; alpine, cen. Ida. and w Mont. to e Oreg., s to the Sierra Nevada of Calif.

C. flava, 4–12", has a basal tuft of bristly leaves, yellow flowers in cylindric inflorescence; grows in sandy soil, Utah and Wyo. to ne Ariz. and nw N.M.

C. virgata has 1 or more stems 10–40" tall, rough-hairy leaves, a cylindrical inflorescence with conspicuous long narrow bracts; from se Wyo. to cen. Colo.

Coldenia
canescens

Anchusa
officinalis

Coldenia
hispidissima

Onosmodium
molle

Myosotis
scorpioides

M. sylvatica

M. verna

Cryptantha
nubigena

Cryptantha
jamesii

Cryptantha
flava

Cryptantha
virgata

BUGLOSS (LYCOPSIS) is Eurasian; *L. arvensis,* a bristly 4–24″ herb with sessile leaves, flowers in leafy clusters, now grows in dry or sandy fields, from Nfld. to Ont., s to Va. and Neb.

HOUND'S TONGUE (CYNOGLOSSUM) Coarse herbs; lower leaves petioled; flowers in panicled racemes, bracted at base, naked above; corolla funnel-form, throat closed by 5 scales; 6 species in N.A. **Common Hound's-tongue** or **Beggar's-lice,** *C. officinale,* 2–4′ high, is soft-hairy; its hooked-bristled fruits cling to cloth and fur; European, now an obnoxious weed, Que. to the Pac., s to S.C. and Ark., in most w states. **Bluebuttons,** *C. grande,* 1–3′ tall, is smooth; basal leaves of 6″ blades on 6″ petioles; grows in woods, at lower elevations, s B.C. to s Calif.

ERITRICHIUM Leaves in dense rosettes, forming low cushions; inflorescence short, bracted; calyx and leaves silky; 6 N.A. species. **King-of-the-Alps,** *E. nanum,* forms cushions 1–4″ wide; alpine, from the Alps to Alaska, s in Rocky Mts. to n N.M.

FIDDLE-NECK (AMSINCKIA) Bristly herbs; leaves veinless, narrow to oval; flowers yellow or orange, in S-shaped spikes, usually bractless; about 14 N.A. species, mostly w. **Tarweed,** *A. lycopsoides,* 12–40″, is erect or reclining, with long spreading branches; grows in open soil, s B.C. to w Mont., s to Nev. and Calif. **Rancher's Fireweed,** *A. intermedia,* 8–40″ high, is erect or widely branched, sparsely bristly, woolly at base of spikes; grows in grasslands, Wash. and Ida. to Baja Calif. and w Tex.

PLAGIOBOTHRYS Delicate mostly soft-hairy herbs, lower leaves opposite in some; white flowers in terminal false racemes; 46 N.A. species, mostly of Calif. **Popcorn-flower,** *P. nothofulvus,* to 2′, grows on open slopes, grassy fields, Baja Calif. to the Columbia River gorge, Wash. *P. scouleri,* 4–12″ high, has racemes bracted to the tip; grows on saline flats, damp sites, B.C. to w Minn., s to Calif. and N.M.; also in Alaska.

STICKSEED (HACKELIA) Low slender to stout herbs with broad veiny leaves, lower ones petioled; white or blue flowers in naked or small-bracted racemes, throat closed by scales; fruits with barbed bristles; about 25 N.A. species. *H. californica* has downy 16–40″ stems, 6″ oval leaves; grows in openings in or near the Cascades, Oreg. to n Calif. *H. jessicae* has many 12–40″ stems, petioled lower leaves to 14″ long; grows in openings and mountain meadows, Alaska; s B.C. to Calif., e to Alta., w Wyo. and Utah. *H. mundula,* 2–3′ tall, is smooth or downy, flowers pink, aging to blue; found in s half of the Sierra Nevada.

Lycopsis arvensis

Cynoglossum officinale

C. grande

Eritrichium nanum

Amsinckia lycopsoides

A. intermedia

Plagiobothrys nothofulvus

P. scouleri

Hackelia californica

H. jessicae

H. mundula

LUNGWORT (MERTENSIA) Smooth or soft-hairy herbs with entire leaves, blue-purple (rarely white) flowers in loose clusters, only the lower one leafy-bracted; 23 N.A. species.

Virginia Cowslip, "Bluebells," or Roanoke-bells, *M. virginica,* 8–28", is smooth, with "bloom" on the leaves; basal leaves long-petioled; blades to 8" long; flowers ⅓–¾" long; in woods, bottoms, N.Y. and s Ont. to Minn., s to S.C., Ark., e Kans.

Languid-ladies, *M. paniculata,* 8–30" tall, is somewhat rough-hairy, loosely branched above; cymes dense at first, becoming loose; corolla short, ⅕–⅓" long; damp woods, shores, Alaska to Que., s to n Mich., Wisc., ne Ia., Mont., Ida., and Oreg.

M. alpina has a clump of stems to 1' high, narrow leaves to 3" long, flowers in tight terminal clusters; alpine meadows, Mont. and Ida. to Colo. and N.M.

M. ciliata, 4–40" tall, has 5" leaves on long petioles; flowers in axillary cymes; in wet sites, foothills to high mts., Oreg. to Mont., s to Calif. and N.M.

M. longiflora, to 10", is often smooth, lacking basal leaves; cymes terminal, crowded; flowers to 1" long; plains and foothills from s B.C. to Calif. and Mont.

VERVAIN FAMILY (VERBENACEAE)

Stems 4-angled; leaves mostly opposite, simple, often toothed or lobed; flowers axillary or terminal, the parts in 4's or 5's; corolla tubular, often 2-lipped; stamens 2, 4, or 5, attached to the tube; 6 genera in N.A. with herbaceous species.

BOUCHEA One herbaceous species, *B. prismatica,* an erect or sprawling 16" plant; leaves opposite, toothed toward the tip; flowers in terminal spikes, pink to blue or purple; in fields, roadsides, w Tex., s Ariz.

VELVET-BUR (PRIVA) is tropical, but **Common Velvet-bur, Bur vervain,** or **Cat's-tongue,** *P. lappulacea,* grows in fields, thickets, roadsides in s Tex.; a prostrate or reclining branched woolly herb to 40"; leaves thin, oval, toothed at the sides, to 6" long; flowers in a many-flowered 2–8" spike; corolla white, pink, blue, or purple.

STACHYTARPHETA One species, *S. jamaicensis,* grows in pinelands and on dunes, Fla. and s Ala.; an herb with widely spread branches, 3" coarsely toothed leaves, long terminal spikes; individual flowers ½" long, emerging from pits in the spike.

TETRACLEA Low erect herbs, woody at base; leaves simple, opposite, toothed or entire; flowers in axillary cymes, mostly 1- to 3-flowered; the 5-lobed corolla is white with a red tint; 2 N.A. species. *T. coulteri,* to 16" high, grows in depressions, on stream banks, dry rocky plains, from w Tex. to Ariz.

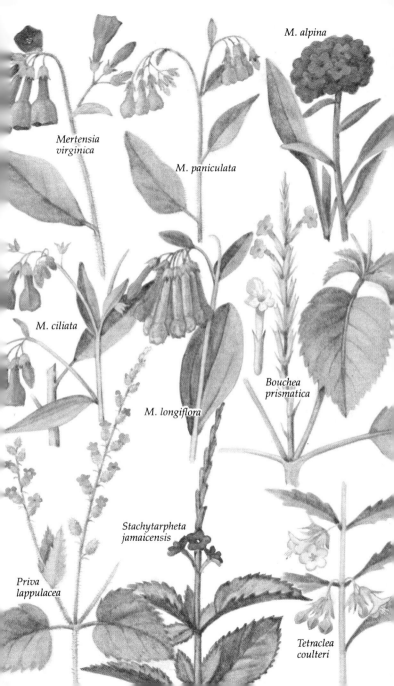

Mertensia virginica

M. alpina

M. paniculata

M. ciliata

M. longiflora

Bouchea prismatica

Stachytarpheta jamaicensis

Priva lappulacea

Tetraclea coulteri

VERVAIN (VERBENA) Flowers sessile, in terminal heads or in single or panicled terminal spikes, each flower subtended by a bractlet; calyx 5-toothed, 1 tooth often shorter than the others; corolla tubular, often curved, somewhat unequally 5-lobed; 2 pairs of stamens, one pair shorter; style slender, stigma often 2-lobed; 47 species in N.A.

Prostrate Vervain, *V. bracteata,* has pinnately cut or 3-lobed leaves on short petioles; in sandy prairies, fields, throughout the U.S., s Canada.

Rose Vervain, *V. canadensis,* has reclining or ascending stems, variable leaves, flowers mostly pink or rose, varying to purple; barrens, prairies, Fla. to Tex., n to se Va., Ia., Kans., Colo.

Gray Vervain, *V. canescens,* has branched hairy stems 6–18", somewhat hairy leaves, glandular-hairy flower spikes; sandy or dry rocky hills, open woods, fields, prairies, s-cen. Tex., s Calif.

Southwestern Vervain, *V. gooddingii,* has hairy glandular branched stems, often mat-forming; leaves 3-lobed, toothed; mts., grasslands, piñon forests, Tex. to s Calif., n to Utah, Nev.

Tuber Vervain, *V. rigida,* 4–24", has sessile sharp-toothed rough leaves, short spikes of purple to magenta flowers; corolla downy outside; native to Brazil and Paraguay, escaped to wastelands, Fla. to e Tex. and N.C.

Hoary Vervain, *V. stricta,* has hairy stems to 6½', simple or branched, leaves nearly sessile, irregularly toothed; flowers in dense foot-long spikes; in prairies and barrens, N.Eng. to ne Wash., s to Del. and Tex.

Moss Verbena, *V. tenuisecta,* has reclining stems with ascending branches to 2', flowers in short dense spikes; S.A., escaped to fields, N.C. to Fla. and Tex.; Ill., Mo., Ky., Ariz., Calif.

Desert Verbena, *V. wrightii,* has branched reclining to erect 2' stems, twice to thrice pinnately lobed leaves; flowers in spikes; Kans. and Colo. to Tex. and Ariz.

White Vervain, *V. urticifolia,* 7½', stiffly erect stems, simple or branched near the base; slender branched spikes of small flowers; e N.A., w to S.D., Tex.

Carolina Vervain, *V. carnea,* a gray downy herb with simple or sparingly branched stems to 32"; leaves rough on upper side; grows in sandy woods, barrens, pinelands, Fla. to Tex. and e Va.

Pink Vervain, *V. pumila,* has hairy stems from a common base, triangular or 3-lobed leaves; in prairies, fields, chaparral, and woods, Tex., Ark., Okla., N.M.

V. simplex has a simple erect 8–24" stem, narrow lance-like irregularly toothed leaves, pencil-like spikes of purple flowers; dry or sandy soil, e N.A., w to Neb.

New Mexican Vervain, *V. macdougalii,* has stout hairy stems to 40", hairy leaves; on flats at high elevations, w Tex.; s Wyo. and cen. Utah to N.M. and Ariz.

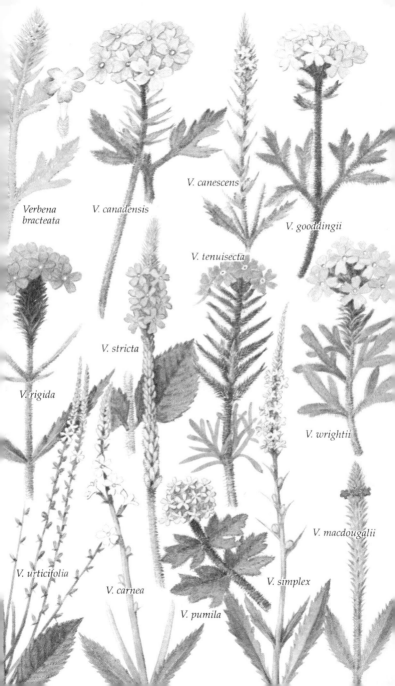

Verbena
bracteata

V. canadensis

V. canescens

V. gooddingii

V. tenuisecta

V. stricta

V. rigida

V. wrightii

V. urticifolia

V. carnea

V. pumila

V. simplex

V. macdougalii

MINT FAMILY (LABIATAE)

Square-stemmed herbs with opposite leaves dotted by oil glands; flowers axillary, in cymes, often combined to form racemes or spikes; corolla tubular, usually 2-lipped; 1 or 2 pairs of stamens, attached to the tube; style 2-lobed; 56 genera in N.A.

BLUE-CURLS (TRICHOSTEMA) Clammy-glandular herbs, some woody at base, with entire leaves, cymes of 1 to many flowers; calyx 5-toothed, upper 3 elongated, at flowering turned upside down; corolla blue, pink, or white; 13 N.A. species. **Forked Blue-curls,** *T. dichotomum,* to 40″ tall, is clad in long straight hairs and round-headed glandular ones; its cymes are leafy-bracted; grows in dry open soil, Me. to Mich., s to Fla. and Tex.

BUGLE-WEED (AJUGA) European herbs; corolla with a large spreading lower lip, the middle lobe notched at the tip; 3 species escaped in N.A. *A. reptans* is a mat-forming herb 4–12″ high; flowers sessile, in whorls of 2–6 in the axils of bracts, producing a leafy terminal spike; grows by roads, in fields, Nfld. to Wisc., s to Pa. and Ohio; also in Tex.

GERMANDER (TEUCRIUM) Leaves simple, toothed or pinnately lobed; flowers in terminal spikes or in the upper leaf axils; upper lip short, cleft, the 2 lobes erect or crossed, lower lip much larger; 5 species in N.A. **American Germander** or **Woodsage,** *T. canadense,* is a variable herb with erect silvery stems to 40″; grows on shores, in thickets and woods, Que. to B.C., s to Fla., Tex., Ariz., and Oreg. but not in Ida. or Mont.

SKULLCAP (SCUTELLARIA) Non-aromatic herbs; flowers 1–3 in the axils or in 1-sided bracted spikes or racemes; upper lip entire or barely notched, lateral lobes mostly with the upper lip; lower lip convex, notched; 42 N.A. species.

S. drummondii, 8–12″, is branched at the base, has entire wavy leaves; in thickets or in open soil, Tex., w Okla., and se N.M.

S. incana, 12″–4′, stem hoary, simple or branched above, leaves oval to oblong; dry woods, openings, se U.S., n to N.Y. and Ia.

Hairy Skullcap, *S. elliptica,* to 28″, has densely hairy stems, oval to triangular leaves; grows in dry woods, Fla. to Tex., n to N.Y., Mich., and Mo.

S. resinosa, 6–8″, has tufts of stems from a caudex, oval to round leaves; on rock, banks, sand, n Tex. to cen. Kans.

Common or **Marsh Skullcap,** *S. epilobifolia,* 4–40″, grows in wet soil, Nfld. to Alaska, s to Del., Mo., Tex., and s Calif.

Rough Skullcap, *S. integrifolia,* 12–28″, has 6–40 flowers per raceme, many recemes in a leafy elongate panicle; borders of woods, bogs, most of e U.S.

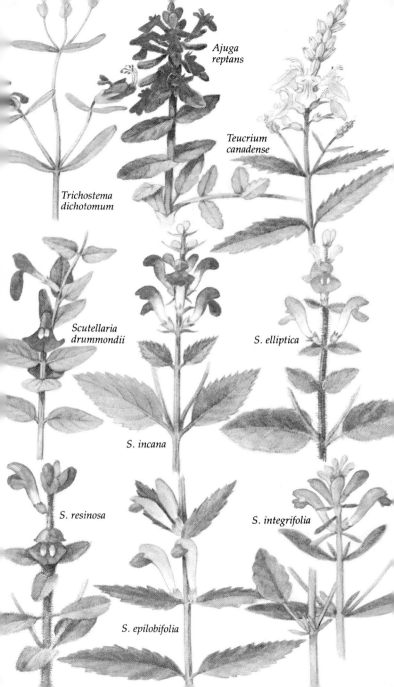

Trichostema dichotomum

Ajuga reptans

Teucrium canadense

Scutellaria drummondii

S. elliptica

S. incana

S. resinosa

S. integrifolia

S. epilobifolia

AGASTACHE Erect herbs with petioled toothed leaves, small flowers in dense whorls that form terminal bracted spikes; 14 N.A. species **Blue Giant Hyssop,** *A. foeniculum,* 2–4' tall, has anise-scented leaves grows in dry soil, Ont. to Mackenz., s to Ill., Ia., S.D., Colo., and Wash.; e in fields to Que. and Del.

MEEHANIA One species, *M. cordata,* a low creeping herb with heart-shaped leaves, flowers in dense terminal spikes on erect 6–8" stems, grows in rich woods, w Pa. to Ill., s to N.C. and Tenn.

CATNIP (NEPETA) Weedy Eurasian herbs; 2 species in N.A. *N. cataria,* a 1–3' erect downy herb with long-petioled toothed leaves, flowers crowded toward the tips of the branches; now widespread in door-yards, by roads, and in wastelands in N.A.

BRAZORIA Erect 1–2' herbs with oblong toothed sessile or petioled leaves, flowers in long narrow racemes or spikes; 4 species, native to Tex. and Okla. **Prairie Brazoria,** *B. scutellarioides,* grows on limestone soil, cen. Tex., s Okla.

GROUND-IVY (GLECHOMA) European creeping and trailing herbs with round toothed leaves, the flowers in their axils. One species, **Gill-over-the-ground** or **Run-away-Robin,** *G. hederacea,* grows by roads, in yards, damp shady sites, e and Pac. N.A.

DRAGONHEAD (DRACOCEPHALUM) Erect herbs with simple or clustered stems, flowers in leafy or bracted terminal heads or spikes; 4 species in N.A. *D. parviflorum,* 4–32", has sharply toothed leaves, spine-tipped bracts; grows in limestone soil, e Que. to Alaska, s to Wash., Ariz., N.M., Neb., Ia., Wisc., N.Y.

FALSE DRAGONHEAD (PHYSOSTEGIA) Similar to *Dracocephalum* but flowers large and showy, in simple or panicled leafless terminal spikes; 16 N.A. species. *P. formosior,* 1–5', grows in wet woods or thickets, Me. to Alta., s to N.Y., Ohio, Mo., and Neb.

SYNANDRA One species, *S. hispidula,* a hairy 1–2' herb; lower leaves long-petioled, the upper ones sessile, becoming bracts, each with a single sessile flower; grows in wet woods, damp thickets, stream banks, from Va. and W.Va. to Ill., s to Tenn.

BALLOTA European; **Black** or **Fetid Horehound,** *B. nigra,* is now a weed of waste places, s N.Eng. and N.Y., s to N.J., Pa., and Md.; an erect 1–3' tall hairy but green herb with oval toothed petioled leaves, flowers in dense clusters in the axils of the upper leaves.

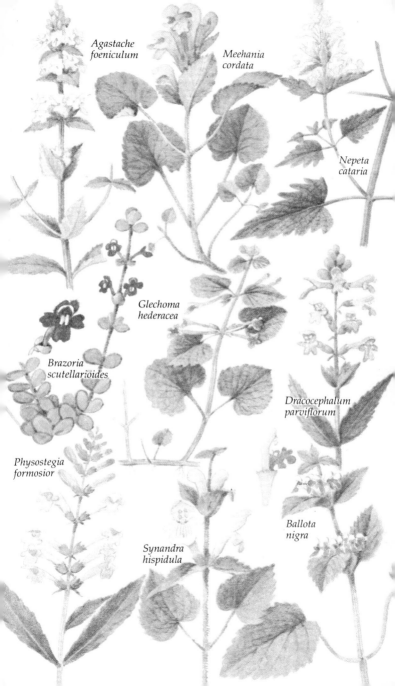

Agastache
foeniculum

Meehania
cordata

Nepeta
cataria

Glechoma
hederacea

Brazoria
scutellarioides

Dracocephalum
parviflorum

Physostegia
formosior

Synandra
hispidula

Ballota
nigra

MOTHERWORT (LEONURUS) Erect Eurasian herbs with lobed and toothed leaves, tight whorls of flowers in their axils; 3 species in N.A. **Common Motherwort,** *L. cardiaca,* to 5' tall, has long-petioled palmately lobed leaves; grows in wastelands, Que. to Mont., s to N.C., Okla., and n Ariz.; also w Wash.

LION'S-EARS (LEONOTIS) One species, *L. nepetaefolia,* is a South African escape, Fla. to Tex., n to Tenn. and N.C.; also Calif.; a tall soft-downy herb to 7' with petioled oval or triangular leaves with scalloped edges, dense globular clusters of flowers.

HEMP-NETTLE (GALEOPSIS) Upright Eurasian herbs with spreading branches, toothed leaves, flowers in whorls in the upper leaf axils; calyx of 5 spine-tipped teeth; 3 species in N.A. *G. tetrahit,* 1–2' high, has bristly stems swollen below the nodes; grows by roads, in wastelands, fields, Nfld. to Alaska, s to N.Y., Mich., Wisc., Ia., S.D., n Ida., and w Wash.

DEAD-NETTLE (LAMIUM) Reclining herbs, lower leaves small and long-petioled, middle leaves heart-shaped and doubly toothed, upper ones bracts with axillary flower clusters; Eurasian, 5 species in N.A. **Henbit,** *L. amplexicaule,* 2–14" high, has sessile upper leaves clasping the stem; **Purple Dead-nettle,** *L. purpureum,* 3–12" high, has short-petioled red or purple upper leaves; both species now in fields and wastelands in much of N.A.

DICERANDRA Delicate erect plants to 16" high with narrow entire leaves, becoming bracts upward, with axillary flower clusters; 5 species, in se U.S. *D. linearifolia* has stalked flower clusters; grows in pinelands, on dunes, Ga., Fla., and Ala.

HEDGE-NETTLE (STACHYS) Erect herbs with diverse foliage, flowers in a bracted terminal raceme or spike; calyx bell-like, of 5 equal spine-tipped teeth; corolla 2-lipped, upper lip erect or arched, lower lip 3-lobed, middle lobe larger and nearly entire. About 30 species in N.A.

S. tenuifolia has branched or simple stems to 4' tall, a few-flowered discontinuous spike; in damp or wet soil, N.Y. to Minn., s to S.C., Tenn., La., and Tex.

S. cooleyae, 2–5', is bristled on the stem angles, has hairy leaves; in swamps, moist soil, e side of the Cascades to the coast, s B.C. to s Oreg.

Texas Betony, *S. coccinea,* has soft-hairy stems to 3' or more, downy leaves, stalked flowers; grows in moist crevices of steep stony mt. slopes, w Tex. to s Ariz.

S. chamissonis, 2–4', is also bristly on the stem angles, has elongated bracted terminal spikes; in moist sites at low elevations, coastal Calif.

*Leonurus
cardiaca*

*Leonotis
nepetaefolia*

*Galeopsis
tetrahit*

*Lamium
purpureum*

*Lamium
amplexicaule*

*Dicerandra
linearifolia*

S. coccinea

S. chamissonis

*Stachys
tenuifolia*

S. cooleyae

SAGE (SALVIA) Herbs of varied form, mostly aromatic; showy flowers in discontinuous spikes or terminal heads; calyx 2-lobed, upper lobe entire or 3-toothed, lower usually 2-toothed; corolla deeply 2-lipped, upper lip entirely or barely notched, lower 3-lobed, the middle one larger; 2 stamens. About 56 herbaceous species in N.A.

S. coccinea, to 40″ tall, sometimes becomes woody at the base; the only red-flowered sage in se U.S., it blooms from May until frost; in sandy soil of open woods, thickets, hammocks, Coastal Plain, Fla. to Tex. and S.C.

Pitcher Sage, *S. spathacea,* has 1–3′ glandular-hairy stems, petioled basal leaves with projecting basal lobes on the blades; upper leaves nearly sessile; on grassy and shady slopes, s Coast Ranges, Calif.

Blue Sage, *S. azurea,* a 2–5′ erect herb, ash-gray from short hairs; lower leaves toothed, upper ones linear, entire; grows on dry prairies, from S.C. nw to Minn. and Colo., s to Fla. and Tex.; escaped e to N.Eng. and N.J.

Thistle Sage, *S. carduacea,* 1–2′, has a basal rosette of pinnately lobed spiny leaves; dense spiny-bracted flower clusters on scapes; lower corolla lip is fringed; inner s Coast Ranges and s Sierran foothills, Calif.

S. pachyphylla is a sprawling herb with small gray-green downy leaves, flowers in dense whorls in a tall spike with purplish bracts; on dry slopes, San Bernadino Mts. to Baja Calif. and Ariz.

Lyre-leaved Sage, *S. lyrata,* has a basal rosette of petioled leaves; spring leaves wavy, pinnately lobed, summer ones often purple-tinged; flowers on an erect scape; grows in sandy open woods, Fla. to Tex., n to Conn., Ill., and Okla.

HORSEMINT (MONARDA) Odoriferous erect herbs with entire or toothed leaves, large showy flowers surrounded by bracts, forming terminal heads or discontinuous spikes; corolla elongated, 2-lipped; 2 stamens; 15 N.A. species.

Oswego-tea or **Bee-balm,** *M. didyma,* to 5′, has sharply angled stems, petioled leaves; in woods, bottoms, N.Y. to Mich., s to Ga. and Tenn.; escaped e to Que. and N.J.; also in Wash.

Lemon-mint, *M. citriodora,* has simple or branching 8–32″ stems, oblong to lance-like awn-tipped leaves, downy bracts, their bases forming a cup around the calyxes, tips ending in long slender awns; Mo. and Kans. s to w Tex.

Wild Bergamot, *M. fistulosa,* to 5′, grows in dry open woods, wet meadows, Que. to Minn., s to Ga. and e Tex.

Plains Bee-balm, *M. pectinata,* to 1′ high, is usually branched from the base to form a globular plant; in dry soil, Neb., Colo., and Utah, s to w Tex. and Ariz.

Spotted Bee-balm, *M. punctata,* 2–40″ high, is in dry or sandy soil, throughout much of e U.S., w to Minn., Kans., Tex., and Ariz.

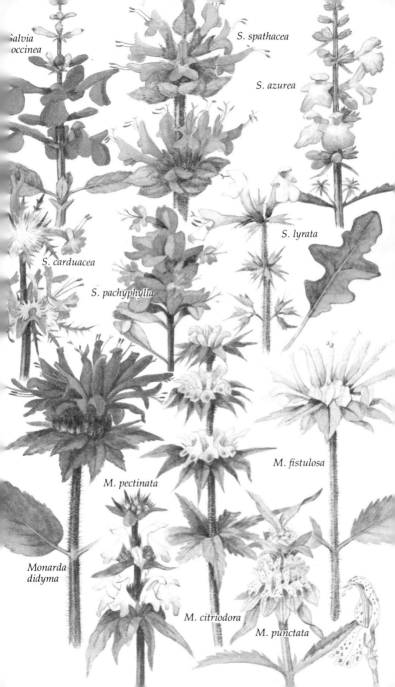

Salvia coccinea

S. spathacea

S. azurea

S. carduacea

S. pachyphylla

S. lyrata

M. fistulosa

M. pectinata

Monarda didyma

M. citriodora

M. punctata

MACBRIDEA Stem erect, simple or branched above, tipped by 1–3 tight-bracted flowers; calyx and corolla 2-lipped; 4 stamens; 2 species, in se U.S. *M. caroliniana,* to 3′ high, grows in marshes, wet woods, Coastal Plain, Fla. to Ala. and se N.C.

POGOGYNE Small erect herbs, flowers in dense terminal spikes; upper 3 calyx teeth short, lower 2 longer; 4 stamens, 2 sometimes sterile; 3 species in Pac. N.A. *P. douglasii,* 6–16″ tall, has hairy bristly-fringed bracts and calyx teeth; grows along the Coast Ranges and Sierra Nevada, Calif.

MONARDELLA Stem simple or branched at base or in clumps from a caudex; flowers in terminal heads; calyx of 5 equal teeth, corolla of 5 nearly equal lobes; 22 species, mostly in s Calif. *M. odoratissima,* 4–20″, has entire leaves, white to purple flowers; grows in open sites, Wash. to Mont., s to s Calif., N.M.

WOOD-MINT (BLEPHILIA) Upright herbs with entire or toothed leaves, small blue-violet flowers crowded in axillary and terminal globular whorls; 2 species, in e N.A. *B hirsuta,* to 4′ high, has a pale corolla spotted with dark purple; grows in moist shady places, w Que. and Vt. to Ga., w to Minn. and Okla.

MOCK PENNYROYAL (HEDEOMA) Low odorous small-leaved herbs, some with a caudex; flowers in loose axillary cymes, usually spaced apart, sometimes combined into leafy terminal spikes; 14 species in e and sw N.A. *H. hispida,* 4–16″, has densely downy stems, crowded linear almost smooth leaves; grows in prairies, plains, and fields, w N.Eng. to s Alta., s to Miss. and Tex. *H. plicatum,* 6–15″, has numerous shoots, many basal branches, 3- to 7-flowered cymes; grows in pine-oak woods, mts., Trans-Pecos, Tex.

SATUREJA Plants of diverse appearance; flowers solitary or in small axillary clusters (a terminal head in one); corolla with an inflated throat, 2 lips, upper lip erect, entire or notched, lower lip 3-parted; 4 stamens; 10 species in N.A. **Yerba Buena,** *S. douglasii,* has slender trailing stems, roundish evergreen leaves; grows in coniferous woods, s Alaska to s Calif., e to n Ida. **Dogmint,** *S. vulgaris,* has flowers in terminal heads subtended by a pair of leaves; inhabits woods, open shores, Nfld. to Man., s to Del., Ind., Wisc., and Minn., upland to N.C.; Colo. to Ariz.

HYSSOP (HYSSOPUS) One species, *H. officinalis,* a 1–2′ Eurasian herb with entire sessile lance-like leaves, flowers in dense terminal spikes and axillary clusters, blue, rose, or white; grows in dry pastures, along roadsides, N.Eng. and Ont. to Mont., s to N.C.

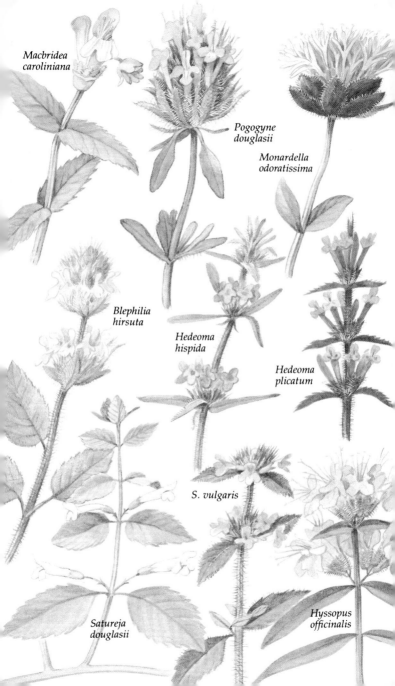

Macbridea caroliniana

Pogogyne douglasii

Monardella odoratissima

Blephilia hirsuta

Hedeoma hispida

Hedeoma plicatum

S. vulgaris

Satureja douglasii

Hyssopus officinalis

MOUNTAIN-MINT (PYCNANTHEMUM) Erect herbs with a mintlike flavor, upper stem branched as a corymb, the leaves with axillary flowers often whitened, flowers in dense whorls crowded with bracts, forming terminal heads or cymes; 4 stamens; 20 species, most in e N.A. *P. virginianum,* 12–40" high, grows on shores, in meadows, thickets, Me. to N.D., s to N.C. and Kans.

WILD MAJORAM (ORIGANUM) is European; *O. vulgare* has escaped to roadsides, old fields, open woods, sw Que. and s Ont. to N.C.; also in nw Oreg. and Santa Cruz Mts., Calif.; a 1–3' hairy herb with nearly entire leaves, purple to crimson flowers and bracts crowded into spikes; one variety has golden leaves.

THYME (THYMUS) is European; **Creeping Thyme,** *T. serpyllum,* a prostrate herb with flat entire oval leaves on short petioles, showy flowers crowded at the branch tips, has escaped to woods and fields, Que. and Ont. to N.C. and Ind.; also in the Pac. NW.

DITTANY (CUNILA) One species in N.A., **Common Dittany,** *C. origanioides,* with 4–16" tufted stems branched above, smooth oval nearly sessile toothed leaves, stalked axillary cymes; purplish to white corolla with 5 nearly equal lobes; grows in open woods and clearings, se N.Y. to se Kans., s to Fla. and Tex.

HORSE-BALM (COLLINSONIA) Lemon-scented herbs with white or yellow flowers in a terminal panicle or spike above the leaves; corolla with a fringed lower lip; 3 species, in e N.A. **Richweed** or **Stoneroot,** *C. canadensis,* a 20–40" erect nearly smooth herb, has pointed toothed petioled leaves 4–8" long; flowers in a loose terminal panicle; grows in moist woods, Fla. to Ark., n to Wisc., Ont., N.Y., Vt., and Mass.

MINT (MENTHA) Erect branching herbs with sessile or petioled leaves, small flowers in bracted axillary clusters or in terminal spikes or heads; corolla almost equally 4-lobed, or upper lobe broader and entire or notched; 4 stamens; all plant parts are strongly aromatic; 1 native and 11 European species in N.A.

Peppermint, *M. piperita,* to 32", with rose-purple to white flowers, has escaped to wet soil throughout s Canada and the U.S.

Apple Mint, *M. rotundifolia,* 1–5' with sticky-hairy herbage; grows by roads, in fields, on wastelands throughout most of U.S.

Field Mint, *M. arvensis,* 6"–3' tall, with leafy bracts many times longer than the flower clusters; circumboreal, s in damp open soil over all but se U.S.

Spearmint, *M. spicata,* to 4' tall, has slender leafless terminal flower spikes; in moist meadows and fields, usually near settlements, throughout N.A.

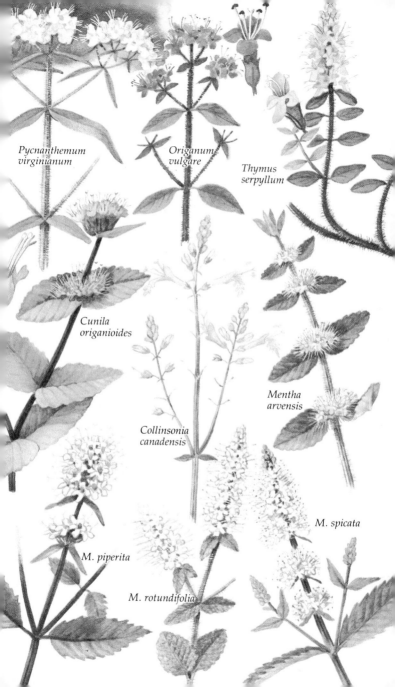

Pycnanthemum virginianum

Origanum vulgare

Thymus serpyllum

Cunila origanioides

Collinsonia canadensis

Mentha arvensis

M. piperita

M. rotundifolia

M. spicata

NIGHTSHADE FAMILY (SOLANACEAE)

Leaves alternate, entire to odd-pinnate; flowers often lateral, solitary or clustered, the parts usually in 5's; calyx and corolla bell-like tubular; 1 style, stigma 2-lobed or entire; 19 genera in N.A. with herbaceous species; many are weedy.

NIGHTSHADE (SOLANUM) Mostly coarse weeds; leaves simple compound, a large and small leaf often together; flowers in cyme some 40 species in N.A. **Buffalo-bur,** *S. rostratum,* to 28" high, is clothed in prickles and stellate hairs; native from N.D. and Wyo. to Tex. and Ariz., now an aggressive weed in n and e U.S. **Purple Nightshade,** *xanti,* 1–3' tall, has inch-wide flowers; grows in chaparral, Ariz. and Calif.

GROUND CHERRY (PHYSALIS) Leaves entire to toothed, petioled flowers often solitary; calyx 5-toothed, inflating to enclose the 2-celled fruit; about 34 species in N.A. *P. virginiana,* 6–24", is a variable herb grows in open woods, on prairies and plains, N.Y. and s Ont. Cascades, B.C., s to Ariz. and Fla. **Purple Ground-cherry,** *P. lobata,* is low or procumbent herb; ranges from w Tex. to Ariz., n to s Nev., Colo., w Kans.

CHAMAESARACHA resembles *Physalis* but the calyx does not inflate 4 N.A. species. *C. grandiflora,* 6"–3', a sticky-hairy herb with 2" flower grows by roads, in open woods, on shores, se Que. to Sask., s to n Vt., s Ont., n Mich. to n Minn. *C. sordida* is basally branched to form clumps to 30" wide; grows on dry plains and mesas, Kans. and Colo. Tex. and se Ariz.

HENBANE (HYOSCYAMUS) is European; **Black Henbane,** *H. niger,* 12–30" tall, a clammy-leaved fetid poisonous narcotic herb with 1–2 sessile flowers in a 1-sided leafy spike; escaped to roadsides, waste lands, s Canada and n U.S.

DATURA Coarse narcotic-poisonous herbs with large funnel-like flowers in the branch forks; 7 species in N.A. **Jimson-weed,** *D. stramonium,* to 5' tall, with 3–4" white to violet flowers; Asian, common in s U.S. local n to s Canada.

PETUNIA One species, **Seaside Petunia,** *P. parviflora,* is a mat-forming herb of wastelands and seabeaches, Fla. to s Calif. and s N.Y.

TOBACCO (NICOTIANA) Rank sticky-downy herbs with large entire leaves, long-tubed fragrant nocturnal flowers in terminal panicles or racemes; 12 species in N.A. **Desert Tobacco,** *N. trigonophylla,* to 3' tall ranges from s and w Tex. to s Calif.

S. xanti

Physalis
virginiana

Solanum
rostratum

Chamaesaracha
grandiflora

C. sordida

Physalis
lobata

Nicotiana
trigonophylla

Datura
stramonium

Hyoscyamus
niger

Petunia
parviflora

FIGWORT FAMILY (SCROPHULARIACEAE)

Herbs with diverse leaves and inflorescences; sepals 4 or 5, free or united; corolla tubular, zygomorphic, of 4 or 5 lobes, often 2-lipped; stamens rarely 5, mostly 1 or 2 pairs, attached to corolla tube; 1 style, stigma entire or 2-lobed; 61 herbaceous genera in N.A.

MULLEIN (VERBASCUM) Tall hairy Eurasian herbs; leaves simple, in a rosette, alternate on the stem; flowers in terminal spikes, racemes, or panicles; calyx and corolla 5-lobed; 5 stamens; 7 species in N.A. **Common Mullein,** *V. thapsus,* to 6' high, has a flower spike to 20" long; **Moth Mullein,** *V. blattaria,* to 3', has doubly toothed leaves, yellow or white flowers in a loose raceme; both now grow throughout temperate N.A.

FLUELLIN (KICKXIA) Prostrate much-branched round-leaved glandular-hairy herbs with axillary flowers; calyx 5-parted; corolla 2-lipped, lower lip spurred; European, 2 species escapes in N.A. **Canker-root,** *K. elatine,* is locally abundant, Mass. to Ind., s to Ga., La. and Kans.; Oreg. and Calif.

TOADFLAX (LINARIA) Erect herbs; leaves entire, lower ones opposite or whorled, upper ones alternate; flowers in racemes or spikes, calyx 5-parted, corolla 2-lipped, lower lip spurred; 12 species in N.A. **Old-field Toadflax,** *L. canadensis,* 4–32" tall; grows in dry or sterile soil, N.S. to s B.C., s to Baja Calif. and Fla.; **Butter-and-eggs,** *L. vulgaris,* to 4½' tall, is a European escape throughout temperate N.A.

SNAPDRAGON (ANTIRRHINUM) Erect to trailing or climbing herbs; leaves simple, opposite or upper ones alternate; flowers in terminal racemes, or solitary and axillary; calyx 5-parted; corolla swollen at base, 2-lipped, not spurred; 4 stamens; 16 species in N.A., mostly w. *A. nuttallianum,* a 4–40" clambering herb, has racemes of ½" flowers; common in dry soil, s Calif. and sw Ariz.

DWARF SNAPDRAGON (CHAENORRHINUM) is European; *C. minus,* a 2–16" tall glandular-hairy branching herb with short-spurred flowers in open leafy racemes; now common on wastelands, Que. and Ont., s to Va. and Mo.

MAURANDYA Prostrate or twining herbs; leaves triangular or heart-shaped, petioled; 2-lipped flowers in the axils of leafy bracts; 4 species, in sw U.S. **Snapdragon Vine,** *M. antirrhiniflora,* with 1" flowers, grows from Tex. to se Calif.

V. blattaria

*Verbascum
thapsus*

*Linaria
canadensis*

*Kickxia
elatine*

*Maurandya
antirrhiniflora*

L. vulgaris

*Antirrhinum
nuttallianum*

*Chaenorrhinum
minus*

COLLINSIA Slender erect herbs with opposite leaves, axillary flower clusters; corolla 2-lipped, upper lip 2-lobed, lower lip of 2 spreading lobes and a middle lobe folded lengthwise; 19 N.A. species. **Blue-eyed Mary,** *C. verna,* 4"–2', grows in woods, from N.Y. to e Ia., s to Va., Ky., Ark., e Kans., and Okla. *C. grandiflora,* 4–16" is found in open sites, n Calif. to s B.C.

FIGWORT (SCROPHULARIA) Tall coarse herbs with 4-angled stems, mostly opposite leaves, dingy flowers in a terminal panicle; globular corolla tube, 5-lobed, the 2 upper lobes pointed forward, the lowest drooping and curved backward; 8 N.A. species. **Carpenter's-square,** *S. marilandica,* to 7', grows in woods, Me. and Que. to Minn., s to S.C., Ga., La., Okla., and Tex.

MONKEY-FLOWER (MIMULUS) Erect or reclining mostly glandular-downy herbs (a few are shrubs) with opposite entire or toothed leaves; flowers usually solitary and axillary or in terminal racemes; calyx tubular, 5-toothed, corolla tube cylindrical, 2-lipped, upper lip 2-lobed, erect or curved backward, lower lip 3-lobed and spreading; all 5 lobes vary from entire to notched; 2 pairs of stamens; style threadlike, 2 platelike sensitive stigmas; 89 N.A. species, mostly w.

Crimson Monkey-flower, *M. cardinalis,* has prostrate or erect 3' stems, 3" toothed clasping leaves, flowers 2" long; grows in shade by streams, Oreg. to Baja Calif., e to Utah and Ariz.

M. guttatus has 2–40" erect or reclining stems, toothed oval 3" leaves, upper ones sessile; in wet soil, Alaska and Yuk. to Baja Calif. and N.M.; naturalized in Conn., Vt., and e N.Y.

M. lewisii has clustered erect 1–4' stems, sticky-hairy sessile leaves, pink to purple 1" flowers, in wet places in mts., Alaska to Calif., e to Alta., Mont., Wyo., Utah.

Musk-flower, *M. moschatus,* is a weak-stemmed clammy-hairy herb to 1'; leaves short-petioled, toothed or entire; in wet soil, s B.C. to Mont., s to Calif., Utah, and Colo.; Nfld. to Ont., s to N.C., W.Va., and Mich.

M. ringens has erect 4-angled stems 1–6" high, sessile toothed leaves, inch-long blue-violet or pinkish flowers; in wet places, C.B. to James Bay and Man., s to Ga., La., ne Tex., and Colo.

M. tricolor, 1–5", sessile elliptic entire or toothed leaves, flowers to 1½" long; in wet clay soil, Central Valley and n Coast Ranges, Calif. to Corvallis, Oreg.

M. barbatus 2–4" high, is glandular-downy, with narrow leaves ½" long; both lips of the flowers can be crimson or yellow; grows in damp sand or gravel, s Sierra Nevada, Calif.

M. bifidus is a sticky-stemmed bushy plant 16–40" high with 1–2" elliptic leaves; deeply notched corolla lobes; foothills of n Sierra Nevada, Calif.; a narrow-leaved var. grows from Monterey Bay to San Luis Obispo.

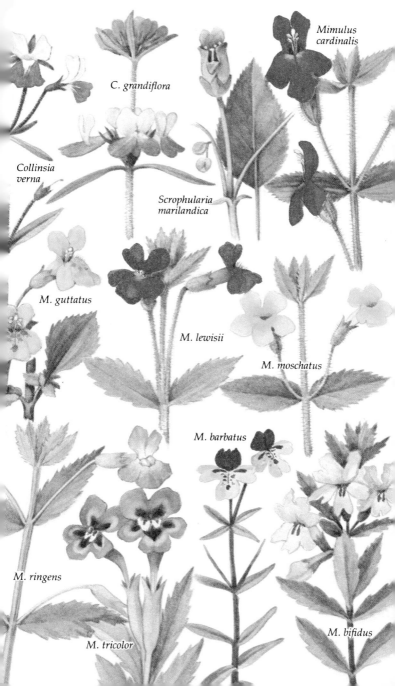

C. grandiflora

Mimulus cardinalis

Collinsia verna

Scrophularia marilandica

M. guttatus

M. lewisii

M. moschatus

M. barbatus

M. ringens

M. tricolor

M. bifidus

BEARD-TONGUE (PENSTEMON) Erect herbs (a few woody) with opposite leaves, each pair at right angles to the pair above or below; lower leaves petioled, upper ones sessile, often clasping the stem; flowers usually in a narrow terminal bracted panicle; 5 sepals; corolla 2-lipped, upper lip 2-lobed, lower 3-lobed; 4 fertile stamens, 1 sterile, its tip often bearded (the "tongue"). About 210 N.A. species.

P. albidus sends up tufts of 6–16″ stems from a caudex; leaves 2–8″ long; herbage downy; on prairies, plains, limestone, Alta. to N.M., e to Man., Minn., Ia., Kans., Okla., and Tex.

P. canescens has an ash-gray downy 1–3′ stem, a basal rosette of saw-toothed leaves, an open panicle, a densely bearded tongue; in woodlands, Pa. to s Ind., s to S.C., Ga., and Ala.

P. cobaea, a downy-stemmed 1–2′ herb, has white, violet or purple flowers; grows on prairies, plains, limestone, Neb. to Mo. and Ark., s to Tex.; introduced elsewhere.

P. palmeri, to 4′ tall, has sharply toothed leaves, bases of upper leaves joined around the stem; the tongue projects from the scented flowers; in sagebrush and piñon regions, Utah and Ariz. to Calif.

P. pseudospectabilis, 2–6′, has leaves coated by a white "bloom," united about the stem, an open panicle of only slightly 2-lipped flowers; common in open land, from sw N.M. to e Calif.

P. angustifolius, 8–20″, has long-pointed leaves, similar smaller bracts on the panicle; on mesas, sandy grasslands, and dunes, N.D. and Mont. to Kans., N.M., and n Ariz.; southern plants have pinkish flowers.

P. rydbergii has 8–20″ stems from a basal rosette, ½″ flowers in a headlike panicle; in moist meadows, slopes, cen. Wash. to sw Mont. and Wyo., s to s Sierra Nevada, n Ariz., N.M.

P. alluviorum, 2–5′, somewhat downy, has lines running down the stem from upper leaf bases, in low ground, s Ohio and s Ind. to Mo., s to Miss. and Ark.

P. australis has a rosette of entire or scalloped leaves, stem leaves entire to double-toothed, 1–3′ gray-downy stems; in sandy pinelands and oak woods, Fla. and Ala. to Va.

P. eatoni is a smooth herb with 2–3′ purplish stems, leathery leaves, flowers on 1 side of a long slender panicle, the corolla scarcely 2-lipped; in sand or clay, s Calif. to sw Colo. and cen. Ariz.

P. richardsonii is woody at the base, with 8–32″ brittle stems; its shiny leaves are doubly toothed or pinnately lobed; flowers rose or lavender; dry rocky sites, s B.C. to Oreg.

P. whippleanus, to 2′, is in alpine meadows or lightly wooded rocky slopes near timberline, from s Mont., e Ida., and Wyo. s to Utah, n Ariz., and N.M. Its flowers vary from dull white or yellowish to deep purple or maroon.

Penstemon albidus

P. canescens

P. cobaea

P. palmeri

P. pseudospectabilis

P. rydbergii

P. angustifolius

P. alluviorum

P. eatoni

P. australis

P. richardsonii

P. whippleanus

TURTLE-HEAD or **SNAKE-HEAD** (CHELONE) Smooth erect branched herbs with toothed leaves, nearly sessile flowers in spikes or clusters, white to rose or purple, shaped like a reptile's head; 4 species, in e N.A. *C. glabra*, 16″–7′, grows in low moist soil, from Nfld. to Ont. and Minn., s to Ga., Ala., and Mo.

STEMODIA Glandular-downy odorous plants, some woody at base, with sessile clasping leaves, 2-lipped flowers, solitary or in leafy-bracted spikes; 3 species, in Tex. and the SW. *S. durantifolia*, a rigidly erect slender-branched herb to 3′, has blue or purple flowers; grows in wet soil, Calif. to Tex.

SCOPARIA Sweet Broomwort or **Goatweed,** *S. dulcis*, grows on wastelands and in open woods, Fla. to Ga. and e Tex.; a smooth much-branched herb to 40″, with short-petioled leaves in pairs or whorls of 3 or 4, to 1½″ long; tiny flowers in most of the upper axils, corolla of 4 equal lobes, the throat bearded.

WATER-HYSSOP (BACOPA) Erect to reclining herbs with sessile leaves; flowers of 5 unequal sepals, corolla 2-lipped or almost equally 5-lobed; style dilated or 2-lobed; 9 N.A. species. *B. rotundifolia* is a mat-forming herb of muddy ponds, with 2′ branches, the rounded leaves clasping at the base; Miss. Valley and Great Plains, w to Mont., Ida., Nev., and Calif.

FALSE PIMPERNEL (LINDERNIA) Low herbs with opposite leaves, axillary flowers of 5 sepals, a 2-lipped corolla, 2 pairs of stamens, upper pair fertile, lower long and sterile; 2 stigmas; 6 N.A. species. *L. dubia*, to 14″ high, grows in damp or wet soil in most of the U.S. and se Canada.

FOXGLOVE (DIGITALIS) Tall European herbs with alternate leaves, showy nodding flowers in a long terminal spike; 4 species escaped in N.A. *D. purpurea*, to 7′ tall, with 2″-long rose-purple to white flowers, is locally abundant in Nfld. and C.B.; s Alaska and B.C. to s Calif., especially near the coast.

CULVER'S-PHYSIC (VERONICASTRUM) One species, *V. virginicum*, to 7′ high; leaves in whorls of 3–7; tiny purple or white flowers in erect panicled 6″ spikes; grows in woods, meadows, and prairies, from N.Eng. to Man., s to nw Fla. and e Tex.

SEYMERIA Erect herbs; lower leaves pinnately dissected, upper ones entire; corolla yellow with 5 nearly equal lobes; 6 species, in e N.A. **Mullein Foxglove,** *S. macrophylla*, 3–6′ tall, grows in woods, on stream banks, Ga. to Tex., n to Ia. and W.Va.

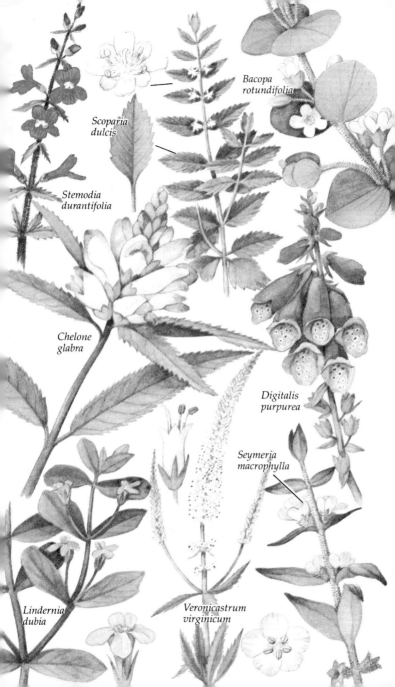

*Scoparia
dulcis*

*Bacopa
rotundifolia*

*Stemodia
durantifolia*

*Chelone
glabra*

*Digitalis
purpurea*

*Seymeria
macrophylla*

*Lindernia
dubia*

*Veronicastrum
virginicum*

BLUE-HEARTS (BUCHNERA) Rough-hairy herbs with opposite leaves or the uppermost alternate; flowers opposite in a terminal bracted spike, corolla with 5 nearly equal lobes; 4 species in s U.S. *B. americana*, 1–3' high, grows in moist sandy soil, w Fla. to Tex., n to N.Y., Ont., Mich., Ill., Mo., and Kans.

MAZUS *M. japonicus*, a 2–8" E Asian escape with coarsely toothed leaves, 2 to 7 blue 2-lipped flowers in loose racemes; in grasslands, on roadsides, Pa. to Mo., La., and e Tex.; also near Portland, Oreg.

SPEEDWELL (VERONICA) Erect or creeping herbs, leaves mostly opposite, flowers blue to white, in axillary or terminal racemes, of 4 or 5 sepals, a 4-lobed corolla, 2 stamens, 1 stigma; 30 species in N.A.

Bird's-eye, *V. persica,* a hairy basally branched herb to 16", has alternate round-lobed leaves with toothed edges; flowers in the axils of leafy bracts; Eurasian, escaped to wastelands and lawns in much of N.A.

V. longifolia has 1–4' stems, 2–6" lance-like doubly toothed leaves in pairs or 3's; herbage is smooth or downy; flowers in long terminal racemes; European, now ranges from Nfld. to w Que., s to N.J., Md., and Ohio.

V. cusickii, a 2–8" alpine herb, has paired sessile entire oval leaves, flowers in a terminal raceme; grows in meadows and moist soil to above timberline, nw Wash. to w Mont., s to cen. Sierra Nevada, Calif.

Brook-pimpernel, *V. anagallis-aquatica,* has stems that creep and root at base, then rise to 40"; sessile leaves, some with clasping bases; axillary small-bracted racemes of many flowers; in wet soil throughout N.A.

GERARDIA (AGALINIS) Erect wiry herbs with narrow opposite leaves, mostly entire, sometimes alternate on the branches, becoming bracts with 1 or 2 flowers per axil, often forming a raceme or spike; calyx 5-toothed or 5-lobed; corolla yellow, pink, purple, or white, bell-shaped or hemispheric, 5-lobed, the upper 2 lobes smaller; 2 pairs of stamens, mostly hairy; 1 stigma; 46 similar species, in e and cen. N.A.

A. pedicularia, 16"–4', with bipinnately lobed leaves, grows in dry deciduous woods, clearings, sw Me. to s Minn., s to n Ill., Ind., Ohio, W.Va., upland to Ga.

Downy False Foxglove, *A. virginica,* 1–4', has petioled leaves, the lower wavy or pinnately lobed; in dry open woods, N.H. to s Mich., s to n Fla. and La.

A. purpurea, to 4' tall, has 4-angled stems, linear 1–2" leaves, 6 to 14 rose-purple or white flowers per raceme; grows in damp mostly acid soils, N.S. to Minn., s to Fla., Neb., and e Tex.

A. fasciculata, to 28", stems fine-bristled, branches angled, 12- to 30-flowered elongated racemes; in dry or moist soil, Fla. to Tex., inland to Ark., Mo., Ga.; Coastal Plain to s Va.

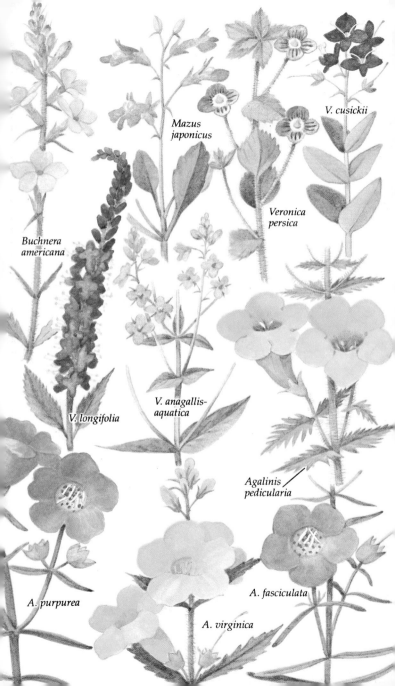

Mazus
japonicus

V. cusickii

Buchnera
americana

Veronica
persica

V. longifolia

V. anagallis-
aquatica

Agalinis
pedicularia

A. purpurea

A. fasciculata

A. virginica

PAINTED-CUP (CASTILLEJA) Small erect simple or branching herbs with alternate entire or pinnately lobed leaves, flowers in bracted terminal spikes, the bracts usually more highly colored than the flowers; calyx 2- or 4-cleft; corolla tube long and narrow, with a hooded upper lip, the lower lip shorter or vestigial; about 109 species in N.A.

Indian Paintbrush, *C. coccinea*, 1–2′, stem leaves and bracts 3–5 lobed; bracts scarlet-tipped or yellow or white; in peat meadows and prairies, or damp sand and gravel, s N.H. to s Man., s to n Fla., n Miss., La., and Okla.

C. levisecta has 4–20″ stems, reclined at base; upper leaves and bracts 2- to 6-lobed near the tip; herbage sticky-hairy; grows in meadows and prairies, at low elevations, w of the Cascades, s B.C. to Linn Co., Oreg.

Great Red Indian Paintbrush, *C. miniata*, 8–32″, may have smooth, downy, or sticky-hairy upper herbage; bracts red, rarely yellow or orange; common at medium and lower elevations, mts. of w N.A., Alaska to Calif. and N.M.

C. pilosa has hairy 6–14″ stems, entire or 3- to-5 lobed leaves; most bracts 3-lobed, tinged with purple or yellow-green; corolla is white or pink, upper lip green; e Oreg. to n Calif. and nw Nev., in grassy meadows with sagebrush.

Indian Paintbrush, *C. linariaefolia*, 1–2′, lower leaves entire, upper 3-lobed; calyx and upper bracts red, rarely yellow; in sagebrush or conifer forests, cen. Oreg. to s Mont., s to N.M. and Ariz., w to s Nev. and Calif. (e of Sierra Nevada).

Downy Painted-cup, *C. sessiliflora*, has a 6–12″ simple stem, 3- to-5 lobed leaves, broader green bracts and calyx; sickle-shaped yellow or pinkish flowers; grows on the Great Plains, s Sask. and s Man. to Ill., s to se Ariz. and w Tex.

OWL-CLOVER (ORTHOCARPUS) resembles *Castilleja* but has showy flowers; the lower lip is usually of 1 or 3 inflated sacs; 24 species, of w N.A., *O. hispidus*, 4–16″, is glandular-hairy, its bracts of 3–7 palmate lobes; grows in moist sites, Alaska to s Calif. **Johnny-tuck,** *O. erianthus*, 2–15″, has leaves and bracts pinnately dissected into thready lobes; flowers violet-scented, upper lip maroon, lower lip white, yellow, or pink; found in open grassy places, s Calif. to s Oreg., introduced near Seattle, Wash. **Escobita,** *O purpurascens*, 4–16″, has pinnately dissected leaves, rose or varicolored bracts; grows in open sites in much of Calif., e to w and s Ariz.

EYEBRIGHT (EUPHRASIA) Low erect herbs of cool climates with opposite toothed or lobed leaves, small flowers, solitary or in spikes; calyx 4-cleft; corolla 2-lipped, upper lip 2-lobed, erect, the sides folded back; lower lip of 3 entire or notched lobes; about 11 species in N.A., *E. americana*, 4–18″ high, is common by roads and in fields from Nfld. to cen. and coastal Me. *E. officinalis* (not shown) is similar, in w Wash.

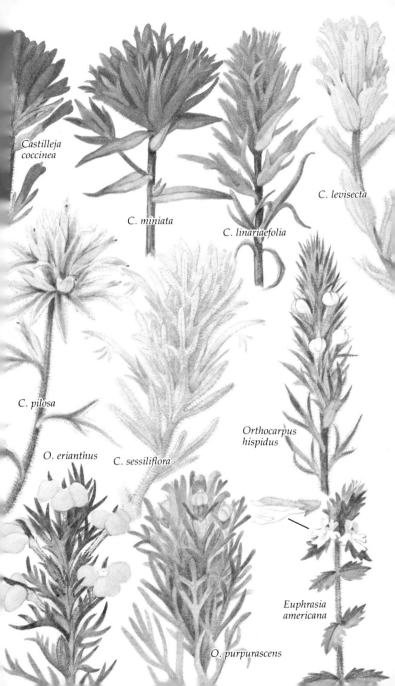

Castilleja coccinea

C. miniata

C. linariaefolia

C. levisecta

C. pilosa

Orthocarpus hispidus

O. erianthus

C. sessiliflora

Euphrasia americana

O. purpurascens

HEDGE-HYSSOP (GRATIOLA) Low herbs of wet soil with opposite sessile leaves, solitary flowers; calyx 5-parted; 1 or 2 bractlets beneath; upper corolla lip entire or 2-lobed, lower 3-lobed; 13 N.A. species. **Golden Pert,** *G. aurea,* 1–16″ high, ranges from se Nfld. to e N.D., s to n Ill., cen. N.Y., on or near Coastal Plain to n Fla. *G. ramosa,* with 1–14″ forked stems, grows in damp sandy pinelands, Fla. to La., n to Md.

COW-WHEAT (MELAMPYRUM) One species, *M. lineare,* a 2–20″ simple to bushy herb; leaves opposite and entire, upper ones often toothed at base, with ½″ solitary flowers; ranges from Nfld. to B.C., s to ne Wash., n Ida., nw Mont., Minn., Wisc., Ohio, Va., mts. to Ga.

YELLOW-RATTLE (RHINANTHUS) Erect herbs with sessile opposite toothed leaves, flowers in 1-sided leafy-bracted racemes; calyx 4-toothed, flattened vertically, inflated in fruit; upper lip hooded, lower small, 3-lobed; 2 N.A. species. *R. crista-galli,* 4–40″ tall, is circumboreal, s to nw Oreg., S.D., N.Y., and N.Eng.; in the Rocky Mts. to Colo. and Ariz.

CHAFFSEED (SCHWALBEA) One species, *S. americana,* with alternate entire sessile leaves, becoming bracts upward on the 1–3′ simple stem; flowers to 1½″ long, in a loose terminal spike; grows in pinelands, oak woods, clearings, from Fla. to e Tex., n to Mass., Conn., N.Y., Ky., and Tenn.

LOUSEWORT (PEDICULARIS) Herbs with mostly pinnately lobed leaves, large flowers in racemes or spikes; corolla 2-lipped, the upper flattened, often beaked at the tip; lower 3-lobed and spreading. There are about 40 N.A. species.

Common Lousewort or **Wood-betony,** *P. canadensis,* has clusters of simple hairy 6–16″ stems; mostly petioled leaves, scattered on the stem; flowers in short racemes, corolla yellow, red, or yellow and red; in woods and clearings, cen. Me. and s Que. to Man., s to Fla. and Tex.

Elephant-heads, *P. groenlandica,* sends up one or more 1–2′ stems from a caudex; basal leaves are long-petioled and pinnate, the pinnae toothed; corolla pink, red, or purple; grows in wet meadows and cold streams at medium to alpine heights, Greenl. to Yuk., s to Calif. and N.M.

P. grayi, to 3′ or more, has twice-pinnate leaves 1–2′ long, a bracted terminal spike, and also axillary flowers; in conifer forests, Wyo. to N.M., Ariz.

P. racemosa, to 2′, has scattered lance-like leaves with finely scalloped edges; corolla pink or white, upper lip with a sickle-like beak; in mts., B.C. and Alta. to Calif. and N.M.

P. centranthera has a low clump of fernlike bronze-green leaves cut into small stiff crinkled lobes; flowers over 1″ long, unbeaked; common in pine forests, Colo. and Utah to N.M. and Ariz.

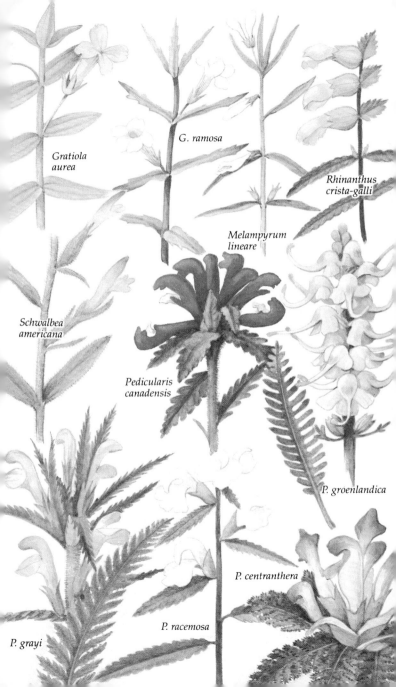

Gratiola
aurea

G. ramosa

Rhinanthus
crista-galli

Melampyrum
lineare

Schwalbea
americana

Pedicularis
canadensis

P. groenlandica

P. centranthera

P. grayi

P. racemosa

PARENTUCELLIA is Eurasian; *P. viscosa* has escaped to moist sandy soil, w of the Cascades, Wash. to n Calif., and in se Tex.; an erect sticky-hairy herb to 20" high, leaves opposite or spiraled, sessile; flowers are sessile, in leafy terminal spikes.

BIRD'S-BEAK (CORDYLANTHUS) Wiry bushy herbs; leaves and bracts small, entire to pinnately lobed; long narrow flowers, in heads or scattered; calyx tonguelike, on the upper side of the corolla, a similar bract sometimes on the underside; corolla 2-lipped, in some beak-like, in others club-shaped; 29 species in w N.A. *C. wrightii*, to 2' tall, has alternate 3- to 5-parted leaves with bristle-like segments; flowers mauve or yellow; grows on dry hills and plains, w Tex. to Ariz. *C. maritimus* is downy-glandular, has 4–8" reclining stems, entire leaves; found in coastal salt marshes, Baja Calif. to Oreg.

BESSEYA Leaves mostly basal, petioled, entire or toothed; flowers in a dense terminal bracted spike; calyx 2- to 4-toothed; corolla (if present) 2-lipped, upper entire, lower 3-lobed; 2 stamens; 6 species, in w N.A. *B. wyomingensis*, to 2' high, grows on open slopes up to subalpine zones, s Alta. s through w Mont. and e Ida. to n Utah, e to S.D., Neb., and Colo.

SYNTHYRIS resembles *Besseya* but may have pinnately lobed leaves; flowers in a spike-like raceme; 4 sepals; corolla always present and as in *Besseya*. *S. missurica*, 4–24" high, grows on moist slopes from se Wash. and w Ida. to ne Calif.

BRACHYSTIGMA One species, *B. wrightii*, to 18" tall; leaves narrow, in pairs or 3's; long-stalked inch-wide flowers in racemes; corolla with 5 nearly equal lobes; 4 stamens; grows on dry slopes and mesas, often among live oaks, sw N.M. and s Ariz.

MOHAVEA Low sticky-downy herbs, leaves alternate, flowers in leafy spikes; corolla of 5 broad lobes; 2 fertile, 3 sterile stamens; 2 species in the SW. **Ghost-flower,** *M. confertiflora*, to 16" high, grows in sand and gravel, s Nev., w Ariz., and s Calif.

UNICORN-PLANT FAMILY (MARTYNIACEAE)

UNICORN-PLANT or **DEVIL'S-CLAW** (PROBOSCIDEA) Erect to decumbent herbs; leaves opposite to alternate, entire to palmately or pinnately lobed; 1–3" 5-lobed flowers in terminal racemes, white or yellow to pink or red-purple; fruit with a long curved beak that splits into 2 claws; 6 species in e and s U.S. *P. louisianica*, with 40" branches, grows on river banks, wastelands, from s Minn. to Tex., e to W.Va. and to Ga.

Parentucellia
viscosa

Cordylanthus
wrightii

C. maritimus

Brachystigma
wrightii

Synthyris
missurica

Besseya
wyomingensis

Mohavea
confertiflora

Proboscidea
louisianica

BROOMRAPE FAMILY (OROBANCHACEAE)

Low fleshy root parasites without chlorophyll, with scales in place of leaves; flowers single or in spikes; corolla 2-lipped, 2 pairs of stamens, 1 style, 1 stigma; 4 genera in N.A.

GROUND CONE (BOSCHNIAKIA) Stems short and thick, covered by overlapping scales, resembling a pine cone; sessile flowers in the axils, 3 species, in Pac. N.A. *B. hookeri*, 3–5″ high, 1″ thick, is found in coastal scrub, n B.C. to n Calif.

SQUAWROOT or **CANCER-ROOT** (CONOPHOLIS) Closely resembles *Boschniakia*; 2 N.A. species. *C. americana*, 1–10″ high, grows in woods, mostly under oaks, N.S. to Wisc., s to Fla. and Ala.

BROOMRAPE (OROBANCHE) Stems glandular-downy, naked or scaly; calyx 5-lobed; upper lip 2-lobed; stigma 2-lipped or cuplike; about 16 species in N.A. *O. fasciculata* has a forking caudex, 6″ stems with 5–10 scales, 4–10 purple or yellow flowers on 1″ stalks; grows in scrub or forest, Alaska to Mich., s to s Calif., Tex., Ill., and n Ind. *O. californica* has thick stems 2–5″ high, purple or yellow flowers; found e of the Cascades, s B.C. to s Calif., e to w Mont. and Utah.

BEECH-DROPS (EPIFAGUS) One species, *E. virginiana*, to 18″ high, often in clumps, stems simple or branched, with tiny scales; calyx 5-toothed, corolla 4-toothed; grows under beech trees, e N.A.

BLADDERWORT FAMILY (LENTIBULARIACEAE)

Flowers on an erect scape; calyx 2-lipped, 2- or 5-lobed; corolla 2-lipped, the lower lip spurred; 2 stamens; 2 N.A. genera.

BUTTERWORT (PINGUICULA) Herbs of moist soil with a rosette of entire greasy leaves, which roll inward from the edge to engulf and digest insects; calyx 5-lobed; 8 N.A. species. *P. vulgaris* has 1–2″ leaves; circumboreal, s to n Calif., Mont., Mich., and N.Y. *P. lutea* has 1′ scapes, 1″-wide flowers; grows in moist sandy soil, Coastal Plain, Fla. to La. and N.C.

BLADDERWORT (UTRICULARIA) Mostly aquatic herbs, leaves finely dissected, bearing little bladders with a lidded mouth rimmed by flagellae; fry, larvae, etc., are swirled in and digested; 21 N.A. species. **Horned Bladderwort,** *U. cornuta*, has 1′ high 3-flowered scapes, grows in swamps and bogs; **Purple Bladderwort,** *U. purpurea*, has submersed 40″ stems, grows in quiet water; both are of e N.A. **Common Bladderwort,** *U. vulgaris*, with 7′ free-floating stems, grows throughout N.A.

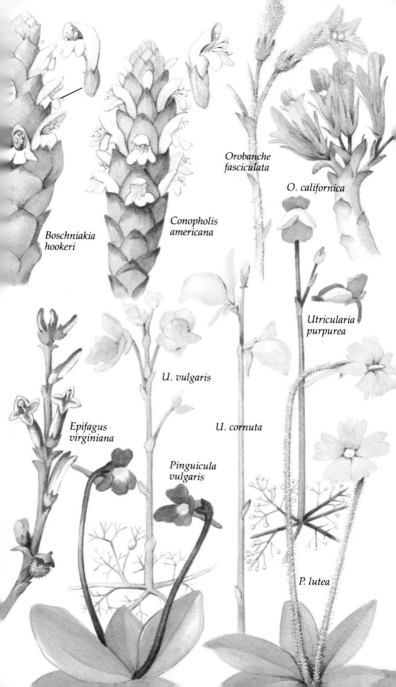

Boschniakia
hookeri

Conopholis
americana

Orobanche
fasciculata

O. californica

Utricularia
purpurea

U. vulgaris

U. cornuta

Epifagus
virginiana

Pinguicula
vulgaris

P. lutea

ACANTHUS FAMILY (ACANTHACEAE)

Herbs with simple mostly entire opposite leaves, flowers often much-bracted; corolla tubular, with 5 nearly equal lobes or 1- or 2-lipped; 1 or 2 pairs of stamens; style slender, stigma entire or 2-lobed; 12 herbaceous genera in N.A.

SCALY-STEM (ELYTRARIA) Leaves in basal or terminal tufts, alternate; flowers blue or white, 2-lipped, in spikes on scaly-bracted scapes; 4 species in s U.S. *E. carolinensis*, to 2′, grows in swampy woods, Fla. to N.C. *E. imbricata*, with 10″ scapes, is found on dry brushy slopes, mountain ledges, w Tex. to Ariz.

STENANDRIUM resembles *Elytraria* but stem leaves are opposite, the scapes may branch, the corolla is 5-lobed; 2 species in s U.S. *S. fascicularis* is almost stemless, the spikes about 1″ long; grows in moist soil, s Fla. and s Tex.

DISCHORISTE Stems prostrate to erect, leaves petioled or sessile, flowers in axillary or terminal cymes, spikes, or heads; corolla tube erect, 5-lobed, barely to clearly 2-lipped; 2 pairs of stamens, stigma 2-lobed; 5 species in sw U.S. *D. linearis*, a 7–16″ erect branched herb, grows in Tex. and N.M.

RUELLIA Leaves petioled, entire to toothed; flowers single or clustered in the axils or in terminal panicles, yellow, white, red, or mauve, with 5 rounded lobes; 4 stamens, stigma 2-lobed; 22 species in e and s U.S. *R. humilis*, to 3′ high, has clustered stems, flowers to 3″ long; grows in open woods and fields, Ia. and Neb. to Mich., W.Va., and Pa., s to Fla. and Tex.

CARLOWRIGHTIA Erect slender-branched herbs, sometimes woody at base, with small narrow entire leaves, cream to purple flowers in loose spikes or racemes, with a slender tube and 4 nearly equal lobes; 2 stamens, 1 round stigma; 5 species in sw U.S. *C. linearifolia*, to 4′ tall, ranges from w Tex. to Ariz.

DICLIPTERA Stems erect or reclined, 6-sided; leaves entire or wavy, petioled; 2-lipped flowers in flattened cymes, combined in spikes or panicles subtended by 2 to 4 pairs of large bracts; 6 species in s U.S. *D. brachiata*, to 28″ high, is found in moist shady sites, Fla. to Tex. n to Mo. and Va.

TUBE-TONGUE (SIPHONOGLOSSA) Bushy herbs, woody at base, with entire leaves; flowers axillary, 2-lipped, the upper 2-lobed or entire, lower 3-lobed; 3 species in the SW. *S. pilosella*, to 1′ tall, grows in rocky soil, s two-thirds of Tex.

E. imbricata

Dischoriste
linearis

Elytraria
carolinensis

Stenandrium
fascicularis

Ruellia
humilis

Dicliptera
brachiata

Carlowrightia
linearifolia

Siphonoglossa
pilosella

WATER-WILLOW (JUSTICIA) Erect simple or bushy herbs of water or wet places, some woody at base, with petioled entire leaves, 2-lipped white, pink, or purple flowers, solitary or in spikes or panicles; upper lip 2-lobed, lower 3-lobed; 2 stamens; 9 species in se U.S. *J. americana* forms colonies to 40″ high; grows in shallow water or mud, Ga. to Tex., n to Ont. and Que.

YEATESIA One species, *Y. viridiflora*, an erect simple or branched herb to 2′ high with simple entire short-petioled leaves to 5″ long, 2″ wide; flowers in compact cylindrical axillary and terminal spikes amid hairy bracts; corolla 3- or 4-toothed; 2 stamens; grows in pinelands, wet soil, Fla. to Tex. n to Ga. and Tenn.

LOPSEED FAMILY (PHRYMACEAE)

LOPSEED (PHRYMA) is the only genus; *P. leptostachya* the one N.A. species; an erect 1–3′ branching herb with coarsely toothed opposite leaves, the lower long-petioled, upper almost sessile; flowers opposite in a slender terminal spike; calyx 2-lipped; corolla tubular, 2-lipped, the upper notched, the lower 3-lobed; 4 stamens, stigma 2-lobed; in open woods and thickets, w N.B. to Man., s to Fla. and Tex.

MADDER FAMILY (RUBIACEAE)

Leaves simple and entire, opposite or whorled, often with stipules that are usually united into a sheath; calyx tubular, 4- to 8-parted; corolla of 3–5 lobes; 3–5 stamens; style slender, often forked. There are 13 herbaceous genera in N.A.

FIELD-MADDER (SHERARDIA) One species, *S. arvensis*, a sprawling square-stemmed Eurasian herb to 16″; leaves pungent, in whorls of 4–6, prickly on the edges; 4–8 flowers in terminal heads subtended by 8–10 long leaflike bracts; corolla 4- to 5-lobed; grows in fields, wastelands, se Canada and e U.S.; Pac. NW to s Calif.

BEDSTRAW and **CLEAVERS** (GALIUM) Slender herbs with 4-angled stems, whorled sessile or short-petioled leaves, leaflike stipules; flowers in small cymes or panicles, corolla 3- to 4-lobed; 4, rarely 3 stamens; 2 stigmas. About 78 species in N.A.

Rough Bedstraw, *G. asprellum,* to 6′, has hooked prickles on the stems; in damp soil, Nfld. to Ont., s to N.C., Ohio and Neb.

Northern Bedstraw, *G. boreale,* 1–3′ tall, has leaves in 4′s; circumboreal, s to Del., Ind., N.D., N.M., Ariz., and Calif.

Wild Licorice or **Cross Clover,** *G. circaezans,* to 18″, leaves in 4′s, grows in woods, Fla. to Tex., n to Mich. and s N.Eng.

G. multiflorum, to 1′, has clustered stems, tiny leaves ⅓″ long; on dry open slopes, Wash. to s Calif., e to Ida. and Ariz.

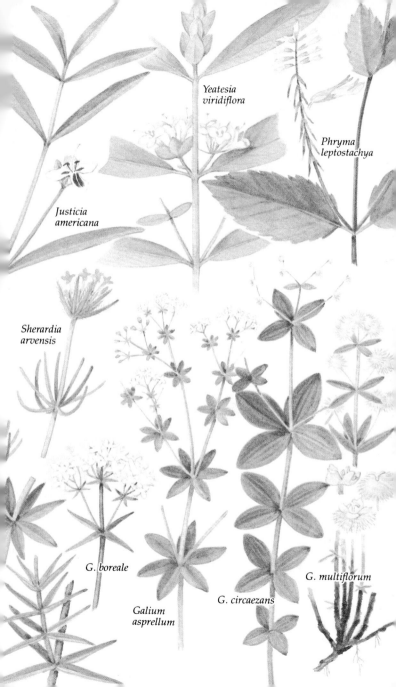

Yeatesia viridiflora

Phryma leptostachya

Justicia americana

Sherardia arvensis

G. boreale

Galium asprellum

G. circaezans

G. multiflorum

WOODRUFF (ASPERULA) is Eurasian; **Sweet Woodruff,** *A. odorata,* occurs sparingly in woodlands, e U.S.; w of the Cascades in the Pac. NW; stems are erect, unangled, 4–12″ high; leaves in whorls of 6–9, flowers and herbage vanilla-scented in drying.

RICHARDIA Branched prostrate to upright herbs with short-petioled leaves, bristled stipules, tiny flowers in terminal heads; corolla 4- to 8-lobed; Trop. Am., 3 species escaped in se U.S. **Mexican Clover,** *R. scabra,* to 3′ high, grows by roads and in fields, from Fla. to Tex., n to se Va., s Ind., and Ark.

PARTRIDGE-BERRY (MITCHELLA) One N.A. species, **Two-eyed-berry** or **Running Box,** *M. repens.* Small trailing evergreen herb; leaves shiny, with white lines; flowers paired, ovaries partly united, corollas 3- to 6-lobed, rarely united and 10-lobed; grows in woods, Fla. to Tex., n to sw Nfld., s Que., s Ont., Minn.

BLUETS (HEDYOTIS) Small and often tufted herbs with entire opposite leaves, joined at base by stipules; flowers solitary or in cymes, calyx and corolla 4-lobed; 4 stamens; 1 style, 2 stigmas; 28 species in e and s N.A. **Innocence** or **Quaker-ladies,** *H. caerulea,* has 2–8″ stems from rosettes, solitary flowers on 2–3″ stalks; grows in open turf, N.S. and N.B. to s Ont. and Wisc., s in thickets and woods to Ga., Ala., and Mo. *H. lanceolata,* 6–16″ high, has funnel-shaped flowers in cymes; grows in dry open woods, pastures, Ala. to Okla., n to s Me., W.Va., Ky., Ill., and Mo. **Star-violet,** *H. minima,* 2–6″, is much-branched, with elongate basal leaves, solitary flowers; found in dry woods, fields, Ill. to Ia. and Kans., s to Ark. and Tex.

KELLOGGIA One species, *K. galioides,* to 2′ high, with opposite lance-like leaves to 2″ long, 4- to 5-lobed flowers in an open terminal panicle, grows on wooded or open mt. slopes up to alpine zones, cen. Wash. to Baja Calif., e to Ida., w Wyo., Utah, Ariz.

BUTTONWEED (DIODIA) Small weak-stemmed herbs with sessile opposite leaves joined by bristly stipules, 1–3 sessile 3- to 4-lobed axillary flowers; 4 N.A. species. *D. teres,* to 32″ long, grows in dry sandy soil, Fla. to Ariz., n to Mo., Mich., and N.Eng.

HONEYSUCKLE FAMILY (CAPRIFOLIACEAE)

TWINFLOWER (LINNAEA) One species, *L. borealis,* is a slender creeping evergreen herb with opposite round-oval wavy-edged leaves, 5-lobed flowers in pairs on an erect forked stalk; grows on peat or in cool woods, circumboreal, s to n Calif., Ariz., N.M. , S.D., Minn., Wisc., n Ind., Ohio, W.Va., and Md.

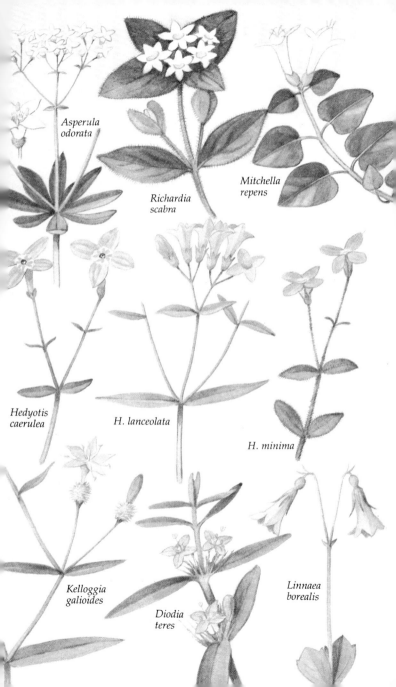

Asperula odorata

Richardia scabra

Mitchella repens

Hedyotis caerulea

H. lanceolata

H. minima

Kelloggia galioides

Diodia teres

Linnaea borealis

MOSCHATEL FAMILY (ADOXACEAE)

MOSCHATEL (ADOXA) is the only genus, *A. moschatellina* the only species; a dwarf herb with a scaly rhizome, long-petioled 1- to 3-ternate leaves, sending up 2–4″ stems with a pair of 3-cleft leaves, a terminal head of tiny flowers; grows in mossy woods, wet rocks, circumboreal, s to Colo., S.D., Ia., and N.Y.

VALERIAN FAMILY (VALERIANACEAE)

Erect herbs with opposite leaves, flowers in cymes or heads; corolla 5-lobed, 1-3 stamens, 1-3 stigmas; 4 genera in N.A.

VALERIAN (VALERIANA) Leaves entire to odd-pinnate; cymes clustered or panicled; calyx of inrolled feathery bristles that spread in fruit; corolla swollen at base; 3 stamens, 3 stigmas; 19 species in N.A. **"Garden Heliotrope,"** *V. officinalis*, a 2–7′ hairy-leaved herb, is a European escape to roadsides and thickets, from Que. to Minn., s to N.J. and Ohio. *V. acutiloba*, 4–24″ high, has entire basal leaves, pinnate-lobed upper ones; grows on open mountain slopes, often by snowbanks, Mont. to Oreg., s to Calif., Ariz., and N.M. *V. arizonica*, 4–12″, also has entire basal and divided upper leaves; found in damp soil, Utah and Colo. to Ariz. and Tex.

PLECTRITIS Leaves simple, the upper ones sessile; pink or white flowers in axillary and/or terminal clusters; no calyx, 3 stamens; 3 N.A. species. *P. congesta*, 4–24″, has a basal spur on the 2-lipped corolla; grows on open slopes, in meadows, s Calif. to s B.C. *P. macrocera*, 4–24″, has nearly equal corolla lobes; found in moist open sites, s B.C. to s Calif., e to Mont. and Utah.

TEASEL FAMILY (DIPSACACEAE)

Leaves opposite or whorled; flowers in dense bracted heads subtended by an involucre; 3 Eurasian genera in N.A.

TEASEL (DIPSACUS) Hairy or prickly herbs with spine-tipped bracts around each 4-lobed flower; 4 stamens; 2 species in N.A. *D. sylvestris*, 2–7′ high, has toothed lance-like leaves, straight-pointed bracts (hook-tipped in var. *fullonum*); grows in old fields, s Canada and n U.S. *D. laciniatus*, 2–7′, has pinnately-lobed leaves, their bases cupped around the stem; ranges from Mass. to Mich.

DEVIL'S-BIT (SCABIOSA) *S. pratensis*, 16″–3′, with mostly basal wavy or entire leaves, is local in fields, from C.B. to Mass.

BLUE-BUTTONS (KNAUTIA) *K. arvensis* grows in fields and wastelands, Nfld. to N.D., Mont. and s B.C., s to Pa.; a hairy 1–4′ herb with pinnately-lobed leaves, 1–2″ flower heads.

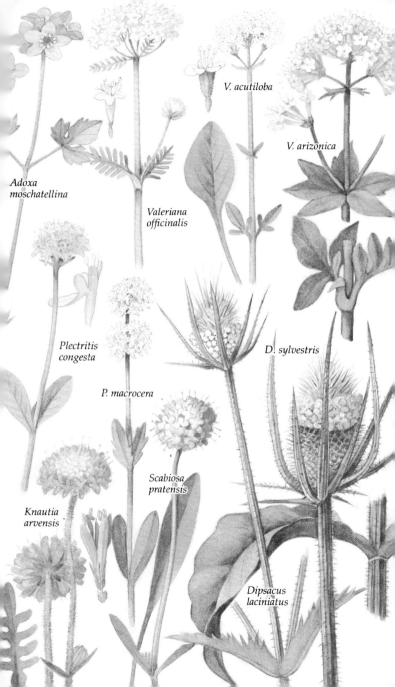

Adoxa moschatellina

V. acutiloba

V. arizonica

Valeriana officinalis

Plectritis congesta

P. macrocera

D. sylvestris

Scabiosa pratensis

Knautia arvensis

Dipsacus laciniatus

GOURD FAMILY (CUCURBITACEAE)

Trailing or climbing vines with tendrils, leaves alternate, petioled, simple or compound; flowers solitary to clustered or in corymbs or racemes, often male or female; corolla 5-lobed, 3 or 5 stamens, 1 style, 2 to 5 stigmas; 21 genera in N.A.

MELON-LOCO (APODANTHERA) One species, *A. undulata*, grows in sand and gravel among shrubs, from w Tex. to s Ariz.; prostrate branches to 10′; leaves kidney-shaped, to 6″ wide, wavy, scalloped, or sparsely toothed; corolla lobes almost separate, to 1½″ long; the hard-shelled 2–4″ oval fruit is ridged lengthwise.

GOURD (CUCURBITA) Running or climbing vines with branched tendrils, entire or lobed hairy leaves; flowers solitary, males with 3 united anthers, females with 3 to 5 3-lobed stigmas; 4 N.A. species. **Fetid-** or **Buffalo-gourd,** *C. foetidissima*, has rampant prostrate branches to 20′ long, malodorous heart-shaped 1′ leaves, 4″-long flowers, 3″ striped fruits; grows in dry or sandy soil, Neb. and Mo. to Ind., s to Tex., w to Calif. **Coyote-melon,** *C. palmata*, has 5-lobed palmate leaves, the 4″ lobes often lobed; flowers 2″ long; 3″ striped fruits; ranges from w Ariz. to Calif.

BRANDEGEA *B. bigelovii*, a delicate vine with palmate 3- or 5-lobed 2″ leaves, the upper side pebbly; grows in sw Ariz. and se Calif.; flowers tiny, the males in corymbs, females single or paired; fruits to ½″, few-spined, with 1 seed.

CYCLANTHERA *C. dissecta*, a slender 10′ vine, grows in rocky soil, Kans. to La., Tex., and Ariz.; tendrils 1–3-forked, palmate leaves of 3–7 toothed leaflets; ¼″ flowers, males in racemes, females single in the same axil; 1″ long-spined fruits.

MELONETTE (MELOTHRIA) *M. pendula*, a slender vine, grows in damp thickets, Fla. to Tex., n to Va., s Ind., Mo., and Okla.; tendrils simple, leaves 5-angled or 5-lobed, rough; ⅓″ flowers, males in racemes, females alone; ½″ black fruits.

CAYAPONIA resembles *Melothria* but has greenish-white flowers, red fruits; 3 species in s U.S. *C. grandifolia* has 3-lobed leaves 4–8″ wide, the basal lobes also lobed; grows in bottomlands, Ga. and Fla. to La., Ark., and se Mo.

WILD CUCUMBER (ECHINOCYSTIS) *E. lobata* has angled stems to 20′ high, 3–5″ heart-shaped 3- to 7-lobed leaves; ½″ flowers, males in long racemes, females alone or clustered in the same axil; 2″ puffy weak-spined fruits; grows on stream banks, e and sw N.A.

*Apodanthera
undulata*

*Cucurbita
foetidissima*

*Brandegea
bigelovii*

*Cucurbita
palmata*

*Cyclanthera
dissecta*

*Melothria
pendula*

*Echinocystis
lobata*

*Cayaponia
grandifolia*

BIG-ROOT or **MAN-ROOT** (MARAH) sends up robust stems from large tubers; leaves 3- to 9-lobed, notched at base; ⅓" flowers, males in racemes, females single in the same axil; the small spiny fruits have several seeds; 6 species in w N.A. *M. oreganus,* to 20', leaves to 8" long; in fields, thickets, on hills, s B.C. to n Calif., e to w Ida.

MOMORDICA Delicate Old World tropical vines; leaves 3- to 7-lobed, the edges toothed; 1" solitary flowers, males on bracted stalks; fruit warty-spined; 2 species in the SE. **Balsam-pear** or **Bitter Gourd,** *M. charantia,* has orange 1½–4" fruits, opening when ripe, exposing the scarlet arils on the brown seeds; grows in thickets, wastelands, Coastal Plain, Fla. to se Tex.

GLOBE-BERRY (IBERVILLEA) Smooth branching vines, leaves entire or with 3–5 coarsely toothed lobes; ¼" flowers, males on separate plants, single to clustered or in racemes; females solitary; fruit a smooth berry; 3 species in s U.S. *I. lindheimeri* has 5–8 glandular-downy males per raceme, 1" fruits; grows in dry woods, open rocky soil, from s Okla. to s-cen. Tex.

BUR-CUCUMBER (SICYOS) Vines with forked tendrils; leaves angular to lobed; flowers tiny, males in racemes, females in a stalked head in the same axil; fruits oval, to ½", smooth to woolly, bristly, or barb-spined, 1-seeded; 5 species in e and s N.A. *S. angulatus* is clammy-hairy, has 8" 5-lobed leaves, long-bristled woolly fruits; grows on river banks, damp soil, from s Me. and w Que. to N.D., s to Fla. and Tex.

BLUEBELL FAMILY (CAMPANULACEAE)

Herbs with milky juice, simple alternate leaves; 2 subfamilies.

I. LOBELIA SUBFAMILY (LOBELIOIDEAE)

Corolla zygomorphic, 5-lobed; 5 stamens, filaments often fused, anthers always fused in a tube around fringed stigma; 7 N.A. genera.

PORTERELLA One species, *P. carnosula,* an erect 2–8" herb with narrow pointed leaves to 1" long, racemes of ½" flowers on 1" stalks; grows in moist soil, se Oreg. to n Wyo., s to Calif. and n Ariz.

DOWNINGIA Small branched herbs with lance-like or narrow leaves, becoming bracts upward; solitary 2-lipped flowers in the axils; upper lip with 2 narrow lobes, lower with 3 broad lobes; 13 species, mostly of wet soil, in Oreg. and Calif. *D. yina,* 1–4" high, leaves to ½" long, grows from w Wash. to nw Calif. and also in se Oreg. *D. elegans,* 4–20" tall, with 1" leaves, ranges from n Calif. to cen. and e Wash., n Ida., and n Nev.

Marah oreganus

Momordica charantia

Ibervillea lindheimeri

Sicyos angulatus

Porterella carnosula

Downingia yina

D. elegans

LOBELIA Mostly tall erect herbs with lance-like leaves, often becoming bracts upward; flowers single or in terminal spikes, racemes, or panicles; corolla tube split on the upper side between 2 erect or turned-back lobes, the 3 lower lobes partly fused in a lip; 2 or all 5 anthers hairy at the tips; 29 N.A. species, mostly e; many contain poisonous alkaloids.

L. appendiculata, to 3', is simple or with a few erect branches; leaves sessile, with broad or clasping bases, to 3" long, 1" wide; ½"-long flowers in a 1-sided raceme to 1' long; in open woods, pinelands, prairies, Ala. to e Tex., n to Ill., Mo., and Kans.

Cardinal-flower, *L. cardinalis,* has a simple stem to 7', leaves lance-like, irregularly toothed; 1–2" flowers in a 4–20" leafy-bracted raceme, deep red to rose or white; in wet open places, Fla. to Nev. and Calif., n to N.B., s Que., s Ont.; Minn., and Okla.

Water-lobelia or **Water-gladiole,** *L. dortmanna,* grows under water on sandy or gravelly pond edges; sending up a naked or bracted hollow scape above the water, with a 1- to 11-flowered loose raceme; Nfld. to Minn., s to N.S., N.J., Pa., Wisc.; sw B.C. to Oreg.

Bay Lobelia, *L. feayana,* is a dwarf less than 1' high, sometimes reclining; leaves long-petioled, the ½" blades nearly round, mostly in a rosette; flowers about ½" long, 2 greenish tubercles at base of lower lip; in Fla. pinelands.

L. elongata, 1–5', has fleshy lance-like sharply toothed stem leaves; 1" flowers in a strongly 1-sided 3–12" raceme; flower stalks are rough, have basal bractlets; in fresh to brackish marshes and swamps, Del. and Md. to Ga.

Indian Tobacco, *L inflata,* 6"–3', is often much-branched; stem leaves sessile or nearly so, toothed, hairy beneath; flowers ⅖" or less, in 4–12" racemes; the bell-like calyx inflates in fruit; in open woods, fields, C.B. to Sask., s to Ga., Ala., Miss., Ark., e Kans.

Purple Dewdrop or **Downy Lobelia,** *L. puberula,* is densely downy; stem simple, to 5' (rarely to 9'), leaves often with callous-tipped teeth, sessile; raceme 1-sided, to 20", with up to 75 1" flowers; in wet soil, se U.S., w to Tex. and Okla., n to N.J., se Pa., Mo.

Blue Cardinal-flower or **Great Blue Lobelia,** *L. siphilitica,* has stems to 4', toothed leaves to 7" long, 2½" wide; flowers over 1" long, in a dense raceme to 20"; in moist soil, Me. to Man., S.D., and Colo., s to Tex., N.C., Ala.

L. dunnii has 12–20" erect or reclining stems, 1–3" toothed leaves, basal ones petioled, upper sessile; flowers to 1" long, few to many amid long narrow bracts; in moist canyons, below 3000', cen. Calif. to n Baja Calif.

Highbelia, *L. spicata,* to 4', is downy at base, smooth above; lower leaves have bristle-edged petioles, upper leaves sessile, their bases running down the stem; in open woods, fields, s N.B. to Minn., s to Ga., Ark., Okla., and Tex.

L. dortmanna

L. cardinalis

L. feayana

Lobelia appendiculata

L. spicata

L. puberula

L. dunnii

L. siphilitica

L. inflata

L. elongata

II. BLUEBELL SUBFAMILY (CAMPANULOIDEAE)

Flowers with radial symmetry; corolla bell-like or wheel-like, 5-lobed; anthers free, filaments sometimes fused; 2 or more stigmas; 7 N.A. genera.

HETEROCODON One species, *H. rariflorum*, 2–12″, is bristly; leaves sessile, rounded, toothed; single axillary flowers, lower ones not opening. Grows in moist soil, s B.C. and Ida. to Calif. and Nev.

TUFTY BELLS (WAHLENBERGIA) is Asian; *W. marginata* has escaped to fields and roadsides, Fla. to Ala. and N.C. Leaves are mostly basal, lance-like, faintly toothed; stems branched, to 18″ high; flowers erect, bell-shaped, solitary, about 1″ wide.

SHEEP'S-BIT (JASIONE) is European. *J. montana* has simple or branching 8–20″ stems, linear to lance-like leaves, flowers in dense heads less than 1″ wide, subtended by involucre bracts. Grows in fields and along roadsides, e Mass. to N.J.

CHICKEN SPIKE (SPHENOCLEA) One species, *S. zeylanica*, a coarse branched hollow-stemmed herb to 3′ or more; leaves to 8″ long, entire, short-petioled; small sessile flowers in dense erect 3″ spikes; Old World tropics, escaped to moist soil, S.C.; e and s Tex. to Miss., Ark.

VENUS' LOOKING-GLASS (SPECULARIA) Flowers axillary, blue or purplish, lower ones not opening; calyx 3- to 5-lobed, corolla 5-lobed, 5 stamens, 3 stigmas; 8 species in N.A. *S. perfoliata*, 20–40″, has clasping leaves and bracts. In open places, Me. to B.C., s to Fla., Tex., Ariz., n Calif.

BELLFLOWER (CAMPANULA) Herbs of diverse appearance; larger, longer-petioled leaves at base; flowers terminal or axillary; calyx 5-lobed; corolla 5-lobed; often bell-like, purplish-blue to blue or white; 5 free stamens; 29 species in N.A.

Tall Bellflower, *C. americana*, to 7′, flowers to 1″ wide. In rich moist soil, s Ont. and N.Y. to Minn. and S.D., s to Fla., Okla.

Marsh Bluebells, *C. aparinoides*, stems 8–24″, 3-angled. Meadows, swales, shores, Me. to Minn., s to Ga., Ky., Ia., Neb., Colo.

Southern Harebell, *C. divaricata*, 1–3′, numerous ⅓″ flowers. Dry woods, rocky hills, w Md. to Ky., s to Ga. and Ala.

C. parryi, to 10″, flowers about ½″ long, 1–2″ narrow stem leaves. Subalpine meadows, Rocky Mts.; Wenatchee Mts., Wash.

Harebell or **Bluebell,** *C. rotundifolia*, 4–20″ (rarely to 40″), 1″ flowers; circumboreal, s to N.J. and Mo., mts. to n Mexico.

Clustered Bluebell, *C. glomerata*, 1–2′, flowers sessile in a leafy head. European, escaped to fields, Que. to Mass. and Minn.

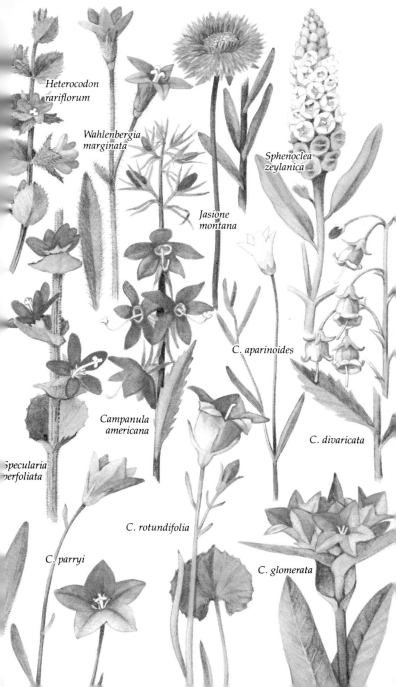

Heterocodon
rariflorum

Wahlenbergia
marginata

Sphenoclea
zeylanica

Jasione
montana

C. aparinoides

Campanula
americana

C. divaricata

Specularia
perfoliata

C. rotundifolia

C. parryi

C. glomerata

COMPOSITE FAMILY (COMPOSITAE)

Leaves opposite, alternate, or whorled, lacking stipules; tiny perfect, unisexual, or sexless flowers, combined into a compact head (the "flower"); the head subtended by involucre bracts, easily mistaken for a calyx. The true flowers, if perfect, consist of a pistil, made up of a 2-celled ovary, 1 style, a 2-lobed stigma; 4–5 stamens, filaments free, anthers fused in a tube around the style; a corolla; no calyx, or of scales, barbs, hairs, or plumes, collectively termed pappus; each flower may be subtended by a scale or bract, the chaff.

Some flowers have a tubular corolla, ending in 4 or 5 even lobes or 2 lips; these are tube-flowers. They compose the central disk of the heads of most Composites. In others, the corolla is a short basal tube and a flat blade, like a single petal of an ordinary flower; these are ray-flowers. One or both kinds of flowers may be present in a single head.

The Compositae is the largest plant family in N.A., represented by 2 sub-families, 11 tribes, and 292 genera.

SUBFAMILY I: TUBULIFLORAE

Juice not milky; all perfect disk flowers tubular, not rayed, evenly 5-lobed (rarely 3- to 4-lobed); ray-flowers, if present, only around the margin of the head, either female or sexless.

I. Ironweed Tribe (Vernonieae)

Leaves mostly simple, in rosettes or alternate; all flower heads alike, of perfect tube-flowers; corolla 5-lobed; pappus double, of hairlike bristles; anthers not tailed; involucre bracts strongly overlapped; 3 N.A. genera.

IRONWEED (VERNONIA) Tall leafy-stemmed herbs; leaves pointed, edges saw-toothed; 15 to many flowers per head, heads in corymb-like cymes; 22 species in N.A., mostly in e and s U.S.

New York Ironweed, *V. noveboracensis,* 3–6', is white-flowered in form *albiflora;* on low ground, Ga. to Miss., n to Mass., Ohio.

V. missurica, 3–5', is downy; in rich low ground, prairies, Ont. and Ohio to Ia., s and sw to Ala., Miss., La., Tex., and N.M.

Plains Ironweed, *V. marginata,* 16"–3', averages 18–21 flowers per head; by streams or in damp soil, Kans., Okla., Tex., N.M.

Woolly Ironweed, *V. lindheimeri,* 8–32" tall, leaves woolly beneath, sometimes also on top; cen. Tex. to Ark. and Mexico.

ELEPHANT'S-FOOT (ELEPHANTOPUS) Mostly short downy herbs; heads of 2 to 5 flowers, clustered in a compound leafy-bracted mass easily mistaken for a single head or flower; 4 species, in se U.S. **Tobaccoweed** or **Devil's-grandmother,** *E. tomentosus,* 6–20" tall, ranges n to Md., Ky.; *E. carolinianus,* 1–3', n to N.J., Ill., and Kans.; both grow in open woodlands.

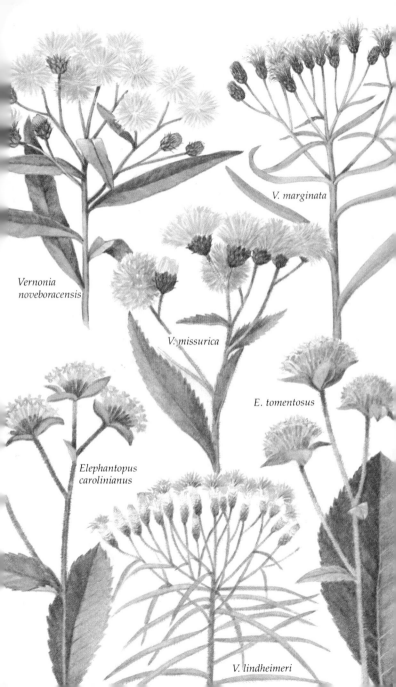

V. marginata

Vernonia noveboracensis

V. missurica

E. tomentosus

Elephantopus carolinianus

V. lindheimeri

II. Thoroughwort Tribe (Eupatorieae)

Leaves mostly simple, opposite, alternate, or whorled; heads alike, of perfect tube-flowers, never pure yellow; anthers not tailed; pappus of scales or bristles; involucre bracts overlapped; 16 N.A. genera.

THOROUGHWORT or **BONESET** (EUPATORIUM) Herbage often resin-dotted; involucre bell-like to cylindric, bracts more than 4, in 2–6 series; corollas 5-toothed, white, blue, rose, or purplish. About 50 N.A. species, mainly in e N.A.

Mist-flower or **Blue Boneset,** *E. coelestinum,* has weak sprawling stems to 6½', petioled downy leaves, blue-violet, red-purple, or white flowers. In damp soil, N.J. to Kans., s to Gulf States.

Joe-pye-weed, *E. dubium,* stems 2–5', purple-dotted; leaves in 3's and 4's, toothed; heads 5- to 12-flowered. Grows in damp acid soil, N.S. and sw Me. to S.C.

Joe-pye-weed, *E. maculatum,* 2–7', leaves mostly in 4's or 5's, heads 8- to 20-flowered; damp rich or lime soil, Nfld. to B.C., s to N.S., N.Eng., Pa., mts. to N.C., Neb., N.M., Ariz., Wash.

Joe-pye-weed or **Trumpet-weed,** *E. fistulosum,* 3–10'; leaves whorled; heads 5- to 8-flowered. In damp soil, Fla. to e Tex., n to sw Me., sw Que., Ia., Okla.

Sweet Joe-pye-weed, *E. purpureum,* to 7', herbage vanilla-scented if bruised; leaves in 2's to 5's; heads 3- to 7-flowered; in dry to moist woodlands, s N.H. to Minn. and Neb., s to Fla., Tenn., Okla.

Thoroughwort or **Boneset,** *E. perfoliatum,* 2–5', stems colonial, hairy; leaves united round the stem; heads 10- to 20-flowered; low woods, swales, wet shores, Que. to se Man., s to Fla., Tex.

E. occidentale, 6–30", stems colonial, leaves single or in pairs, petioled, toothed; heads 9- to 12-flowered, red, lilac, or white; rocky places, mts., cen. Wash. and Ida. to Calif., Utah.

E. incarnatum, 1–7', sprawling, much-branched; leaves paired; heads 20- to 25-flowered; rich woods and wooded swamps, Fla. to s Ariz., n to se Va., Mo., Okla.

White Snakeroot, *E. rugosum,* 2–4', few-stemmed; leaves paired, petioled; heads 15- to 20-flowered. In woods or clearings, lime soil, e N.A., w to Sask., Tex.

Upland Boneset, *E. sessilifolium,* 2–6', leaves paired, rarely in 3's, sessile, fine-toothed; corymb a dense cluster of 5-flowered heads; woodlands, Mass. to Ind., s to Ga., Ala., Mo.

Yankee Weed, *E. compositifolium,* to 10', leaves mostly alternate, pinnately segmented or upper ones entire; heads 3- to 5-flowered; fields, open woods, mostly in sandy soil, Fla. to s Tex., N.C.

Late Boneset, *E. serotinum,* 2–5', stems colonial; leaves mostly opposite, toothed, downy; heads 12- to 15-flowered, crowded in cymes; thickets, fields, se U.S., n to Mass., W.Va., Wisc., Kans.

E. maculatum

E. dubium

E. fistulosum

Eupatorium
coelestinum

purpureum

E. perfoliatum

E. occidentale

E. incarnatum

E. sessilifolium

E. rugosum

E. compositifolium

E. serotinum

CLIMBING HEMPWEED (MIKANIA) Twining vines with opposite leaves; heads 4-flowered, involucre of 4 bracts, otherwise like *Eupatorium* (p. 270); 3 species in e N.A. *M. scandens* has milk-white to purplish flowers. Found in swamps, thickets, stream banks, Fla. to Tex., n to se Me., s N.H., Mass., N.Y., s Ont.

FALSE BONESET (KUHNIA) Stems erect to decumbent; most leaves alternate; heads 1 to few, or in panicles; involucre bracts in 4–7 series, outer 2–4 series graduated in size; corollas white to yellowish or reddish; pappus 1 row of 10, 15, or 20 feathery bristles; 3 N.A. species. *K. eupatorioides*, 1–4', is erect; leaves narrow to oval, entire to toothed; heads 7- to 33-flowered; grows in open woods, plains, Mont. to N.J., s to Ariz., Fla.

TASSEL-FLOWER (BRICKELLIA) resembles *Kuhnia* but leaves are often opposite, involucre bracts more numerous, pappus rough or barbed, rarely feathery; 12 herbaceous species, of w N.A. *B. grandiflora*, 1–2', with long-petioled mostly alternate leaves, heads 20- to 30-flowered, grows in dry or limestone soil, B.C. to Mexico, e to Neb., Mo., Ark., w Tex.

BRISTLEHEAD (CARPOCHAETE)· One species, *C. bigelovii*, 8–20", bushy, woody at base; narrow entire resin-dotted leaves to 1", opposite or in tufts; solitary sessile 4- to 6-flowered heads at branch tips; pappus about 10 bristly scales; w Tex. to Ariz.

SCLEROLEPIS One species, *S. uniflora*, a creeping herb of swamps, shores, shallow water; erect 4–12" flowering stems, narrow entire leaves in whorls of 4–6; terminal solitary many-flowered heads to ½" wide; 1–2 series of equal involucre bracts; pappus 1 row of 5 horny scales. Ranges from Ala. and Fla. to N.H.

BLAZING-STAR and **BUTTON-SNAKEROOT** (LIATRIS) Stems simple, erect; narrow entire leaves alternate, resin-dotted; heads in spikes, racemes, or cymes, 4- to many-flowered; corolla lobes slender, rose-purple (rarely white); pappus 12–40 plumed or barbed hairs; 34 species, in e N.A. *L. spicata*, 1–6', grows in damp soil, s N.Eng. and Ont. to Wisc., s to Fla., La.; *L. pycnostachya*, to 6', heads 5- to 12-flowered, in damp prairies, Wisc. to S.D., s to Ky., La., and Tex.; *L. elegans*, 1–4', heads 5-flowered, in sand, S.C. to Tex., inland to Ark. and Okla.

CARPHEPHORUS resembles *Liatris* but outer flowers subtended by chaff; 4 species, of se U.S. *C. bellidifolius*, 8"–2', has an elongate corymb with up to 100 or more heads; dry sandy barrens, woods, Coastal Plain, Fla. to se Va.

Mikania scandens

Kuhnia eupatorioides

Brickellia grandiflora

Carpochaete bigelovii

Liatris spicata

L. pycnostachya

L. elegans

Sclerolepis uniflora

Carphephorus bellidifolius

III. Aster Tribe (Astereae)

Leaves alternate (rarely opposite); heads only of tube-flowers or also with marginal ray-flowers; tube-flowers mostly yellow, rays 3-lobed or 3-toothed; anthers not tailed; involucre bracts unequal, in few to many series; 49 genera in N.A.

GUMWEED (GRINDELIA) Coarse, often gummy herbs; leaves sessile or clasping, entire to toothed; heads terminal, many-flowered; involucre bracts with slender spreading tips, in 4–8 series; rays none to 45, yellow; pappus 2–10 scale-like to slender awns; 33 N.A. species, chiefly in w U.S. **Curly-cup,** *G. squarrosa,* 8–40″, rays 25–40 (none in var. *nuda* of s U.S.), grows in dry soil over most of U.S. except the SE.

BROOM-SNAKEROOT (GUTIERREZIA) Herbs or shrublets, usually resinous; leaves narrow, entire; heads of few to several flowers, with 1–10 yellow rays; involucre of about 3 graduated series; pappus 5–9 bristly or chaffy scales, shorter in ray-flowers; 11 N.A. species. *G. sarothrae* is many-branched, 6″–3′; heads of 3–6 tube-flowers, 3–7 rays; heads in small cylindric clusters. On dry plains, Man. to Alta., s to Calif. and Tex.

GOLDEN ASTER (CHRYSOPSIS) Low downy to woolly or sticky herbs; heads many-flowered, tube- and ray-flowers yellow; involucre bracts narrow, overlapped, in 3–9 graduated series; pappus of all flowers double, outer row short scale-like or fringed bristles, inner row long, hairlike; 39 N.A. species.

C. mariana, 1–2′, has gland-dotted herbage, silky when young. In woods and openings, Fla. to Tex., n to se N.Y., s Ohio.

C. oregona, 6–30″, is woody at base; leaves bristly-hairy; lacks ray-flowers. On sand and gravel bars, Wash. to s Calif.

Silkgrass, *C. graminifolia,* 8″–3′, leaves grasslike, is clothed in silvery silk. Grows in pine or oak woods, openings, Del. to n Fla., w to ne Okla., e Tex.

C. villosa, 8–30″, has both fine and coarse hairs; heads 3–63 per aerial stem, with 35–100 flowers per head. In open sunny places, B.C. to Sask., s to Mexico.

CAMPHORWEED (HETEROTHECA) is like *Chrysopsis* but ray-flowers lack pappus; 4 N.A. species. *H. subaxillaris,* 1–3′, has clasping upper leaves, basal leaves with lobed petioles. Grows in sandy soil, N.J. and Del. to Fla., w to Ill., Kans., and Ariz.

LAZY-DAISY (APHANOSTEPHUS) Leaves simple to pinnately lobed; heads solitary on the branch tips, disk hemispheric or conical, tube-flowers numerous, yellow; rays present, white to lavender or rose-purple, never yellow; 6 N.A. species. *A. skirrhobasis,* to 20″, grows in open sandy soil, Fla. to Okla., Tex.

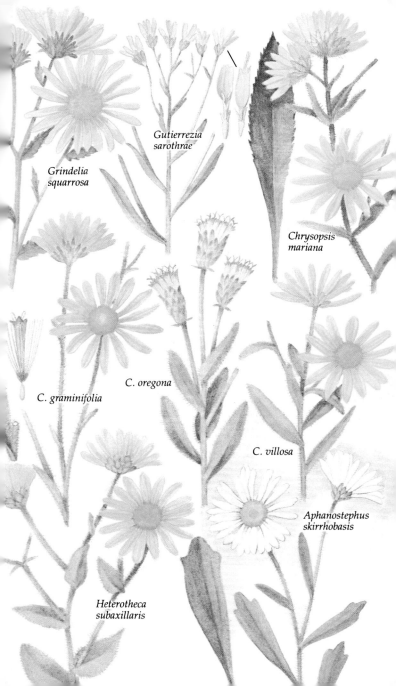

Grindelia squarrosa

Gutierrezia sarothrae

Chrysopsis mariana

C. graminifolia

C. oregona

C. villosa

Aphanostephus skirrhobasis

Heterotheca subaxillaris

DESERT STAR (MONOPTILON) Tiny herbs, forming tussocks; leaves narrow, entire; heads solitary at branch tips; involucre bracts in 1 series; tube-flowers yellow or purplish, rays white or pinkish; pappus many unequal bristles and short scales, or 1 feathery bristle; 2 SW species. *M. bellioides* forms clumps 10″ wide. In sandy or rocky soil, s Calif. to s Utah, w Ariz.

CHAETOPAPPA Low, often bushy herbs; leaves simple, entire and mostly sessile; heads solitary at branch tips; involucre bracts in 2–6 series; tube-flowers yellow; rays none to 70, rosy, bluish, white, or yellow; pappus absent or of scales, sometimes with a few awns; 11 sw species. *C. asteroides*, 2–12″, is common in dry soil, sw Mo., e Kans., and Ark. to Tex.

WESTERN DAISY (ASTRANTHIUM) Low branching plants; leaves blunt, entire; upper part of branches naked, heads at tips; involucre 1 series of bracts; many tiny yellow tube-flowers, many white rays; no pappus; 2 species, in s U.S. *A. integrifolium*, 4–12″, grows in sandy soil, nw Ga. to Tex., n to Kans., Ky.

DAISY (BELLIS) is European; **English Daisy,** *B. perennis*, 3–6″, is locally escaped, Nfld. to B.C., n U.S.; petioled downy leaves in a rosette; heads single, 1–2″ wide, on hairy stalks; tube-flowers yellow, rays numerous, narrow, white or rose.

BOLTONIA Slender wiry-branched herbs with small sessile entire leaves; heads small, at branch tips; involucre bracts in 2–5 series; tube-flowers yellow, on a hemispheric disk; rays white or lilac; pappus tiny pointed scales or broad bristles plus 2 awns (3 awns in ray-flowers); 4 N.A. species. **Doll's-daisy,** *B. diffusa*, 20–40″, grows in woods, fields, Fla. and sw Ga. to Tex., n to Ky., s Ill., Mo., and Okla.

TOWNSENDIA Low, few-branched gray-downy herbs; leaves sessile, entire; heads solitary at branch tips; involucre 3–5 series of bracts; tube-flowers yellow, often tinged pink or purple; rays numerous, white to bluish or purplish (yellow in *T. aprica* of s Utah); pappus 1 row of broad barbed bristles (in ray-flowers sometimes united in a scaly corona); 22 species of w N.A. *T. montana*, a dwarf tufted plant, has 12–30 white, pink, or bluish rays; in gravel or stony soil, mts., ne Oreg. to sw Mont. and w Wyo., s to Utah. *T. florifer*, to 10″, has 15–30 white or pink rays; grows in dry open sites at low elevations, cen. Wash. to w Wyo., s to Nev., Utah. *T. condensata* has sessile heads, 12–100 white, pink, or lilac rays; alpine, w Mont., e Ida., nw Wyo.

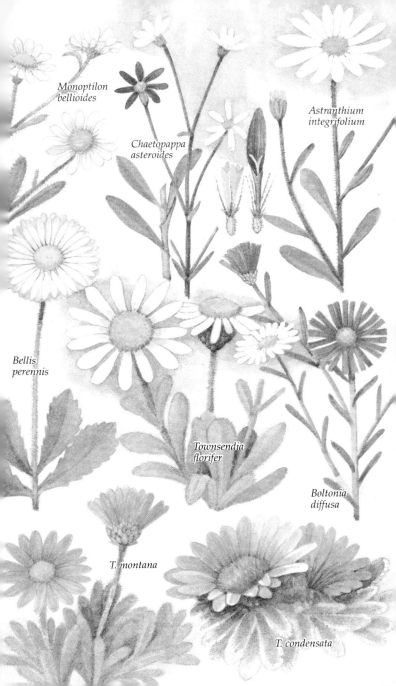

Monoptilon
bellioides

Chaetopappa
asteroides

Astranthium
integrifolium

Bellis
perennis

Townsendia
florifer

Boltonia
diffusa

T. montana

T. condensata

ASTER Leafy-stemmed herbs; leaves always alternate, usually sessile, never pinnately lobed, becoming small upward; heads at branch tips, mostly clustered; involucre bracts in several series, overlapped, unequal, outer ones green; tube-flowers yellowish, or tinged with blue, rose, or violet; ray-flowers in 1 or 2 series, white, bluish, violet, or rosy, never yellow; pappus 1 or 2 rows of many hairlike bristles. About 150 species in N.A., mostly showy, a few weedy.

Large-leaved Aster, *A. macrophyllus,* 8″–5′, has heart-shaped toothed basal leaves to 1′ wide; rays violet or pale blue, rarely white; open woods, clearings, se Que. to n Minn., s to Del., N.C., Ill.

Showy Aster, *A. spectabilis,* 1–3′; pale-green toothed leaves tapering to petioles, basal leaves tufted; involucre bracts in about 6 series; around 20 violet rays ½–¾′ long; in sandy open woods, clearings, e Mass. to N.C.

Prairie Aster, *A. turbinellus,* 2–4′; narrow entire leaves 2–5″ long; panicle to 2′ high, very open; heads with 15–25 violet rays; open woods, dry prairies, bluffs, Ill. to Neb., s to La., Kans.

New England Aster, *A. novae-angliae,* to 8′, leaves hairy, toothed, sessile and clasping; 40–50 violet-purple, rose, or white rays; damp thickets, meadows, shores, sw Que. to Alta., s to Del., w N.C., Ky., Ark., Kans., and Colo.; escaped elsewhere.

A. chilensis, 2–3′, leaves rough, fine-toothed or entire, lower ones sessile, clasping; heads with 15–40 white, pink, or violet rays; grows in various habitats, commonly in dry open places, mts., Sask. to Wash., s to s Calif., n Ariz., and s Colo.

A. alpigenus, a dwarf alpine plant to 18″ high, narrow entire leaves, basal ones in a tuft, to 10″ long; heads with 10–40 rose-purple rays; in mts., Wash. to w Mont. and w Wyo., s to s Calif., ne Nev.

A. curtissii, 2–5′, has long-petioled basal leaves, toothed or entire; stem leaves tapering to petioles; involucre bracts narrow, leaflike, curved outward; tube-flowers aging to magenta; in mt. woods, Ga. to N.C., Tenn.

Bristle-leaved Aster, *A. linariifolius,* stems in tussocks 4″–2′ high; narrow sharp-tipped leaves; heads solitary on bracted stalks; rays violet-blue; dry open soil or sandy pine-oak woods, se Canada and e U.S., w to Minn. and Tex.

Heath Aster, *A. ericoides,* 8″–7′, bushy, hairy, lower branches erect to reclined; leaves narrow, sessile; heads in 1-sided racemes, tube-flowers white, rarely blue, rose, or violet; rays white; dry open soil, Me. to s B.C., s to Ga., Ark., Tex., Ariz.

New York Aster, *A. novi-belgii,* 8–40″, leaves narrow, fine-toothed or entire, upper ones partly clasping; rays typically blue-violet, but rosy and white forms occur; damp thickets, meadows, shores, mostly within 100 miles of the sea, Nfld. to Ga.

A. spectabilis

Aster macrophyllus

A. turbinellus

A. alpigenus

A. chilensis

A. novae-angliae

A. linariifolius

A. curtissii

A. ericoides

A. novi-belgii

MACAERANTHERA is like *Aster* (p. 278) but most species have pin-nately or bipinnately lobed spine-tipped leaves; pappus of many brown unequal bristles, in some species the ray-flowers lack pappus; about 35 N.A. species. **Tahoka-daisy,** *M. tanacetifolia,* 4–16″, leaves bipinnate, heads 2″ wide, grows on plains and hills, Alta. to S.D., s to Mexico. **Hoary-** or **Piñon-aster,** *M. canescens,* 8–30″, is densely hairy, sticky on upper stem; in dry soil, s B.C. to Sask. and w N.D., s to w Kans., Ariz., Calif. *M. linearis,* 12–40″, with white, bluish, or violet-tinged rays, grows in open desert, Utah and Colo. to Ariz. and w Tex.

FLEABANE (ERIGERON) Daisylike usually downy herbs; leaves mostly sessile, entire or toothed, pinnately lobed or dissected in a few; heads solitary on naked stalks at branch tips; involucre bracts in 2–3 series, nearly equal; tube-flowers yellow; rays narrow, often in 2 series, white, pink, or purple; pappus lacking, or 1 row of hairs, or with a second row of short scales; about 140 N.A. species; some are unattractive weeds.

E. speciosus, 6–32″, has lance-like or oval leaves; up to 12 heads per stem; rays slender, 75–150 per head; open woods, to moderate heights in mts., s B.C. to S.D., s to Ariz., n N.M.

Daisy Fleabane, *E. philadelphicus,* 4–40″, basal leaves toothed or scalloped, stem leaves with basal "ears"; 100 or more rays per head; in damp soil, throughout the U.S. and most of Canada.

Running Fleabane, *E. flagellaris,* 2–16″, trails; leaves entire to toothed or lobed; heads on erect stalks; 50–100 white, pink, or blue rays; in open places, S.D., Wyo., and Nev., s to Tex. and Ariz.; also s B.C.

Robin's-plantain, *E. pulchellus,* has long whiplike runners, ro-settes of leaves at the tips; leaves scalloped or toothed; heads 2–7 per corymb, with about 50 broad blue-purple to whitish rays per head; se Canada, e U.S.

HAPLOPAPPUS Plants of diverse modes of growth; herbaceous, or with a caudex, or partly woody, or shrubs; leaves simple and entire to toothed, pinnately lobed, or dissected, spiny in some; heads many-flowered, solitary on scape-like stalks to clustered in corymbs; involu-cre of overlapped bracts; disk flat, tube-flowers yellow; rays none to many, yellow (white in 1 woody species); pappus 1 row of many unequal bristles; about 70 N.A. species, mostly in w N.A. *H. armer-ioides,* 2–8″, has narrow entire mostly basal leaves to 4″ long, solitary heads with 7–15 rays; inhabits dry hills, plains, Mont. and Sask. to Neb., N.M., and Ariz. *H. spinulosus,* 1–2′, with pinnately or bipinnately cleft leaves, bristle-tipped involucre bracts, grows on prairies, plains, Alta. and Sask. to Minn., s to Tex., Baja Calif. **Jimmy-weed,** *H. hetero-phyllus,* 8–32″, has narrow entire leaves, rayless heads in corymbs; in open, often alkaline soil, from Tex. to Ariz.

Macaeranthera tanacetifolia

M. canescens

M. linearis

Erigeron speciosus

E. flagellaris

E. philadelphicus

E. pulchellus

Haplopappus armerioides

H. heterophyllus

H. spinulosus

GOLDENROD (SOLIDAGO) Stems long and slender, branched in the upper head-bearing portion; leaves alternate, narrow to lance-like, rarely heart-shaped, entire to toothed; never lobed; basal leaves sometimes petioled, other chiefly sessile; heads small, few- to many-flowered, in racemes or clusters; ray-flowers 1–20 or so, both tube- and ray-flowers yellow (rarely cream-color). About 90 N.A. species.

S. altissima, 2–6′, often has numerous stems; leaves crowded, lance-like; herbage downy-gray; heads in a pyramidal panicle 2–12″ high, of long curving branches; Que., Ont., and e U.S., w to Minn., Wyo., Ariz.

Blue-stem Goldenrod, *S. caesia*, 8–40″, has smooth green or purple stems covered by waxy bloom; smooth sharply toothed leaves; heads in a leafy panicle or in loose axillary clusters; rays 3–4 per head; in woods and clearings, Fla. to Tex., n to Wisc., N.S.

S. decumbens, 6–12″, has erect or reclined stems, solitary or in tufts; leaves toothed or scalloped, rounded, tapering to petioles; panicle spike-like; Alaska and Mackenz. to Sask., s in mts. to Mexico; also n Mich.; Va. mts.

S. missouriensis has solitary 4–40″ stems, narrow entire or toothed leaves with ciliated edges; a terminal panicle 1–8″ wide, heads 15- to 25-flowered; dry prairies, rocky slopes, s B.C. to Mich., s to Oreg., Ariz., Tex., Mo., Tenn.

Silver-rod, *S. bicolor*, 8–32″, has scalloped or fine-toothed basal leaves; herbage with ash-gray down; heads in a spike-like panicle; tube-flowers yellow; 7–9 rays, whitish or cream; dry open sterile soil, Ga. to Ark., n to s Ont., sw Que., Me., N.B., C.B.

Early Goldenrod, *S. nemoralis*, has clumped 1–2′ stems from a caudex; heads in a 1-sided panicle, of 3–5 tube-flowers, 5–9 rays; dry open soil, P.E.I. and N.B. to Alta., s to Ga., the Gulf States, N.M., and Ariz.

S. occidentalis, 2–7′, a smooth herb, has narrow 2–4″ leaves not much smaller upward; heads in small tight clusters toward the tips of an open leafy panicle; moist low ground, s B.C. to Alta., s to Calif., Ariz., N.M., and w Neb.

Sweet Goldenrod, *S. odora*, 20–40″, has narrow lance-like sessile leaves with pellucid dots, anise-scented if bruised; heads in 1-sided racemes combined in a 1-sided panicle; heads 6- to 8-flowered, rays 3–4; in dry open sites, e U.S., w to Mo., Okla., Tex.

S. squarrosa, 8″–5′ tall, rosette leaves coarsely toothed, 3–12″ long, 1–4″ wide; upper leaves small, entire; heads in a spike, rays 12–16; in dry open woods, clearings, se Canada, s to Del., W.Va., Ky., upland to N.C.

Seaside Goldenrod, *S. sempervirens*, 8″–8′, has thick entire sessile stem leaves, lower ones clasping; wide-petioled basal leaves; heads large, mostly stalked, with 12–40 tube-flowers, 8–10 rays, in a loose panicle; saline to fresh marshes, near coast, Fla. to Nfld., se Tex.

Solidago
altissima

S. caesia

S. missouriensis

S. decumbens

S. bicolor

S. nemoralis

S. occidentalis

S. sempervirens

S. odora

S. squarrosa

IV. Everlasting Tribe (Inuleae)

Leaves are alternate or basal, mostly entire; heads only of tube-flowers, or with marginal ray-flowers; tube corollas often threadlike, unlobed, anthers tailed at base; involucre bracts usually dry scales, in several series, sometimes leafy or petal-like; 16 genera in N.A.

MARSH-FLEABANE (PLUCHEA) Aromatic silky herbs; leaves fine-toothed or scalloped; heads in terminal clusters; involucre bracts overlapped, barely scaly; heads many-flowered, all tubular, central ones 5-lobed, all others threadlike; pappus 1 row of hairlike bristles; 6 herbaceous species in N.A. *P. purpurascens*, 2–4' high, grows in saline or fresh marshes, mud, s half of U.S. **Stinking-fleabane,** *P. foetida*, 20–32", is chiefly coastal, in mud, wet sand, Fla. to Tex., n to s N.J., se Mo.

TRAIL-PLANT (ADENOCAULON) One species, *A. bicolor*, 1–3' tall; most leaves basal, triangular, smooth above, woolly beneath; a few small heads in a loose glandular panicle; involucre bracts in 1 series; heads of 5–10 tube-flowers; no pappus; grows in moist woods, upper Great Lakes to S.D.; s B.C. to w Mont., s to Calif.

BLACKROOT (PTEROCAULON) Stems simple, erect; narrow sessile entire leaves, woolly beneath, bases winged down the stem; heads in a dense terminal spike, only tube-flowers, central ones 5-lobed, the others threadlike; pappus 1 row of bristles; 2 N.A. species. **Rabbit-tobacco,** *P. undulatum*, 1–3' tall, grows in pinelands, Coastal Plain, Fla. to Miss. and N.C.

FACELIS One species, *F. retusa*, 2–8" high, decumbent gray-woolly branches, sessile spatula-shaped leaves, has heads in tight leafy clusters at the branch tips, all tube-flowers, central ones 5-lobed and perfect, outer ones threadlike, female; pappus many feathery bristles; S.A., now wide-ranging in sandy soil, se U.S., n to N.C., w to e Tex.

EVERLASTING (ANAPHALIS) One species in N.A., **Pearly Everlasting,** *A. margaritacea*, 1–3', erect, leaves narrow, woolly; heads in corymbs, bracts pearly-white, no rays; grows in dry sand or gravel, to subalpine areas, Nfld. to Alaska, s to N.C., S.D., N.M., Calif.

INULA is Eurasian; **Elecampane,** *I. helenium*, 2–6' tall, escaped to roadsides and fields, N.S. to N.C., Mo.; w Oreg. Leaves are large, unequally toothed, velvety beneath, rough above, basal ones petioled, upper sessile, clasping; heads 2–4" wide; involucre bracts leafy; numerous long narrow marginal ray-flowers.

*Pluchea
foetida*

*Pluchea
purpurascens*

*Pterocaulon
undulatum*

*Adenocaulon
bicolor*

*Facelis
retusa*

*Anaphalis
margaritacea*

Inula helenium

COTTON-ROSE (FILAGO) Low branching woolly herbs; leaves entire; disk raised, chaffy; only tube-flowers, the central ones 5-lobed, with hairlike pappus, no chaff; outer ones threadlike, chaffy, no pappus; 11 species in N.A. **Herba Impia,** *F. germanica,* to 1' high, is European, naturalized in dry fields, from s N.Y. to Ohio, s to Ga. *F. californica,* 2–12" tall, is common in dry open soil, from Utah to s Ariz. and s Calif.

PUSSY'S-TOES and **EVERLASTING** (ANTENNARIA) Woolly or silky herbs with simple stems from a rhizome; leaves entire; heads usually clustered, rarely single, all of tube-flowers; males and females are borne on separate plants; involucre bracts dry, scaly, in males with petal-like tips; pappus a ring of hairlike bristles in females, the tips thickened in males; disk not chaffy. About 85 N.A. species.

Rosy Everlasting, *A. rosea,* has mat-forming basal branches; flowering stems erect, 2–12"; tiny heads in 1" terminal clusters, bracts white or rosy; in dry open soil, Alaska to n Ont., s in mts. to Calif., Ariz., N.M.

A. plantaginifolia forms close or open mats, basal shoots end in rosettes; flowering stems in females 2–12" high with 3–30 heads, corollas often red; males 1–7" high. In fields, open woods, Me. to Minn., s to Ga., Mo.

A. parvifolia is a low matted herb with crowded ascending basal offshoots; flowering stems erect, 1–6"; bract tips whitish, long in female heads, broad in males; Great Plains and e base of Rocky Mts., w to B.C., Ariz.

A. solitaria creeps by long threadlike runners tipped by rosettes; heads single at the tips of 1–14" erect stems, male and female plants alike; in rich woods, clearings, Md. and w Pa. to Ind., s to Ga. and La.

CUDWEED (GNAPHALIUM) Woolly herbs; leaves sessile, bases often winged down the stem; heads many-flowered, all whitish or yellowish tube-flowers, outer ones threadlike; involucre bracts overlapped in several rows, dry, white or colored; 29 species in N.A.

Cotton-batting, *G. chilense,* has several erect or reclining stems to 2', clasping aromatic leaves, heads in round clusters; in open moist sites, w Wash. and sw B.C. to Mont., s to s Calif., Tex.

Purple Cudweed, *G. purpureum,* 4–12", often several-stemmed, has heads in a terminal spike, lower part leafy; involucre bracts brown to purple; in dry soil, Fla. to Calif., n to s N.Eng., Oreg.

Catfoot, *G. obtusifolium,* 4"–5', has sessile leaves, not winged on stem; young herbage densely woolly; heads in dense globular corymbs; grows in dry open soil, Gulf States, n to e Canada.

Clammy Cudweed, *G. macounii,* 1–3', stem glandular below, sometimes to tip; leaves winged down the stem; dry open soil, s B.C. to Que., widespread s in U.S. except SE.

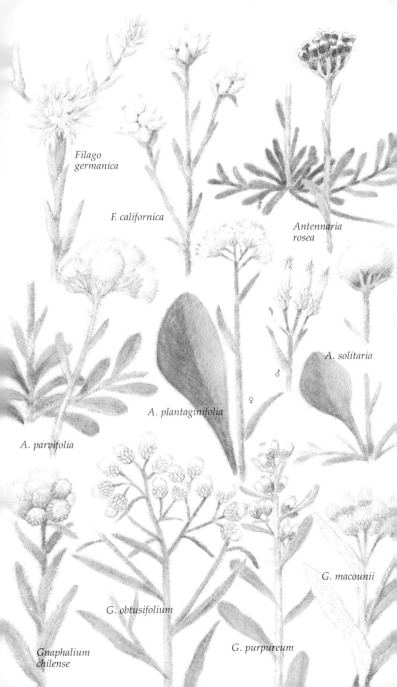

Filago
germanica

F. californica

Antennaria
rosea

A. solitaria

A. plantaginifolia

♂

♀

A. parvifolia

G. macounii

G. obtusifolium

Gnaphalium
chilense

G. purpureum

V. Sunflower Tribe (Heliantheae)

Lower leaves are often opposite; heads mostly with both tube- and ray-flowers; involucre bracts usually herbaceous, in 1 to many series; all or outer tube-flowers with chaff; anthers not tailed; pappus never of hairlike bristles; style branched or simple; 79 genera in N.A.

BLACK-FOOT (MELAMPODIUM) Stems forking; leaves paired, sessile, entire or lobed; heads solitary, stalked, arising at middle or upper forks; outer involucre cuplike, of 5 bracts; each inner bract encloses the base of a ray-flower; few to many tube-flowers, yellow, 5-lobed; 5 species in SW. *M. longicorne*, to 1', has long coiled tips on inner involucre bracts; in limestone canyons, s N.M., se Ariz. *M. leucanthum*, 6–20", has entire to pinnately lobed glandular-hairy leaves, heads 1–1½" wide; grows in limestone soil, Ariz. to Tex., n to Colo. and Kans.

GREEN-EYES (BERLANDIERA) Stems branched, decumbent to erect; leaves alternate, simple, sessile to long-petioled; herbage downy to rough-hairy; involucre bracts in about 3 series, inner ones larger; tube-flowers red to maroon, with chaff; rays 2–13, usually 8; virtually no pappus; 5 species in s U.S. *B. lyrata*, to 4', has velvety leaves, the lower ones long-petioled; heads ½" wide; grows in dry limestone soil, Tex. to Ariz., n to Colo., Kans. *B. pumila*, to 28", is sometimes woody at base, heads to ¾" wide; in sandy soil, Fla. to Tex. and S.C.

ENGELMANN DAISY (ENGELMANNIA) One species, *E. pinnatifida*; 1 to several stems, 8–20" tall; leaves pinnately lobed, basal ones 8–12" long; upper 4" of plant much branched, each ending in a head; tube-flowers yellow, 5-toothed, chaffy; rays usually 8, each subtended by an involucre bract; ray pappus a few scales; open limestone soil, Neb. and Colo. to Tex. and N.M.

PARTHENIUM Bitter aromatic plants; leaves alternate, entire to toothed, lobed, or divided; heads small, woolly, many-flowered, single or in terminal panicles; involucre cuplike, of 2 series; tube-flowers white, male, with chaff; rays none or 5, with short broad corollas; pappus 2 or 3 awns, 2 scales, or absent; 9 herbaceous species in N.A. **Santa Maria,** *P. hysterophorus*, 1–3', has a hairy single stem from a rosette; leaves once- or twice-pinnately lobed, hairy; pappus 2 petal-like scales; a Trop. Am. immigrant, in wastelands from Fla. to Tex., n to Mass., Mich., and Okla. **Wild Quinine,** *P. integrifolium*, 16"–4', has unlobed toothed leaves; in dry open woods, prairies, Ga. to Tex., n to Mass., se N.Y., W.Va., Mich., Wisc., and Minn.

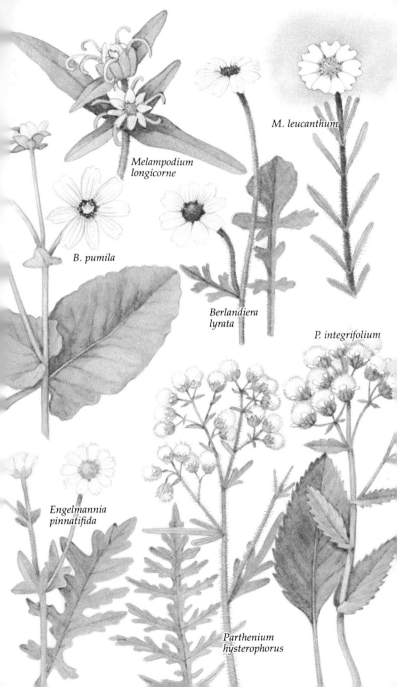

Melampodium longicorne

M. leucanthum

B. pumila

Berlandiera lyrata

P. integrifolium

Engelmannia pinnatifida

Parthenium hysterophorus

ZINNIA Low bushy plants; entire sessile leaves in pairs; heads at stem and branch tips; involucre bracts overlapped, dry; tube-flowers 5-toothed, 1 tooth elongated; rays present; disk chaffy; pappus of awns; 4 species, in SW. **Desert Zinnia,** *Z. acerosa,* to 6″, grows in desert or desert grasslands, Tex. to Ariz. *Z. grandiflora,* 3–9″, is common in dry limestone areas, Kans. to Nev., s to Tex. and Ariz. *Z. multiflora,* to 12″, is a tropical species ranging n to Ariz.; Fla.

SANVITALIA Low downy herbs; leaves paired, petioled to sessile, sheathing stem at base; heads terminal; disk conical, chaffy; tube-flowers 5-lobed; rays entire or 2-lobed; pappus 1–4 awns or none; 2 SW species. *S. albertii,* to 10″ tall, with 5 to 9 2-lobed rays, grows in mts. at about 4000′, from w Tex. to Ariz.

DESERT-SUNFLOWER (GERAEA) Leaves alternate, petioled to sessile, entire to toothed; herbage both downy and hairy; heads large, terminal, rayed or rayless; involucre bracts in 2 to 3 series; tube-flowers 5-lobed, chaffy; pappus 2 slender awns; 2 SW species. *G. canescens,* 8–24″, heads 2½″ wide with about 20 rays, is common in sandy soil, s Utah to se Calif., Ariz.

CROWN-BEARD (VERBESINA) Downy herbs; leaves opposite or alternate, toothed, base often winged down the stem; clustered or solitary heads; involucre bracts in 2 to several series, overlapped; disk conic to globular, chaffy; tube-flowers 5-toothed, yellow or white; rays none to many, tips 3-toothed or 3-lobed, yellow or white; pappus 2 awns or absent; 15 N.A. species.

Wingstem, *V. alternifolia,* 3–6′, stem somewhat hairy, winged above; leaves opposite, alternate, or in 3's; rays irregular, 2–8; in thickets, woodland borders, Fla. to Tex., n to e Ont., Ia.

Yellow Crown-beard, *V. occidentalis,* 3–6′, stem 4-winged; leaves opposite, toothed; heads slender, in compound corymbs; rays 1–5; grows in woods, openings, Fla. to Miss., n to Pa., Ill.

Cowpen Daisy, *V. encelioides,* 4″–3′, much-branched, downy; leaves mostly paired, toothed, often clasping; heads 1″ wide; in open soil, Mont. to Ariz., e to Kans., Tex.; local to N.Eng.

Tickweed or **Frostweed,** *V. virginica,* 3–6′, stem 4- to 5-winged below, not in head-bearing part; rays 1–5; tube- and ray-flowers are whitish. In dry open woods, Fla. to Tex., n to Kans., Pa.

COSMOS One species, *C. parviflorus,* an erect 1–3′ branching herb with opposite twice-pinnately dissected leaves; heads solitary, to 1″ wide, on 4–12″ stalks; usually 8 spreading outer involucre bracts, inner ones shorter; tube-flowers 5-toothed, yellow; about 8 white to rosy rays, tips 3-toothed; pappus 2–4 erect barbed awns. Grows in moist meadows, Tex. to Ariz., n to Colo.

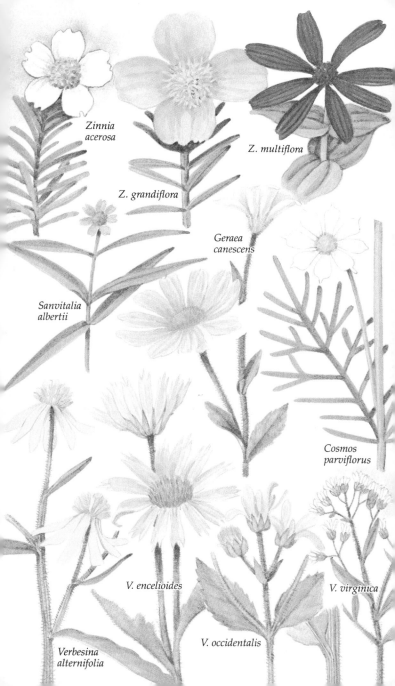

Zinnia acerosa

Z. grandiflora

Z. multiflora

Geraea canescens

Sanvitalia albertii

Cosmos parviflorus

V. encelioides

V. virginica

V. occidentalis

Verbesina alternifolia

NERVE-RAY (TETRAGONOTHECA) Leaves are paired, toothed to lobed, sessile or fused at base; single terminal heads; outer 4 involucre bracts leafy, inner ones small, each subtending a ray-flower; disk conic, chaffy; tube-flowers 5-toothed; rays 6–15, yellow, veins often red; no pappus; 4 species, in s U.S. **Pineland-ginseng,** *T. helianthoides,* has 1–3' simple stems, 3"-wide heads; in sandy soil, Fla. to Miss., n to Va. and Tenn.

ROSINWEED (SILPHIUM) Tall coarse herbs; juice resinous; leaves alternate or paired, entire to pinnately lobed, upper ones sessile; heads many-flowered; involucre of few series, outer broad, leafy; disk flat, with narrow chaff; tube-flowers 5-toothed; rays in 2–3 rows; pappus 2 teeth or none; 17 species in e, cen. U.S. **Compass-plant,** *S., laciniatum,* 2–12' tall, is rough-bristly; leaves alternate, pinnately lobed, petioles dilated, clasping, lower leaves 1–3' long; heads 2–5" wide; inhabits prairies, Mich. to N.D., s to Ala. and Tex. **Cup-plant,** *S. perfoliatum,* has 4–8' 4-angled stems, toothed 6–12" opposite leaves, bases of upper ones united in a cup; heads 2–3" wide; in woods, prairies, s N.Eng. and s Ont. to S.D., s to Ga. and Okla.

LEAF-CUP (POLYMNIA) Tall branched sticky-hairy herbs of rank odor; leaves large, lobed, lower ones opposite; heads in panicled corymbs; involucre in 2 rows, outer larger; disk flat, chaffy; tube-flowers yellow; rays in 1 row, 5–15 (rarely none), yellow or white; no pappus; 3 species, e N.A. **Bear's-foot,** *P. uvedalia,* 3–10', lower leaves palmate on winged petioles, upper almost sessile, angled and toothed, has heads to 3½" wide. Grows in woods, N.Y. to Fla., w to Ill., Okla., and Tex.

BARBARA'S-BUTTONS (MARSHALLIA) Low smooth herbs with alternate entire leaves, solitary terminal heads, only of 5-lobed tube-flowers; involucre bracts in 1–2 rows, leafy; disk chaffy, convex to conic; pappus 5–6 scales; 8 species, in SE. *M. caespitosa* has white, cream, or pink-tinged 1" heads on 6–16" stems; in prairies, openings, from Miss. to Tex., n to Okla., s Mo. *M. graminifolia,* 12–18", with grasslike leaves, grows in wet pine barrens, plains, Coastal Plain, Fla. to La. and N.C.

GOLDEN-STAR (CHRYSOGONUM) One species, *C. virginianum,* 1–2', is at first low or stemless; leaves paired, long-petioled, edges scalloped, rarely toothed, blades 1–2" long; heads solitary on long stalks, to 1½" wide; involucre of 5 leafy bracts and 5 inner scales; disk flat, with narrow scaly chaff; tube-flowers 5-lobed; rays about 5, broad; pappus a 2- to 3-toothed crown; rich woods, shaded rocks, Pa. and W.Va. to Fla., La.

*Tetragonotheca
helianthoides*

*Silphium
laciniatum*

S. perfoliatum

*Polymnia
uvedalia*

*Marshallia
caespitosa*

M. graminifolia

*Chrysogonum
virginianum*

HIERBA DEL CABALLO (CALYPTOCARPUS) One species, *C. vialis*; stems low, sprawling, to 2' long; paired fine-toothed petioled leaves; small solitary heads on axillary stalks; involucre about 5 bracts; disk chaffy; tube-flowers 5-toothed; rays about 5; pappus 2 awns; inhabits wastelands, lawns, from Fla. to Tex.

SEA OX-EYE (BORRICHIA) has many stiffly ascending branches; leaves nearly entire, paired; heads stalked, solitary, terminal; involucre bracts overlapped; disk flat, with rigid chaff; tube-flowers 5-lobed, anthers blackish; rays 15–30, 3-toothed; pappus a low 4-toothed crown; 2 species, in SE. *B. frutescens*, 1–3', has fine-silky 1–4" leaves, often toothed near base; chaff spiny; in salt marshes, Fla. to Tex., n to e Va.

OX-EYE (HELIOPSIS) Simple or loosely branched herbs with opposite petioled leaves, coarsely toothed, 3-veined; heads terminal; involucre bracts overlapped, in 2–3 rows; disk conic, with narrow chaff partly enclosing the yellow to brown or purple tube-flowers; rays 10 or more, notched at tip; no pappus; 3 N.A. species. *H. helianthoides*, 3–5' high, heads 3" wide, rays 12–14, grows in open woods, on dry banks, s Ont. to B.C., s in e U.S. to Ga., w to the Dakotas, Neb., Colo., and N.M.

BUR-MARIGOLD (BIDENS) Leaves opposite, entire to toothed or variously dissected, upper leaves sometimes alternate; heads in most many-flowered; involucre double, outer bracts leafy; disk flat or convex, chaffy; tube-flowers 5-toothed; 3–10 or no rays, tips 3-lobed; pappus 1–8 awns, often barbed, or absent; about 30 N.A. species, some weedy.

Tickseed-sunflower, *B. aristosa*, 1–5', has pinnate or bipinnate petioled toothed leaves; heads 1–2" wide, rays 6–10; in low soil, N.Eng. to Minn., s to Ala., Tex.

Spanish-needles, *B. bipinnata*, 1–5'; leaves bi- or tripinnate; heads ¼" wide, rays tiny, entire or 2–3-lobed; in woods, wastelands, SE, n to Mass., Kans.

Water-marigold, *B. beckii*, has finely divided submersed leaves, simple aerial ones with comblike lobes; heads 1½" wide; ponds, slow streams, C.B. to Minn., s to N.J., Mo.; also Wash., Oreg.

Stick-tight, *B. cernua*, 1"–6'; leaves entire to toothed; heads rayed or rayless, erect, nodding in fruit; low wet sites, Alaska and temperate Canada, s over n U.S. to N.C., Okla., Colo., Calif.

TIDY-TIPS (BLEPHARIPAPPUS) One species, *B. scaber*, 4–12" tall, with narrow alternate leaves; heads single or clustered at branch tips, few-flowered; involucre bracts in 1–2 rows, sticky-hairy; disk chaffy; 2–7 broad white 3-lobed rays, purple-veined below; pappus of narrow fringed scales, or lacking. Grows on grassy prairies, foothills, from se Wash. and Ida. to n Calif. and nw Nev.

Calyptocarpus
vialis

Borrichia
frutescens

Heliopsis
helianthoides

Bidens
aristosa

Bidens
beckii

Blepharipappus
scaber

Bidens
cernua

Bidens
bipinnata

PRAIRIE-CONEFLOWER (RATIBIDA) Erect herbs, often branched above; leaves alternate, pinnately divided; heads single at tips of naked branches; involucre bracts in 2 rows; "disk" a grayish column, chaffy; tube-flowers 5-lobed; rays few, drooping, faintly 3-toothed; pappus 2 teeth or none; 4 N.A. species. *R. pinnata*, 3–5', has disk ½–1" long; anise-scented if bruised; rays 5–10, yellow, 1–2" long; grows in dry soil, s Ont., s to Ga., Ark., and Okla. *R. tagetes*, 6–16", is bushy; heads short-stalked, often in clusters; disk ⅓–½" high; rays 5–7, maroon at base or all over; on dry plains, Tex. to Ariz., n to Kans. and Colo. **Mexican Hat**, *R. columnifera*, 8"–4', is basally branched; disk 1–2" long; rays 3–7, yellow or maroon; grows in dry soil, Man. to se B.C., s to Mexico.

PURPLE-CONEFLOWER (ECHINACEA) has stout erect stems, simple alternate leaves, entire to toothed, lower ones petioled; upper stem naked, a single large head at tip; involucre bracts in 3–4 series; disk conic, its spine-tipped chaff longer than the yellow or purple 5-lobed tube-flowers; rays mostly drooping, 2- or 3-lobed, rose, purple, white, or yellow; pappus a small toothed rim; 7 N.A. species. **Black Sampson**, *E. angustifolia*, 4–20", rays about 1" long; grows on dry prairies, Minn. to Sask., s to Tex. *E. pallida*, 16"–3', rays 2"–3" long, inhabits prairies, barrens, Mich. to Mont., s to Ga. and Tex. *E. purpurea*, 2–6', rays 1–2" long, in dry open woods and prairies, ranges from Ga. to La., Okla., and ne Tex.; n to Ia., Ohio, and Va.

CONEFLOWER (RUDBECKIA) Leaves alternate, simple or compound; heads terminal; involucre leafy; disk conic to columnar, chaffy; tube-flowers 5-toothed, brown; rays long, vaguely 3-toothed, yellow, rarely reddish; no pappus; 24 N.A. species.

R. amplexicaulis, 8–32" tall, has sessile heart-shaped leaves that clasp the stem; disk ½–1" long; grows in moist ground, Ga. to Tex., n to Mo. and Kans.

Black-eyed Susan, *R. hirta*, 1–3', is rough-hairy; leaves simple, upper ones sessile; disk hemispheric; open woods, fields, Nfld. to Fla., w to B.C., Calif.

R. laciniata, 2–10', has pinnate leaves of 5–7 lobed leaflets, upper leaves sessile; disk dome-like, to 1" wide; on low ground, Que. to Mont., s to Fla., Ariz.

Orange Coneflower, *R. fulgida*, 1½–4', has runners tipped by tufts of leaves; moist or dry, open or shady sites, N.J. to Mo. and Okla., s to N.C., Ark., Tex.

R. occidentalis, 2–6', has entire to toothed or lobed leaves to 10" long; no ray-flowers; in woods, on stream banks, Wash. to n Calif., e to sw Mont., Utah.

R. bicolor, 8"–3', has small mostly sessile leaves; bristle-tipped chaff; base of rays purple or brown; in dry soil, Ala. to La., n to s Ind., s Mo., Okla.

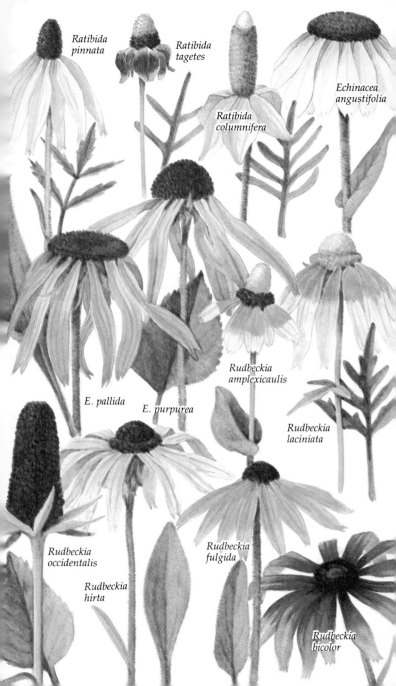

Ratibida pinnata

Ratibida tagetes

Ratibida columnifera

Echinacea angustifolia

E. pallida

E. purpurea

Rudbeckia amplexicaulis

Rudbeckia laciniata

Rudbeckia occidentalis

Rudbeckia hirta

Rudbeckia fulgida

Rudbeckia bicolor

BALSAMROOT (BALSAMORHIZA) Leaves in basal rosettes, petioled, entire to pinnate; heads solitary or few, on scape-like stems; involucre bracts in several rows, outermost sometimes leafy; disk convex, chaffy; tube-flowers 5-toothed, yellow; rays yellow (rosy in 1); no pappus; 11 species, in w N.A. *B. hookeri* has pinnately lobed 4–16″ leaves, solitary heads to 3″ wide on 2–16″ stems, 10–16 rays; on dry plains, w-cen. Ida. to sw Wyo. and nw Colo., s to Calif., Utah; also cen. Wash. *B. sagittata* has entire leaves to 1′ long, silvery when young; heads solitary, 2½–4″ wide, on 4–32″ stems, 8–25 rays; in open hills, flats, s B.C. to s Calif., e to S.D. and Colo.

MULE'S-EARS (WYETHIA) Heads similar to *Balsamorhiza* but stem very leafy, with or without basal rosettes; leaves simple, alternate; 14 species, in w N.A. *W. angustifolia*, 8″–3′, is hairy; leaves entire to toothed, petioled to sessile; heads 2–4″ wide, rays 13–21; grows in meadows, moist open hills, n Oreg. to San Luis Obispo Co., Calif. *W. helianthoides*, 8–32″, is sparsely to densely hairy; leaves entire or nearly so, petioles often winged; rays about 16, white, cream, or yellow; in moist mountain meadows, cen., e Oreg. to sw Mont., nw Wyo., and n Nev.

HELIANTHELLA Leafy-stemmed; leaves simple, entire, all or lower ones opposite; heads terminal, often solitary; involucre bracts in several rows; disk flat or convex, chaffy; tube-flowers 5-toothed, yellow or maroon; rays yellow; pappus a row of scales and 2 awns; 6 species, in w N.A. *H. quinquenervis* has several 2–5′ stems from a caudex; long-petioled lower leaves, upper ones sessile; heads 3–5″ wide, rays 13–21; in mountain meadows, woods, e Ida. and sw Mont. to S.D., s to N.M. and Ariz.

ENCELIOPSIS Silvery or woolly herbs; simple petioled leaves in basal tufts from a caudex; heads as in *Helianthella*, solitary (in 1 species without rays); 3 species, in arid w U.S. *E. nudicaulis*, 4–20″, heads 2¾–4¾″ wide, rays about 21, ranges from Ida. to n Ariz., Nev.

GOLDEN-EYE (VIGUIERA) Lower or all leaves opposite, simple, entire to toothed, sessile or nearly so; heads terminal; involucre bracts in 2–5 rows, bases ribbed; disk conic to flat, with keeled chaff; tube-flowers 5-toothed, yellow or brownish; rays yellow; pappus 2 awns and a few short scales, or none; 11 herbaceous species in N.A. *V. porteri*, 1–4′, is bristly, with narrow pointed leaves to 6″ long; heads 3″ wide; on granite, Ga. mts. *V. multiflora*, 1–4′, has rough 1–3″ leaves, heads ¾–1½″ wide; dry hills, from Mont. to N.M., Ariz., and e Calif.

Balsamorhiza
hookeri

W. helianthoides

Wyethia
angustifolia

B. sagittata

Enceliopsis
nudicaulis

V. porteri

Helianthella
quinquenervis

Viguiera
multiflora

SUNFLOWER (HELIANTHUS) Rather coarse herbs; stem simple or branched; leaves simple, in most rough-textured, lower ones always opposite, the others often alternate; heads terminal, solitary or in corymbs, on nearly naked stalks; involucre bracts in 2–4 rows, green, sometimes leafy; disk flat to low-conical, chaffy; tube-flowers numerous, 5-toothed, yellow to red, brown, or purple; rays in 1 series, yellow, 3-toothed at tip; about 50 N.A. species.

Common Sunflower, *H. annuus,* 3–12', leaves mostly alternate, long-petioled, heart-shaped to oval, toothed; heads 3–6" wide in wild plants, rays 12–35; in open rich soil, s Canada, U.S.

Showy Sunflower, *H. laetiflorus,* 2–8', is stiffly erect; leaves slightly toothed, sessile; stem and leaves rough but shining; heads 2–4" wide, rays 15–20; in open woods, prairies, Que. to Sask., s to Ga., N.M.

Jerusalem Artichoke, *H. tuberosus,* has 5–10' grooved branching stems, upper leaves alternate, fine-toothed, petiole winged; heads 2–3½" wide, 10–20 rays; in damp soil, Ont. to Sask. and Mont., s to Ga., Ark., n-cen. Tex., Colo.

H. maximiliani has 2–12' stems, simple below the heads; leaves alternate, downy, narrow, often infolded; heads 2–3" wide, rays 10–25; dry open places, Man. to se B.C., s, e of Rocky Mts., to Mo., Tex.; escaped in e U.S.

Dark-eyed Sunflower, *H. atrorubens,* has 2–5' stems, forked above; large oval toothed or scalloped leaves near base on long winged petioles; middle and upper leaves tiny, alternate; heads in corymbs, about 2" wide; open woods, Fla. to La., n to Va.

Swamp Sunflower, *H. angustifolius,* 2–5', stem bristly, paniculately branched above; leaves sessile, alternate, narrow, 4–8" long, edges rolled down; heads 2–3" wide; in moist acid soil, bogs and pinelands, Fla. to Tex., n to L.I., e Pa., Ind., and Ia.

H. nuttallii, 2–7', stem erect, often with "bloom"; short-petioled mostly opposite leaves, entire or nearly so; heads 1½–3¼" wide, rays usually 10–16; in moist places, Sask. to se B.C., s to N.M., Ariz., Nev., ne Oreg.

Blue-weed, *H. ciliaris,* has 1 to several 20–28" stems; leaves lance-like, mostly opposite, entire to pinnately lobed; herbage smooth, with "bloom"; heads 1¼–1¾" wide grows in fields, desert, Tex. to Calif., n to Kans.

H. divaricatus, 2–5', stem simple or branched at top, erect, smooth, with "bloom"; leaves lance-like, broad at base, sessile or nearly so, opposite; heads about 2" wide; dry open woods, Fla. to Ark., n to Me., sw Que., Sask.

Beach Sunflower, *H. debilis,* 2–7', stem prostrate to weakly ascending, with long lower branches; leaves alternate, entire to toothed, on long petioles; heads 1¾–2¾" wide, rays 11–20; in sandy soil, Fla. to Tex., S.C.; local to Me.

H. laetiflorus

Helianthus annuus

H. tuberosus

H. maximiliani

H. atrorubens

H. angustifolius

H. nuttallii

H. divaricatus

H. debilis

H. ciliaris

TARWEED (MADIA) Odorous sticky herbs; leaves entire or slightly toothed, lower opposite, upper alternate; heads axillary and terminal, few- to many-flowered; involucre bracts in 1 row, each bract enclosing a ray-flower's base; disk flat or convex, 1 row of bracts between ray- and tube-flowers; rays 1–20 (rarely none), yellow; no pappus or of tiny scales; 17 species, of w N.A. *M. sativa*, 8"–5', has heads from ¼–½" wide in racemes or clusters, rays 5–13; ranges from n Wash. to s Calif.; Que. to Del., Ind. *M. elegans*, 8"–4', has heads to 2" wide in open cymes, rays mostly 13, yellow or with a maroon basal spot; from sw Wash. and w Oreg. to s Calif. Both prefer dry open soil.

TARWEED (HEMIZONIA) resembles *Madia* but has 3–45 notched or 3-lobed rays per head, yellow or white; involucre bracts clasp only outer side of ray-flowers; disk may be chaffy; 27 species, in w N.A. **Spike-weed**, *H. pungens*, 4"–3', has pinnately lobed lower leaves, upper ones small, rigid, spine-tipped; heads ½" wide; inhabits fields, wastelands, from Wash. to Calif. and Ariz.

LAYIA is also like *Madia*, but lower leaves are pinnately lobed; heads have 1–13 yellow or white rays; tube-flowers with pappus of 10–35 bristles; 15 species, in w N.A. *L. glandulosa*, 2–16", heads 1½" wide, rays white or yellow, grows in dry open desert, foothills, s B.C. to s Calif., Ariz., and w N.M.

GREEN-THREAD (THELESPERMA) Smooth erect herbs; leaves paired, mostly dissected; long-stalked solitary heads; involucre bracts in 2 rows, outer green, inner fused halfway up, scaly; disk flat, chaffy; tube-flowers 5-lobed; rays none or 8–10; pappus 2–3 awns or teeth; 13 N.A. species. *T. longipes* has many stems, forming clumps or mats 8–15" high; heads ½" wide, no rays; in limestone soil, Tex. to Ariz. *T. filifolium*, 8–28", is simple to bushy-branched; heads 1–2" wide, 8 3-lobed rays; grows on plains, n Mo. to Colo., s to La. and N.M.

TICKSEED (COREOPSIS) Most leaves opposite, entire to dissected; heads stalked, single or panicled; involucre bracts in 2 rows of 8; disk flat or convex; rays usually 8, tips entire to lobed or toothed, yellow (rarely pink or white), often marked with maroon; pappus 2 awns or teeth, or none; about 40 species in N.A. *C. atkinsoniana*, 1–4', has once- or twice-pinnate leaves; heads ¾–2" wide; grows on moist banks, plains, B.C. and Sask. to N.D., s to Oreg., n Ariz. *C. tinctoria*, 2–4' tall, has pinnate lower leaves, upper entire; heads ¾–2" wide; on low ground, w N.A., escaped e to Atl. *C. bigelovii*, 1–2', has pinnate leaves in basal tufts, 1–2" heads; in Calif. deserts.

M. elegans

Hemizonia pungens

Madia sativa

Layia glandulosa

T. longipes

Thelesperma filifolium

Coreopsis atkinsoniana

C. tinctoria

C. bigelovii

VI. Sneezeweed Tribe (Helenieae)

Leaves often gland- or resin-dotted; heads usually with rays; involucre in 1–3 rows, outer bracts green; disk not chaffy; anthers not tailed; pappus never hairlike; 46 genera in N.A.

PAPER-FLOWER (PSILOSTROPHE) Woolly or smooth herbs, often in clumps; lower leaves petioled, paired, entire to lobed; upper ones alternate, sessile; heads stalked or sessile, solitary or crowded; involucre bracts in 2–3 rows, outer hairy, inner scaly; tube-flowers 5-toothed or 5-lobed; 3–7 papery yellow rays; pappus 4–5 scales; 6 species, in SW. *P. cooperi*, 8–20" tall, is bushy, woody at base; heads solitary, 1¼" wide; common on mesas and plains, w N.M. and Utah to s Calif.

DESERT-MARIGOLD (BAILEYA) Woolly herbs with alternate leaves, lower pinnately lobed, upper entire; heads stalked; involucre 2–3 rows of woolly bracts; rays 5–50, yellow, becoming papery; no pappus; 3 species, in SW. *B. multiradiata* has 1 or more 8–12" stems, heads to 2" wide, 25–50 rays; ranges from Tex. to Calif., n to Utah and Nev. *B. pauciradiata*, 4–24", has heads ½–1" wide, 5–8 rays; grows in sw Ariz. and se Calif.

ROCK-DAISY (PERITYLE) Leaves paired or alternate, smooth to hairy, entire to dissected; heads stalked, single to densely clustered; involucre bracts in 2 rows; tube-flowers 4-lobed, white, yellow, or purple-tinged; rays none to 20, white or yellow; pappus of 1 to many bristles, or none; 25 species, in SW, many rare; most grow from bare rock crevices. *P. emoryi*, 4–16", has 7–13 rays; sw Ariz. to the Channel Is., s Calif.

PERICOME One species, *P. caudata*, 2–4', a widely branched odorous herb; leaves paired, long-petioled, blades halberd-shaped, tip and lobes long-tailed; heads about ½" wide, in corymbs, only of 5-lobed yellow tube-flowers; involucre bracts 16–20 in 1 row; pappus a few scales. Grows in mountain canyons, coniferous forests, from w Tex. to Ariz., n to Nev. and Colo.

PALAFOXIA Stems nearly simple below, branched at top; leaves mostly alternate, lance-like, entire; heads in corymbs; tube-flowers 5-toothed or 5-lobed; rays, if present, 3-lobed, rosy; pappus 7–10 scales; 11 species, in s U.S. *P. callosa*, 8–32", has heads of 7–12 tube-flowers, no rays; grows in limestone areas, Mo., Ark., Okla., and Tex. *P. sphacelata*, 1–2', has heads with 5–10 rays; inhabits sandy plains, dunes, from Kans. and Colo. to Tex. and N.M. **Spanish-needles,** *P. linearis*, 8–30", has heads only of 10–20 tube-flowers; in sand, s Utah and Ariz. to Calif.

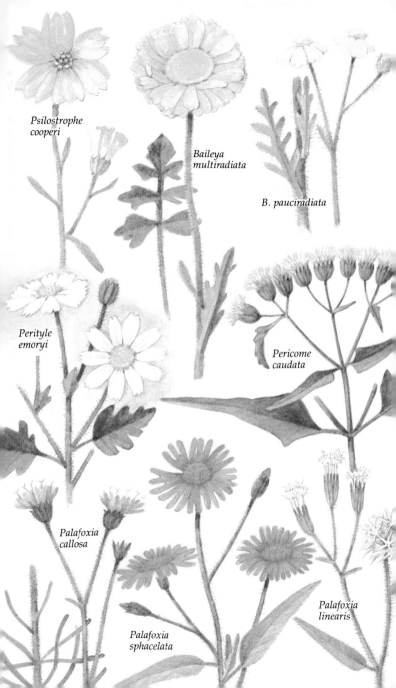

*Psilostrophe
cooperi*

*Baileya
multiradiata*

B. pauciradiata

*Perityle
emoryi*

*Pericome
caudata*

*Palafoxia
callosa*

*Palafoxia
linearis*

*Palafoxia
sphacelata*

HYMENOPAPPUS Stems erect; leaves pinnately dissected, woolly beneath, in a rosette, alternate on stem; heads stalked, in corymbs; involucre 6–14 bracts in 2–3 rows, often petal-like; disk flat to domed; tube-flowers 5-lobed, white, yellow, or rosy; no rays (except in *H. biennis*); pappus 12–22 scales, or none; 12 N.A. species. *H. filifolius* has 1–3′ stems from a caudex, few to many heads, yellow or pink involucre tips; in dry soil, Sask., Alta., and cen. Wash., s to s Calif., Tex.; *H. scabiosaeus*, 1–3′, has single stems, many heads, white- or green-tipped involucres; ranges from Fla. to Tex., n to S.C., Ind., and Neb.

HYMENOTHRIX Erect 12–28″ herbs; leaves 2- to 3-ternately lobed; heads in corymbs; involucre 1–2 rows of scales; tube-flowers of 5 unequal white or pink lobes; rays cream if present; pappus 12–18 scales, in some bristle-tipped; 3 sw species. *H. wrightii* has 1 or more 1–2′ stems, alternate leaves, a basal rosette; heads of 15–30 tube-flowers; ranges from w Tex. to Calif.

TRICHOPTILIUM One species, *T. incisum*; stems several, woolly, 2–8″ high; leaves alternate, petioled, spine-toothed; heads axillary, long-stalked, all of 5-lobed tube-flowers; involucre 2 rows of bracts; pappus 5 scales; grows in deserts, w Ariz., s Calif.

MARIGOLD (TAGETES) Aromatic herbs; leaves mostly paired, pinnate; heads single or clustered; involucre fused in a tube; tube-flowers 5-toothed; rays 1 to several; pappus 3–6 scales, 1–2 often awned; 5 species in N.A. *T. lemmoni*, 20–40″ high, bushy; leaves of 3–7 toothed segments; heads 1″ wide, rayed; grows in moist canyons, se Ariz.; **Licorice-marigold,** *T. micrantha*, 4–12″, has threadlike leaves, heads usually of 6 tube-flowers, 1 ray; grows in moist mountain canyons, from w Tex, to se Ariz.

PECTIS Low odorous herbs; leaves mostly opposite; heads stalked, single or clustered, few-flowered; involucre 1 row of 3–12 bracts; rays yellow, usually as many as bracts; pappus of scales, awns, or bristles; 13 species, in s U.S. *P. angustifolia*, 4–8″, has leaves with 6–10 bristle-tipped lobes; heads of 10–15 tube-flowers, 8–10 rays; grows in dry limestone uplands, Neb. and Colo. to w Tex., Ariz. *P. filipes*, 4–20″, has leaves with 1–5 pairs of basal bristles; heads of about 5 tube-flowers, 5–6 rays; ranges from w Tex. to Ariz.

JAUMEA One species, *J. carnosa*, in N.A.; a sprawling succulent to 1′ tall, with paired entire leaves; heads solitary, ½–1″ wide; involucre 3 rows of broad pink-tipped bracts; tube-flowers 5-toothed; rays 6–10, entire to 3-toothed; tidal flats, s B.C. to s Calif.

Hymenopappus filifolius

Hymenothrix wrightii

Hymenopappus scabiosaeus

Trichoptilium incisum

Tagetes lemmoni

Tagetes micrantha

Pectis angustifolia

P. filipes

Jaumea carnosa

FETID-MARIGOLD (DYSSODIA) Strong-odored herbs; leaves mostly opposite, entire to pinnate; heads terminal; involucre bracts fused in a cup, a few loose bracts below; tube-flowers 12–100; 5-lobed; rays few, rarely none; pappus 5–22 scales, sometimes split into bristles; 15 species in N.A. *D. papposa*, 4–28″ high, has pinnate leaves, ½″ heads, up to 8 short rays; grows in dry open places, from Me. to Mont., s to Ohio, La., and Ariz. **Parralena**, *D. pentachaeta*, 4–8″ tall, has stiff pinnate leaves, ½″ heads, 8–13 rays; n-cen. to s Tex., w to s Utah, Nev., and Calif. **Tiny-Tim** or **Dahlberg-daisy**, *D. tenuiloba*, 4–12″, forms dense clumps 6–20″ wide; most leaves are alternate, pinnate; heads with 10–21 rays; ranges from cen. to se Tex.; s Fla.

CHAENACTIS Most leaves pinnately or irregularly divided; heads stalked, of 5-lobed tube-flowers, large outer ones suggesting rays; involucre bracts narrow, in 1–2 rows; pappus 4–20 scales; 22 species in w N.A. *C. douglasii*, 4–24″, is downy; leaves 1–3 times pinnately lobed, lobes curled; heads 1″ long, white or pink; inhabits dry open places, B.C. to Mont., s to Calif. and N.M. **Golden Girls**, *C. glabriuscula*, 6–16″, heads 1½″ wide, grows on wooded or open slopes, n-cen. to s Calif.

WOOLLY-DAISY (ERIOPHYLLUM) Woolly bushy herbs, some woody at base; leaves paired or alternate, entire to pinnately lobed; heads single or in corymbs; involucre 1 row of bracts; rays few (rarely none), yellow; pappus of scales, or none; 11 species, in w N.A. *E. lanatum*, 4–24″ high, has variable leaves, 1–2″ heads; dry open sites, B.C. to Mont., s to Calif., Utah.

BAERIA Low herbs with opposite entire to pinnately lobed leaves; heads solitary; involucre bracts few; disk convex or conic; rays few, yellow; pappus of awns, scales, or none; 12 species, in w N.A. **Gold-fields**, *B. chrysostoma*, to 16″, has downy threadlike leaves, heads to 1½″ wide; inhabits grassland, from Oreg. to s Calif. and Ariz. *B. maritima* is a 4–20″ sprawling succulent; heads are ½″ wide; grows along the coast, s B.C. to s Calif.

BAHIA Erect hairy herbs; leaves paired or alternate, in most ternately dissected; heads stalked, in cymes; involucre bracts in 1–3 rows; tube-flowers 5-toothed; rays 5–20, yellow; pappus 8–15 scales, or none; 11 species, in SW. *B. absinthifolia*, 4–16″, has erect basal branches ending in 1–5 heads 1½″ wide; entire to pinnate or ternate leaves; ranges from sw Tex. to Ariz.; *B. dissecta* has single 8–32″ stems panicled at top, many ¾″ heads; grows from Wyo. to w Tex., w to Calif. *B. oppositifolia*, 4–12″, much-branched stems, ½″ heads; N.D. to Mont., s to Okla., N.M.

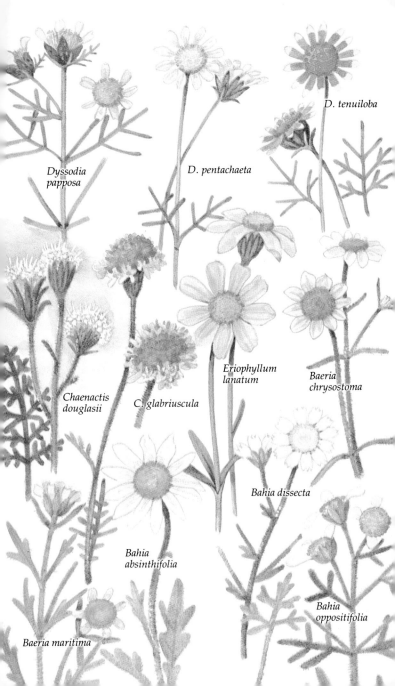

*Dyssodia
papposa*

D. pentachaeta

D. tenuiloba

*Chaenactis
douglasii*

C. glabriuscula

*Eriophyllum
lanatum*

*Baeria
chrysostoma*

*Bahia
absinthifolia*

Bahia dissecta

Baeria maritima

*Bahia
oppositifolia*

HULSEA Sticky-hairy aromatic herbs; leaves alternate, entire to pin-nately lobed; heads single or in racemes; disk flat; rays 10–60, yellow to purple; pappus of thin scales; 8 species, in w N.A. *H. algida*, 4–16″, has toothed leaves in tufts from a caudex; heads 1–2½″ wide, rays 25–55; alpine, on talus, rock crevices, ne Oreg. to sw Mont.; ne Nev.; e mts. of Calif.

GAILLARDIA Leaves entire to pinnately lobed, alternate or basal; heads stalked, solitary; involucre bracts green in 2–3 rows; disk convex; tube-flowers with 5 hairy teeth; ray tips 3-lobed; pappus 5–10 awned scales; 14 N.A. species. *G. aristata* has several 8–28″ stems, hairy herbage, heads 3–4″ wide; grows in dry meadows, prairies, B.C. to Sask., s to n Oreg., n Utah, Colo., and S.D. **Indian Blanket** or **Fire-wheel,** *G. pulchella*, 1–2′, is soft-downy; heads 2″ wide, rays 6–10; in dry open places, sandy soil, ranges from Fla. to Ariz., n to Colo., Neb., Minn., and Va. *G. pinnatifida*, 12–16″, heads 1¾″ wide, grows in grass-land, Utah, Colo., and Okla., s to Mexico.

BITTERWEED (HYMENOXYS) Leaves narrow, entire to pinnate, both in a rosette and alternate, or all basal; heads stalked, solitary or clus-tered; outer involucre bracts fused halfway up; disk domed, pitted; rays yellow, tips 3-lobed or 3-toothed, in age papery, down-curving; pappus 5–10 pointed scales; 22 species in N.A., only on soils derived from basic rocks. *H. acaulis*, a variable species, is stemless; silky entire leaves in tufts from a caudex; heads solitary, 1–2″ wide on 2–14″ scapes, rays 8–16, rarely none; grows on plains, dry rocky slopes to alpine areas, Alta. and Sask., s to se Calif., Tex.; e on plains to Kans. and Ohio. *H. odorata*, 3″–2′, is bushy; leaves of 3–15 pinnate lobes; aromatic if crushed; heads ½–1″ wide, rays 6–13; in limestone soil, Tex. to Calif., n to Colo. and Kans.

SNEEZEWEED (HELENIUM) Erect herbs; leaves alternate, sessile, bases in some running down stem, entire to pinnately lobed; heads solitary or in corymbs; involucre bracts spreading, in 2–3 rows; disk globular to oblong; rays 3- to 5-lobed, often drooping; pappus 5 awn-tipped scales; 20 N.A. species. *H. flexuosum*, stems 1–3′, winged below, branched at top, has rosetted offshoots at base; leaves entire to pin-nately cut; heads numerous, 1–2″ wide; tube-flowers mostly 4-toothed; rays, if present, yellow, umber, or striped with both; grows in damp plains, meadows, fields, originally se U.S., now n to N.Eng., Ohio, Mich., and Okla. **Owl-claws,** *H. hoopesii*, 1–3′, has entire leaves, 3″-wide heads; ranges from Wyo. to Oreg., s to N.M. and Calif. *H. amarum*, 4–20″, bushy at top, has grooved stems; grows in sandy soil, se U.S.

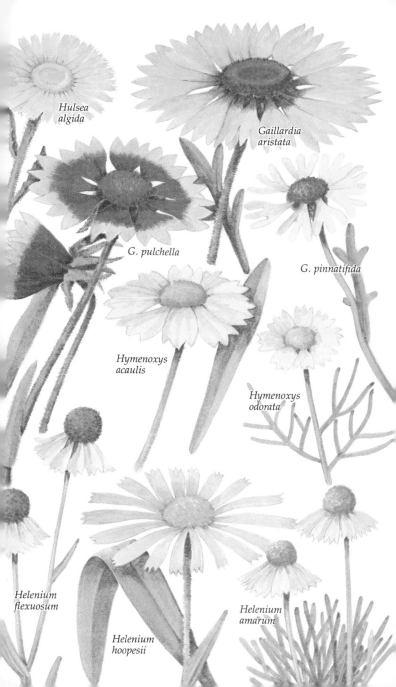

*Hulsea
algida*

*Gaillardia
aristata*

G. pulchella

G. pinnatifida

*Hymenoxys
acaulis*

*Hymenoxys
odorata*

*Helenium
flexuosum*

*Helenium
hoopesii*

*Helenium
amarum*

VII. Mayweed Tribe (Anthemideae)

Strong-scented herbs; leaves alternate; heads with or without rays;
involucre bracts in 1–4 rows, overlapped, papery or dry; anthers no
tailed; pappus a low crown or none; 12 N.A. genera.

YARROW (ACHILLEA) Erect herbs; leaves simple to finely divided
tiny heads in corymbs; disk convex, chaffy; tube-flowers 10–75; rays 3–
12, white, pink, or yellow; 5 species in N.A. *A. millefolium* has 1 or more
8–40″ stems, fernlike leaves, 5–12 rays; grows on open ground
throughout nearly all of N.A.

CHAMOMILE (ANTHEMIS) Leaves finely divided; stalked heads at
branch tips; disk conic, chaffy; rays white or yellow; Old World; 8
species in N.A. **Mayweed** or **Dog-fennel,** *A. cotula,* 8″–2′, heads ½–1″
wide, rays 10–20, disk chaffy only at summit; grows in fields, waste
lands, from Nfld. to Alaska, s throughout N.A.

WILD CHAMOMILE (MATRICARIA) has herbage like *Anthemis;* heads
single or in corymbs; disk not chaffy; rays white or none; Old World; 5
species in N.A. *M. maritima,* to 2′ tall, has spreading branches, ½–1″
stalked heads at branch tips; tube-flowers 5-toothed; rays 12–25; sea
shores, wastelands, Nfld. to Ont., s to Pa., Kans.; Pac. Coast; **Pineap
ple Weed,** *M. matricarioides,* 2–16″ high, has rayless heads with 4
toothed tube-flowers; herbage pineapple-scented if bruised; in fields
and along roadsides, most of N.A.

CHRYSANTHEMUM Leaves toothed or divided; heads single or clus
tered; disk flat or convex, chaffless; tube-flowers 3- to 5-toothed; rays
many or none, white, yellow, or pink; 18 species in N.A. **Ox-eye-daisy,**
C. leucanthemum, 8–32″, has 1–2″ solitary heads at branch tips, 15–30
rays; Eurasian; grows in fields, most of temperate N.A. **Feverfew,** *C.
parthenium,* 1–3′ tall, a bushy herb, has ½–1″ heads in corymbs, 10–20
rays; European, escaped to wastelands, much of U.S. **Tansy** or **Gold
buttons,** *C. vulgare,* 2–5′, has 20–200 rayless ¼–½″ heads in a flat corymb;
European, escaped to fields, Nfld. to B.C., s in most of the U.S.

COTULA Low herbs; leaves toothed to divided; heads stalked, of 4
toothed tube-flowers; S. Hemisphere; 2 species in N.A. **Brass-buttons,**
C. coronopifolia, 2–12″ high, heads ⅕–⅖″ wide; on tidal flats, salty soil, from
Que. to Mass.; B.C. to w Ariz.

WORMWOOD (ARTEMISIA) Herbs or low shrubs; leaves entire to
divided; tiny heads in spikes, racemes, or panicles; rays 1/25″ long; about
100 N.A. species. **White Sage,** *A. ludoviciana,* 1–3′, is the most wide
spread; ranges from B.C. to Mexico, e to Ont. and Ark.

*Achillea
millefolium*

*Anthemis
cotula*

*Matricaria
maritima*

*Chrysanthemum
parthenium*

*Chrysanthemum
leucanthemum*

*Matricaria
matricarioides*

*Cotula
coronopifolia*

*Chrysanthemum
vulgare*

*Artemisia
ludoviciana*

VIII. Groundsel Tribe (Senecioneae)

Leaves are mostly alternate or basal; heads single or in corymbs or panicles, often rayed; involucre 1–2 rows of green bracts, not over-lapped or only slightly so; disk not chaffy; anthers not tailed; pappus of hairlike bristles; 18 genera in N.A.

BRITTLE-STEM (PSATHYROTES) Low branching moundlike herbs; leaves rounded, woolly or scurfy, petioled, entire or toothed; heads single, stalked, of 5-toothed tube-flowers; involucre cuplike, in 2 rows; 4 SW species. *P. ramosissima,* to 5" high, 1' wide, has ½" heads; ranges from sw Utah and w Ariz. to se Calif.

INDIAN-PLANTAIN (CACALIA) Tall smooth herbs; leaves entire to pinnate, mostly petioled; heads of 5 to many 5-toothed tube-flowers, in corymbs; involucre 1 row of erect bracts; 10 N.A. species. **Pale Indian-plantain,** *C. atriplicifolia,* 3–6' tall, grows in dry open woods, from N.Y. to Minn., s to Fla., Ala., and Okla.

COLT'S-FOOT (TUSSILAGO) is European; one species, *T. farfara,* has escaped to damp clay soils, Nfld. to Minn., s to N.J. and Ohio. Heads are single, about 1" wide, on scaly 2–13" scapes from horizontal root-stock; toothed heart-shaped leaves appear later.

FALSE BROOMWEED (HAPLOESTHES) is Mexican. *H. greggii* ranges n in alkaline soil to Colo., Kans., and Okla.; basal stems few to many, 12–20", many erect parallel branches, narrow entire leaves in pairs; heads in dense corymbs; 3–5 short rays.

LUINA Stems simple, erect, from a woody rhizome or caudex; leaves alternate, entire to deeply cut; heads only of 5-toothed tube-flowers, in racemes or corymbs; involucre bracts in 1 row; 4 species, in Pac. N.A. **Silverleaf,** *L. hypoleuca,* 6–16", has silky herbage, entire sessile leaves, 10- to 17-flowered heads; grows in rocky places, cen. B.C. to cen. Calif. **Silver-Crown,** *L. nardosmia,* 16–40", has long-petioled mostly basal leaves, palmately lobed and toothed, to 10" wide, silky beneath; heads of 30 or more flowers; grows in mountain meadows, open woods, Wash. to cen. Calif.

CROCIDIUM One species, *C. multicaule;* stems several, 4–12"; leaves alternate and basal, entire or few-toothed; heads about 1" wide, rays 5–13; dry open low elevations, s B.C. to Calif.

RAILLARDELLA Leaves alternate or basal, simple, entire; heads sin-gle or few, yellow, sometimes rayed; involucre 1 row of bracts; 5 species; mountains of Calif., w Nev., and Oreg. *R. scaposa* has silky leaves in basal tufts, single heads on 1–5" scapes.

Psathyrotes
ramosissima

Cacalia
atriplicifolia

Tussilago
farfara

Haploesthes
greggii

Luina
hypoleuca

Crocidium
multicaule

Raillardella
scaposa

L. nardosmia

GROUNDSEL (SENECIO) Leaves alternate or basal, entire to pinnate; heads solitary or clustered; involucre bracts in 1–2 rows, often a few tiny extras at base; tube-flowers 5-toothed; rays mostly present, entire or 3-toothed; 120 species in N.A.

Golden Ragwort or **Squaw-weed,** *S. aureus,* has creeping rhizomes, erect 8″–4′ stems, 1″-wide heads in clusters; grows in meadows, woods, swamps, e N.A.

Stinking-Willie, *S. jacobaea,* 1–4′, stem simple below the broad corymb; European; heads 1″ wide; in fields, Nfld. to N.J., Ont.; Pac. Coast, w of Cascades.

S. douglasii, 2–6′ high, several stems from base, bushy above; lower or all leaves pinnate with threadlike lobes; abundant in the driest parts of w N.A.

Butterweed, *S. glabellus,* has soft hollow 8–40″ stems; pinnate leaves, leaflets blunt-toothed; grows in wet woods, swamps, ditches, se U.S., w to Mo., e Tex.

S. werneriaefolius has several 1–6″ decumbent stems from a caudex; leaves mostly basal, entire; alpine; in rocky places, Calif. to Mont., Colo., w Ariz.

S. resedifolius has 2–8″ stems from a caudex; blunt-toothed leaves; (rarely 2) 1–2″ heads; alpine, Alaska to Nfld., s to Wash., Mont. nw Wyo., se Que.

S. triangularis has several 2–5′ stems, triangular sharp-toothed leaves, few to many 1″ heads, rays 5–8; moist sites, mts., Alaska and Yuk. to Sask., Calif., N.M.

German-ivy, *S. mikanioides,* is a African high-twining vine; heads rayless, ⅓″ wide, in tight corymbs escaped to gullies and canyons coastal Calif.

ARNICA Stems simple, from a rhizome or caudex; leaves basal or paired, entire to toothed; heads stalked, in corymbs or single; involucre bracts in 1–2 rows; tube-flowers 5-lobed; rays present in most, often toothed at tip; 32 N.A. species. **Leopard's-bane,** *A. acaulis,* 1–3′ tall, has glandular hairs; a basal rosette of broad sessile leaves; stem leaves small and far apart; heads 2½″ wide, 2–16 per corymb; in sandy woods, from se Pa. and Del. to Fla. *A. mollis,* 2–24″ high, has entire to toothed leaves; herbage downy to glandular-hairy; heads about 2″ wide, 1–10 per corymb; alpine, subalpine moist places, Alaska and Yuk. to Calif. Utah, Colo.; Gaspé Pen., Que. to mts. of Me. and N.H. *A. sororia,* 1–2′ has entire leaves, 1 to few heads, to 4″ wide; open dryish places, foothills to moderate heights, B.C. and Alta. to Calif., Wyo., Utah.

FIREWEED (ERECHTITES) Rank-odored erect herbs; leaves alternate, entire to pinnate; heads in panicles, only of tube-flowers, outer ones threadlike, inner ones 4- to 5-toothed; 4 species in N.A. *E. hieracifolia* to 8′ tall, has sharp-toothed leaves, often irregularly lobed; few to many whitish heads; damp thickets, shores, wastelands, e N.A., w to Minn. Tex.; also in w Wash.

*necio
reus*

S. jacobaea

S. douglasii

S. glabellus

S. werneriaefolius

S. resedifolius

S. triangularis

S. mikanioides

A. sororia

A. mollis

*Arnica
acaulis*

*Erechtites
hieracifolia*

IX. Thistle Tribe (Cynareae)

Leaves alternate, often spiny; heads only of tube-flowers, corollas of 4 or 5 equal or irregular long lobes; involucre bracts in many rows, overlapped, spiny or fringed; base of anthers tailed; pappus mostly bristles; 11 genera in N.A.

STAR-THISTLE (CENTAUREA) Leaves entire to pinnate, not spiny; heads solitary or panicled; involucre sometimes spiny; disk bristly; outer flowers often enlarged, suggesting rays; 27 species in N.A. **Basket-flower,** *C. americana,* 3–5' tall, has sessile entire leaves, single heads at branch tips, 1½–3" wide; grows on plains, SE and SW, n to Mo. **Bachelor's-button** or **Cornflower,** *C. cyanus,* 1–2', heads 1½" wide, blue, purple, pink, or white; European, escaped to wastelands, temperate N.A. **Barnaby's-thistle,** *C. solstitialis,* 1–3' high, is downy; leaf bases winged down stem; heads ½–¾" wide, involucre spines to ¾" long; Eurasian; Fla. to Calif., n to Wash., Ia., s Ont., and Mass.

SAUSSUREA usually has several simple erect stems from a woody rhizome or caudex; leaves entire to toothed, not spiny; heads in terminal corymbs; 5 species, in NW. *S. americana,* 2–4' high, grows in moist open sites, Alaska and n B.C. to Oreg. and n Ida.

BLESSED THISTLE (CNICUS) One species, *C. benedictus,* to 2' tall, a European escape to wastelands, s Canada and the U.S.; leaves spine-toothed or spine-lobed; heads sessile, 1" wide, surrounded by clustered leafy bracts; outer involucre bracts tipped by simple spines, the inner ones by pinnately branched spines.

SCOTCH THISTLE (ONOPORDUM) is Eurasian; one species, *O. acanthium,* is now local, N.B. to Ont., s to Ala., se Mo.; n-cen. Tex.; Snake River Canyon, Ida., Wash.; a much-branched 3–10' spiny herb, sparsely to densely woolly; stems winged; involucre bracts all spine-tipped; heads 1½–2" wide.

MILK THISTLE (SILYBUM) is Old World; one species, **St. Mary's-** or **Holy Thistle,** *S. marianum,* 3–6' tall, has escaped to wastelands, fields, in much of U.S. (a noxious weed in Calif.); leaves white-mottled, bases clasping; heads 1–2" wide, single at tips of branches, often nodding; involucre bracts spine-tipped.

PLUMELESS THISTLE (CARDUUS) has spiny-winged stems; pappus rough, not feathery; Old World; 5 species in N.A. *C. acanthoides,* 1–5', has 1" erect heads, single or clustered at branch tips; **Musk Thistle,** *C. nutans,* 1–3', has single 1–2" nodding heads; both widespread but local, s Canada and the U.S.

ntaurea
ericana

Centaurea
cyanus

Centaurea
solstitialis

Cnicus
benedictus

Onopordum
acanthium

Silybum
marianum

Saussurea
americana

Carduus
acanthoides

Carduus
nutans

PLUMED THISTLE (CIRSIUM) Leaves sessile, spine-toothed or spine lobed; heads 1 to many, sessile or stalked, terminal, in some also axillary; involucre bracts mostly spine-tipped; disk densely soft-bristled; pappus feathery; 92 species in N.A.

Bull Thistle, *C. vulgare,* 2–6′, heads 2–3″ high; European; an aggressive weed of pastures, ranges from Lab. to Alaska, s to s Calif., Colo., Mo., mts. to Ga.

Yellow Thistle, *C. horridulum,* 4″-3′, mostly solitary heads subtended by a false leafy involucre grows in sandy or peat soil, Coastal Plain, Me. to Tex.

Canada Thistle, *C. arvense,* 1–5′, heads about 1″ high, single or 2–4 together; Eurasian, now a noxious field weed, Alaska to Lab., s over U.S. except SE.

Swamp Thistle, *C. muticum,* has hollow 2–10′ stems; heads long stalked; involucre with tiny spine or none; in acid soil, se Canada, U.S., s to N.C., La.

X. Mutisia Tribe (Mutisieae)
Leaves entire to lobed, all basal or sessile and alternate; heads single or clustered; involucre bracts in 2–5 rows, overlapped; flowers zygomorphic, 2-lipped, upper (inner) lip 2-lobed or 2-toothed, lower often raylike, 3-lobed or 3-toothed; anthers tailed at base; pappus of bristles 5 N.A. genera.

CHAPTALIA Leaves entire to pinnately lobed, in a basal rosette; heads solitary on scape-like stalks; involucre bracts in 4–5 rows; disk flat, outer flowers lack upper lip; 5 species in s U.S. **Sunbonnets,** *C. tomentosa,* 6–12″ tall, heads 1″ wide; grows in moist pinelands, Coastal Plain, N.C. to Fla. and Tex.

PEREZIA Leaves spine-toothed or spine-lobed; heads solitary or clustered; involucre bracts in 3–5 rows; disk flat; all flowers 2-lipped, lower lip raylike, 3-toothed; 5 species in SW. **Peonía,** *P. runcinata,* has pinnately lobed leaves in a rosette; 8–13″ scapes, 1 or 2 terminal heads 1″ high, 40- to 50-flowered; grows in brush, limestone soil, cen. and s Tex. **Brownfoot,** *P. wrightii,* has rusty wool at base of 2–4′ erect stem; unlobed leaves with clasping bases; heads 8- to 11-flowered, in terminal clusters; ranges from cen. Tex. to s Utah, Ariz. **Desert Holly,** *P. nana,* is colonial; stems erect, 1–8″ high, often zigzag; leaves hollylike; heads single at stem tips, 15- to 24-flowered; Tex. to Ariz.

TRIXIS Weak somewhat sprawling shrubs; leaves entire to fine-toothed; heads ½–1″ wide, in irregular groups at branch tips, a few leaves clustered beneath in a false involucre; involucre of 8 narrow bracts; heads 12- to 14-flowered; flowers yellow, lower lip raylike; 2 species in SW. *T. californica,* to 3′ tall, leaves downy and densely resin-dotted beneath; frequent in canyons, ranges from w Tex. to s Calif.

Cirsium vulgare

Cirsium arvense

Cirsium horridulum

Cirsium muticum

Perezia runcinata

Chaptalia tomentosa

P. nana

P. wrightii

Trixis californica

SUBFAMILY II: LIGULIFLORAE

Juice milky; stem leaves mainly alternate; heads all of perfect ray flowers, rays 5-toothed at tip; one tribe.

XI. Chicory Tribe (Cichorieae)

Involucre bracts in 1 to many rows: anthers eared at base, not tailed pappus of scales, bristles, or none; 37 genera in N.A.

DWARF DANDELION (KRIGIA) Leaves mostly basal, entire to toothed heads at tips of scapes or branches; involucre 1–2 rows of bracts; pappus double, outer of scales, inner bristles; 5 N.A. species. **Potato-dandelion,** *K. dandelion*, has single 1½" heads on 6–20" scapes; grows or prairies, Gulf Coast, n to N.J., Kans.

MOUNTAIN DANDELION (AGOSERIS) Leaves basal, long, entire to pinnately lobed; heads solitary on scapes; involucre bracts in 2–3 rows, overlapped; pappus of hairlike bristles; 8 N.A. species. *A. glauca* has 2- to 14"-long narrow leaves, 2" heads on 1–2' scapes; grows in oper places, all elevations, w N.A., e to Ont., Minn., S.D., N.M. *A. aurantiaca* flowers age to pink or purple; grows in meadows, open woods, moderate to alpine heights, w N.A., e to Alta., N.M.; also Gaspé Co., Que.

MICROSERIS resembles *Agoseris* but may have more than 1 head per stalk; pappus of 5 to many bristle-tipped scales; 17 species in w N.A. **Silver-puffs,** *M. linearifolia*, 4"–2' tall, has single 70- to 100-flowered heads; pappus 5 awn-tipped scales; inhabits low elevations, Wash. to s Calif., e to Ida., Utah, w Tex. *M. nutans*, to 2' high, 1 to few heads per stalk; pappus 15–20 plume-tipped scales; all elevations, B.C. to Mont., s to Calif., Utah, and Colo.

MALACOTHRIX Leaves pinnately divided; heads at stem and branch tips, yellow, white, or pink; involucre bracts in 2 rows; pappus a ring of white hairs; 14 species in w N.A. **Desert Dandelion,** *M. glabrata*, 6–12" tall, leaf-lobes threadlike, 2" heads; common on plains, mesas, from Ida. to Ariz., Calif.

HAWKBIT (LEONTODON) Leaves in a rosette, toothed or pinnately lobed; 1 or more heads on simple or forking scapes; disk not chaffy; European; 4 species in N.A. **Fall Dandelion,** *L. autumnalis*, has forking scaly 4–32" scapes, heads to 1⅓" wide; grows in fields, Ntfld. to Ont., s to Pa., Mich.; Alaska to Wash.

CAT'S EAR (HYPOCHAERIS) Like *Leontodon* but disk is chaffy, flower stems sometimes leafy below; European and S.A.; 3 species in N.A. *H. radicata*, 6–24", is often branched above; heads to 1½" wide; inhabits fields, lawns, s Canada and the U.S.

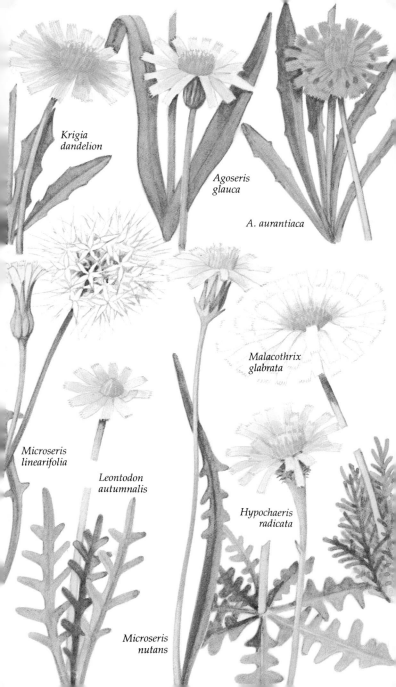

*Krigia
dandelion*

*Agoseris
glauca*

A. aurantiaca

*Microseris
linearifolia*

*Leontodon
autumnalis*

*Malacothrix
glabrata*

*Hypochaeris
radicata*

*Microseris
nutans*

HAWKWEED (HIERACIUM) Leaves entire to toothed or unevenly lobed, often downy or hairy; heads single, or in panicles or corymbs on scapes or leafy stems; pappus of sordid to brownish rough hairs; 5∞ species in N.A. **Devil's Paint-brush,** *H. aurantiacum,* has many-leaved basal rosettes, ¾" heads in corymbs on 8–28" scapes; European; grows in fields, Nfld. to Minn., s to Va., Ia.; Juneau, Alaska; w Wash., n Oreg. **Mouse-ear,** *H. pilosella,* forms carpets of dwarf rosettes by runners; 1 single heads on 2–10" scapes; European; in pastures, fields, from Nfld. to Minn., s to N.C. and Ohio. *H. scouleri* has leafy 1–3' stems, few to many 1" heads in terminal panicles; grows in open places, mountains from B.C. to s Calif., e to w Mont., nw Wyo.

HAWK'S-BEARD (CREPIS) resembles *Hieracium* but the pappus is of soft white hairs; 22 species in N.A. *C. nana* is a dwarf tufted mat forming herb 1–2" high; heads are crowded on short branches or among the leaves; arctic N.A., s in mountains to nw Nfld., Calif., Utah. *C. occidentalis* has several 2–16" leafy stems from a caudex, 2–25 heads in a corymb at top; grows in dry open places, plains, s B.C. to Sask., s to s Calif., N.M., S.D.

RATTLESNAKE-ROOT (PRENANTHES) Erect leafy-stemmed herbs; heads 5- to 35-flowered, in racemes or panicles, often nodding, white to yellow, pink, or purple; involucre bracts in 1 row, a few bractlets at base; pappus of rough bristles, white to yellow or brown; 12 N.A. species. *P. alba* has a 2–5' purplish stem, variable leaves, 8- to 12-flowered heads in a terminal panicle; grows in woods, Que. to Sask., s to Ga., Tenn., Mo., and S.D.

RUSH PINK or **SKELETON-WEED** (LYGODESMIA) Erect branched herbs; stem leaves awl- or scale-like, or none; heads as in *Prenanthes* but erect, rose-purple, terminal or scattered; 7 N.A. species. *L. juncea,* 6"–2' tall, has terminal mostly 5-flowered heads; inhabits plains, Man. to s B.C., s to Ark., Tex., Ariz., Nev., w Wash. *L. grandiflora,* to 1' high, heads 10- to 12-flowered, is common on sandy plains, Wyo. to Ida., s to N.M. and cen. Ariz.

RUSH PINK or **SKELETON-WEED** (STEPHANOMERIA) Like *Lygodesmia* but has feathery pappus; flowers white to rose; 13 N.A. species. *S. tenuifolia* has multiple 8–28" stems from a caudex; grows on dry rocky sites, s B.C. to w Mont., s to Calif. and Ariz.

CHICORY (CICHORIUM) is Eurasian; **Common Chicory** or **Blue-sailors,** *C. intybus,* is an escape to fields, by roads, Nfld. to B.C., s in much of U.S.; stems 1–5', rigidly branched above, 1½" sessile heads, 1–3 together, in upper leaf axils.

Hieracium aurantiacum

H. pilosella

H. scouleri

Crepis nana

Crepis occidentalis

Lygodesmia juncea

Prenanthes alba

L. grandiflora

Stephanomeria tenuifolia

Cichorium intybus

GOAT'S-BEARD (TRAGOPOGON) Smooth erect Old World herbs with grasslike clasping leaves; large solitary heads, yellow, reddish, or purple; involucre 1 row of bracts; pappus 1 row of feathery bristles, united at base; 5 species in N.A. *T. dubius* is bushy, 1–3' high, young leaves downy; heads to 1½" high, 100- to 200-flowered; dry open sites, N.Y. to Wash., s over U.S. except SE. **Salsify** or **Oyster-plant,** *T. porrifolius,* 2–4' tall, has fewer branches, leaves to 1' long; heads 84- to 117-flowered, closing by noon; grows in fields, by roads, much of s Canada, U.S.

CALYCOSERIS Several stems from base, with tack-shaped glands above; basal leaves pinnately lobed, upper ones bracts; heads single at branch tips, yellow or whitish; inner involucre bracts long, in 2 rows, outer ones tiny, in 2–3 rows; pappus a ring of slender bristles; 2 species, in SW. **White Cup-fruit,** *C. wrightii,* 4–20" high, has white flowers aging to pink; fruits with a tiny cup around base of pappus; ranges from w Tex. to Calif. and Utah.

PLUME-SEED (RAFINESQUIA) Similar to *Calycoseris* but flowers are purplish-white to pale pink; pappus of 8–15 bristles, plumed at sides but tips naked or barbed; 2 species, in SW. *R. neomexicana,* 6–20", has each ultimate branch tipped by a 1" head; grows in deserts, w Tex. to Calif., n to Utah, Nev.

GLYPTOPLEURA Low tufted or matted herbs with pinnately lobed spiny-toothed leaves, the edges white-encrusted; flowers as in *Calycoseris,* white, yellow, or pinkish; 2 SW species. *G. setulosa* has 1" cream or yellow flowers, aging to pink; grows on sandy desert flats, sw Utah and nw Ariz. to s. Calif.

ANISOCOMA One species, *A. acaulis,* with pinnately lobed leaves in a rosette, several to many 2–10" naked scapes tippped by solitary flowers to 3" wide; involucre cylindrical, of 3–5 rows of bracts; pappus of 10–12 long feathery bristles; inhabits sandy desert washes, cen. Nev., e Calif., nw Ariz.

TOBACCO-WEED (ATRICHOSERIS) One species, *A. platyphylla;* stems erect, solitary, branched at top, from a flat rosette of broad leaves with unequal teeth; 1½" flowers at branch tips, white or pinkish; desert, ranging from sw Utah and w Ariz. to se Calif.

PINAROPAPPUS Clump- or mat-forming herbs; leaves mostly basal, entire to lobed; heads solitary on scape-like branches; involucre bracts overlapped; disk slightly convex, chaffy; pappus of rough buff-white bristles; 2 SW species. **Rock-lettuce,** *P. roseus,* 4–12" tall, grows in open limestone areas, Tex., Ariz.

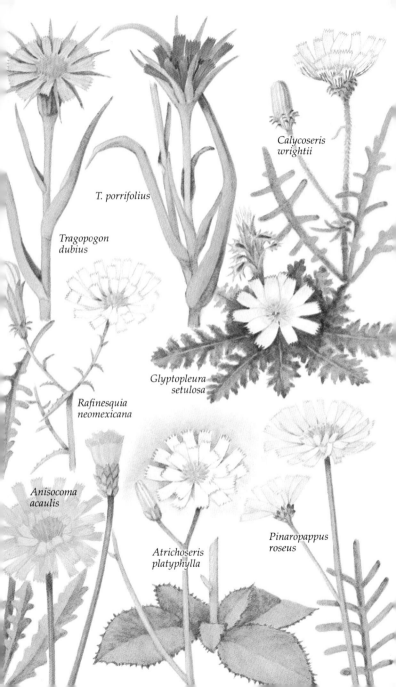

*Calycoseris
wrightii*

T. porrifolius

*Tragopogon
dubius*

*Glyptopleura
setulosa*

*Rafinesquia
neomexicana*

*Anisocoma
acaulis*

*Atrichoseris
platyphylla*

*Pinaropappus
roseus*

GEOGRAPHICAL ABBREVIATIONS USED IN TEXT

Ala. Alabama
Alta. Alberta
Ariz. Arizona
Ark. Arkansas
Atl. Atlantic
B.C. British Columbia
Calif. California
C.B. Cape Breton Island
cen. central
Co. county
Colo. Colorado
Conn. Connecticut
D.C. District of Columbia
Del. Delaware
e east, eastern
Fla. Florida
Ga. Georgia
Greenl. Greenland
I. Island
Ia. Iowa
Ida. Idaho
Ill. Illinois
Ind. Indiana
Is. Islands
Kans. Kansas
Ky. Kentucky
La. Louisiana
Lab. Labrador
L.I. Long Island, New York
Mackenz. Mackenzie District
Man. Manitoba
Mass. Massachusetts
Md. Maryland
Me. Maine
Mich. Michigan
Minn. Minnesota
Miss. Mississippi
Mo. Missouri
Mont. Montana
mt., mts. mountain, mountains
n north, northern
N.A. North America, north of Mexico
N.B. New Brunswick
N.C. North Carolina
N.D. North Dakota
ne northeast, northeastern
NE the Northeast
Neb. Nebraska
N.Eng. New England
Nev. Nevada
Nfld. Island of Newfoundland
N.H. New Hampshire
N.J. New Jersey
N.M. New Mexico
N.S. Nova Scotia
nw northwest, northwestern
NW the Northwest
N.Y. New York
Okla. Oklahoma
Ont. Ontario
Oreg. Oregon
Pa. Pennsylvania
Pac. Pacific
P.E.I. Prince Edward Island
Pen. Peninsula
Que. Province of Quebec
R. River
s south, southern
S.A. South America
Sask. Saskatchewan
S.C. South Carolina
S.D. South Dakota
se southeast, southeastern
SE the Southeast
sw southwest, southwestern
SW the Southwest
Tenn. Tennessee
Tex. Texas
Trop. Am., Tropical America
U.S. the 48 conterminous states
Va. Virginia
V.I. Vancouver Island
Vt. Vermont
w west, western
Wash. State of Washington
Wisc. Wisconsin
W.Va. West Virginia
Wyo. Wyoming
Yuk. Yukon Territory

SELECTED REFERENCES

Abrams, LeRoy. *Illustrated Flora of the Pacific States.* vols. 1–3, 1940–1951; vol. 4 (with Roxana S. Ferris) 1960; Stanford University Press, Stanford, Calif.

Bailey, L. H. *Manual of Cultivated Plants.* rev. ed. The Macmillan Co., New York, 1949.

Correll, Donovan Stewart and **Helen Butts Correll.** *Aquatic and Wetland Plants of Southwestern United States.* 2 vols. Stanford University Press, Stanford, Calif., 1972.

Correll, Donovan Steward and **Marshall Conring Johnston.** *Manual of the Vascular Plants of Texas.* Texas Research Foundation, Renner, Texas, 1970.

Fernald, Merritt Lyndon. *Gray's Manual of Botany.* 8th ed. American Book Co., New York, 1950.

Gleason, Henry A. *The New Britton and Brown Illustrated Flora of the Northeastern United States and Adjacent Canada.* 3 vols. Hafner Publishing Co., New York & London, 1963.

Hitchcock, C. Leo, Arthur Cronquist, Marion Ownbey, and **J. W. Thompson.** *Vascular Plants of the Pacific Northwest.* In 5 parts. University of Washington Press, Seattle, 1955–1969.

Hultén, Eric. *Flora of Alaska and Neighboring Territories.* Stanford University Press, Stanford, Calif., 1968.

Jepson, Willis Lynn. *A Manual of the Flowering Plants of California.* University of California Press, Berkeley, 1923–1925.

Kearney, Thomas H. and **Robert H. Peebles.** *Arizona Flora.* 2nd ed. University of California Press, Berkeley, 1960.

Long, Robert W. and **Olga Lakela.** *A Flora of Tropical Florida.* University of Miami Press, Coral Gables, Fla., 1971.

Muenscher, Walter Conrad. *Aquatic Plants of the United States.* Cornell University Press, Ithaca, N.Y., 1944.

Munz, Philip A. and **David D. Keck.** *A California Flora.* University of California Press, Berkeley, 1968.

Polunin, Oleg. *Flowers of Europe, a field guide.* Oxford University Press, London, 1969.

Radford, Albert E., Harry E. Ahles, and **C. Ritchie Bell.** *Manual of the Vascular Flora of the Carolinas.* University of North Carolina Press, Chapel Hill, N.C., 1964.

Rickett, Harold William. *Wild Flowers of the United States.* 6 vols. McGraw-Hill Book Co., New York, 1966–1973.

Steyermark, Julian A. *Flora of Missouri.* Iowa State University Press, Ames, Ia., 1962.

INDEX

The numbers following the common names and the generic scientific names in this index refer to text pages; illustrations are on the facing page. The scientific names of individual species treated within each genus are given in the text pertaining to the genus.

MEASURING SCALE (IN INCHES)

o